GLENCOE

VOCABULARY BUILDER

Peter Fischer, Editorial Consultant

National-Louis University

Course 4

Glencoe

New York, New York   Columbus, Ohio   Chicago, Illinois   Peoria, Illinois   Woodland Hills, California

Acknowledgments
The pronunciation key used in the glossary has been reproduced by permission
from *The American Heritage Dictionary of the English Language, Fourth Edition.*
Copyright © 2000 by Houghton Mifflin Company.

Printed in the United States of America

Send all inquiries to:
Glencoe/McGraw-Hill
8787 Orion Place
Columbus, OH 43240

SE ISBN: 0-07-861666-2
ATE ISBN: 0-07-861667-0

8 9 10   QDB   15 14 13 12 11

Contents

The Surrender Speech of Chief Joseph

Name _____

It has been called the outstanding example of Native American oratory. Its simplicity and expressiveness stand in sharp contrast to the **harangues** so commonly delivered by orators of the late nineteenth century.

5 Chief Joseph had led hundreds of Nez Perce men, women, and children on a 1,500-mile **trek** over mountains and rivers in the winter of 1877. Driven from their home along the Snake River, these native inhabitants of present-day Idaho and Oregon sought the safety of Canada. However, just a few miles from the Canadian border, the Nez Perce were attacked by United States troops led by General Nelson Appleton Miles.

10 Facing the total **annihilation** of his sick and exhausted people, Chief Joseph accepted the promise of General Miles that the Nez Perce would be returned to their home if they surrendered. Chief Joseph spoke the following words to his people:

I am tired of fighting. Our chiefs are killed. Looking Glass is
15 dead. The old men are all dead.

It is the young men who say no and yes. He who led the young men is dead. It is cold and we have no blankets. The little children are freezing to death. My people, some of them have run away to the hills and have no blankets—no food. No one knows
20 where they are—perhaps they are freezing to death.

I want to have time to look for my children and see how many of them I can find. Maybe I shall find them among the dead. Hear me, my chiefs, I am tired, my heart is sad and sick. From where the sun now stands, I will fight no more forever.

25 This brief but **eloquent** speech by Chief Joseph is considered one of the most moving and memorable in American literature. In a few sincere and moving sentences, it **succinctly** expressed the suffering and **anguish** of the Native American and the **ferocity** of war.

In the end, General Miles's promise was only a **ruse.** Chief Joseph and
30 the surviving Nez Perce were not allowed to return. Until his death in 1904, Chief Joseph **petitioned** the U.S. government repeatedly to allow the Nez Perce to return to their ancestral home, but his pleas were met with **indifference.** The Nez Perce never saw their home again.

Words
anguish
annihilation
eloquent
ferocity
harangue
indifference
petition
ruse
succinct
trek

Unlocking Meaning

Each word in this lesson's word list appears in dark type in the selection you just read. Think about how the vocabulary word is used in the selection, then write the letter for the best answer to each question.

1. A *harangue* (line 2) can best be described as _____ .
   (A) quiet thoughtfulness   (B) a clever speech
   (C) a cruel trick   (D) a long, wordy speech

1. _____

2. A *trek* (line 5) is a(n) _____ .
   (A) sea voyage   (B) wilderness trail
   (C) long, difficult trip   (D) adventure

2. _____

3. Which word could best replace *annihilation* in line 10?
   (A) starvation   (B) release
   (C) destruction   (D) rejection

3. _____

4. Which word could best replace *eloquent* in line 25?
   (A) complex   (B) expressive
   (C) musical   (D) loud

4. _____

5. A *succinct* speech (line 27) is one that is _____ .
   (A) short and to the point (B) confusing
   (C) historic   (D) convincing

5. _____

6. Which word or words could best replace *anguish* in line 27?
   (A) agony   (B) cooperative spirit
   (C) hostility   (D) stupidity

6. _____

7. Which word could best replace *ferocity* in line 28?
   (A) gallantry   (B) wisdom
   (C) excitement   (D) savagery

7. _____

8. Which word or words could best replace *ruse* in line 29?
   (A) trick   (B) insult
   (C) solemn promise   (D) courtesy

8. _____

9. Which word or words could best replace *petitioned* in line 31?
   (A) visited   (B) asked
   (C) attacked   (D) prayed to

9. _____

10. Which word or words could best replace *indifference* in line 33?
    (A) unconcern   (B) enthusiasm
    (C) agreement   (D) strange behavior

10. _____

Applying Meaning

Follow the directions below to write a sentence using a vocabulary word.

1. Describe a sporting event you have seen or would like to see. Use any form of the word *annihilate*.

   _____

   _____

   _____

2. Describe a speech or sermon. Use any form of the word *harangue*.

   _____

   _____

   _____

3. Tell how you feel about something or someone. Use any form of the word *indifference*.

   _____

   _____

   _____

4. Describe a trip you or someone you know took. Use any form of the word *trek*.

   _____

   _____

   _____

5. Tell how your class might go about asking the principal for a special favor. Use any form of the word *petition*.

   _____

   _____

   _____

Read each sentence or short passage below. Write "correct" on the answer line if the vocabulary word has been used correctly. Write "incorrect" on the answer line if the vocabulary word has been used incorrectly.

6. Even though the question was long and complicated, the teacher gave a very *succinct* answer.

   6. _____

7. The banquet table was set with the most *eloquent* dishes.

   7. _____

8. The contest turned out to be just a *ruse* for getting people to visit the store.

8. _____

9. I wrote a *petition* to Aunt Mary thanking her for my birthday present.

9. _____

10. The storm struck with a *ferocity* never before seen in that part of the country.

10. _____

11. The *anguish* caused by the sudden death of her pet took years to overcome.

11. _____

12. When he did not return my phone calls or answer my letters, I decided that he was *indifferent* about the proposal.

12. _____

13. I considered his annoying stares to be very inappropriate. I do not want this kind of *haranguing* while I am working.

13. _____

14. In trying to find the perfect college, we ended up *trekking* around the entire country.

14. _____

For each word used incorrectly, write a sentence using the word properly.

_____

_____

_____

_____

_____

_____

_____

_____

_____

_____

Mastering Meaning

Think about the events surrounding Chief Joseph's surrender speech. If you had been a newspaper reporter observing the surrender, how would you describe what you saw and heard? Write an article for your newspaper about what happened that day in 1877 near the Canadian border. Include a headline. Use some of the words you studied in this lesson.

Name _____

How many speakers have you heard in your lifetime? You have no doubt heard speakers and speeches that left you bored and weary. A few may have changed the way you thought or may have moved you to take some action. There are as many types and styles of speeches as there are speakers. In this lesson you will learn ten words that describe speakers and how they speak.

Unlocking Meaning

Read the sentences or short passages below. Write the letter for the correct definition of the italicized vocabulary word.

Even though the subject was complicated and difficult, the teacher was quite *articulate* in her explanation. By the end of the period, everyone understood the problem.

1. (A) able to express thoughts well
   (B) argumentative
   (C) often misunderstood
   (D) loud and talkative

The captain's defiant call for action was only *bravado*. When the fighting started, he was nowhere to be found.

2. (A) a deep sense of courage and commitment
   (B) mechanical
   (C) showy behavior without courage behind it
   (D) a very interesting speech

No one was fooled by the newspaper's *effusive* praise of the football coach. Everyone knows Coach Riley is the editor's brother-in-law.

3. (A) disguised
   (B) excessive; gushing
   (C) commonplace; ordinary
   (D) moving and sincere

Arthur's *garrulous* behavior at the party caused many people to leave early. Once he gets started there is no stopping him. After a while your ears start to hurt.

4. (A) excessively talkative
   (B) quiet and shy
   (C) embarrassing
   (D) cordial and engaging

Words

articulate

bravado

effusive

garrulous

glib

histrionics

laconic

polemic

trite

verbosity

1. _____

2. _____

3. _____

4. _____

The politician's *glib* response to my question convinced me she would not get my vote. That subject is far too important to be dismissed with such a simple answer.

5. (A) intelligent and perceptive
   (B) impressive
   (C) untruthful
   (D) superficial and insincere

5. _____

When the candidate held up the flag and tearfully reminded us that he was a veteran, the audience began to feel uneasy. Such *histrionics* do not usually get votes.

6. (A) powerful arguments
   (B) childish behavior
   (C) excessive emotional appeals
   (D) patriotism

6. _____

It is hard to believe that Phil, one of the most talkative and friendly people in school, has such a *laconic* brother.

7. (A) speaking briefly and to the point
   (B) angry and hostile
   (C) dull and lazy
   (D) foolish

7. _____

I hated to see Roberto take his seat in the auditorium. He was certain to engage the speaker in some *polemic*. No matter what her opinion might be, Roberto was certain to take the opposite view.

8. (A) unusual behavior
   (B) controversy or argument
   (C) lengthy discussion
   (D) false praise

8. _____

I had hoped to hear something fresh and interesting at last night's career forum. However, in the end the speakers offered the same *trite* advice I have heard again and again: Stay in school. Study hard. Good things will start to happen.

9. (A) exciting and interesting
   (B) humorous
   (C) logical; sensible
   (D) overused; meaningless

9. _____

Jackie bragged about having written the longest term paper in the class. It was twice as long as the assignment required. If the teacher gives grades for *verbosity*, Jackie will get an A.

10. (A) wordiness
    (B) sincerity
    (C) humility
    (D) neatness

10. _____

Applying Meaning

Read each sentence or short passage below. Write "correct" on the answer line if the vocabulary word has been used correctly. Write "incorrect" on the answer line if the vocabulary word has been used incorrectly.

1. In their day, Benjamin Franklin's proverbs were considered quite clever, but after more than two hundred years, they have become some of the *tritest* expressions in the language.

   1. _____

2. Because it was late and we were all eager to get home, we asked the speaker to give a *verbose* answer to the final question.

   2. _____

3. It is little wonder that Colonel Stern is so greatly admired. His *bravado* is apparent in every speech.

   3. _____

4. Her ability to *articulate* how we all felt about the problem made Juanita the obvious choice for chairperson.

   4. _____

5. Ruben shook everyone's hand vigorously as he greeted each guest *effusively*.

   5. _____

6. His *garrulous* manner made conversation difficult. Every question or comment got a one-word answer.

   6. _____

7. Political advertisements prove nothing. The ten-second sound bite can provide only *glib* answers to complex problems.

   7. _____

8. The movie cowboy was often a man of few words. He was portrayed *laconically* answering "yup" or "nope" to every question someone asked.

   8. _____

9. Maria's *polemics* made her unpopular with the audience. Everyone had come to hear the mayor's proposals, not Maria's constant objections.

   9. _____

10. Next year my brother will receive his degree in *histrionics*. He has done a great deal of research on the French Revolution.

    10. _____

11. We were not sure that the ring was a genuine antique. It might be a cleverly done *articulate*.

    11. _____

12. In the distance we saw a faint *glib* of sunlight shining through the thick forest.

    12. _____

For each word used incorrectly, write a sentence using the word properly.

_____

_____

_____

_____

_____

_____

_____

_____

_____

_____

_____

_____

_____

_____

_____

Cultural Literacy Note

Silence Is Golden

There is a popular proverb that says, "Silence is golden. Speech is silver." It suggests that while speech is admirable, complete silence can be more valuable. Do you agree?

Cooperative Learning: Work with a partner to list some situations in which silence is preferable to speaking. Are there times at school or at home when the more you talk, the worse things become? List some ways of talking that get you into trouble, like glib answers or histrionic outbursts. Use words from this lesson.

Name _____

One of the most easily recognized Latin roots is -*bell*-, which comes from the Latin word *bellum*, meaning "war." The Latin word *caedere* means "to cut" or "to kill." This root often appears in English words as -*cis*- or -*cid*-. Another Latin word, *vincere*, means "to conquer" or "defeat" and usually appears as -*vinc*- in English words. However, it can also appear in other forms, such as -*van*-. The vocabulary words in this lesson all have one of these roots.

Root	Meaning	English Word
-bell-	war	belligerent
-cid-	to kill, to cut	genocide
-cis-		incisive
-vinc-	to conquer	evince
-van-		vanquish

Words

bellicose

belligerent

concise

evict

evince

fratricide

genocide

incisive

invincible

vanquish

Unlocking Meaning

Write the vocabulary word that fits each clue below. Then say the word and write a short definition. Compare your definition and pronunciation with those on the flash card at the back of the book.

1. This word is always used as an adjective. It might be used to describe a person who always wants to start a fight or an argument.

   concise - Some one who is very arguementitive

2. This word is a combination of two Latin roots. One of the roots comes from the Latin word *frater*, meaning "brother."

   fratricide - fratricide can be used to discribe o blangr

3. This adjective has a prefix that means "not." If a football team is this, it never loses.

   invinsibe - can never be taken down.

4. This word is a synonym for eject and suggests that before you can throw someone out you have to defeat the person.

_____

_____

5. According to this word, if you can say a lot with a few words, you "cut" straight to the important information.

_____

_____

6. The Greek word *genos,* meaning "race," can be seen in this word.

_____

_____

7. This word is related to incision, but it usually refers to a sharp mind instead of a sharp knife.

_____

_____

8. This word is always a verb. You would not be able to do this to someone who is invincible.

_____

_____

9. This verb came into English through the Latin word *evincere,* meaning "to win a point," or "to prove." Today it is a synonym for "show."

_____

_____

10. This word is similar in meaning to the answer for number 1, but it can be used as a noun or an adjective and can refer to a country or a person.

_____

_____

Applying Meaning

Decide which word in parentheses best completes the sentence. Then write the sentence, adding the missing word.

1. Before attempting to climb that steep mountain cliff, we must condition our bodies and _____ our fear. (evince; vanquish)

   _____

   _____

2. The doctor's careful attention to the patients' explanations _____ her personal interest in their welfare.

   _____

   _____

3. The brothers never liked each other very much, but lately their relationship had turned utterly _____. (fratricidal; genocidal)

   _____

   _____

4. The _____ actions of the South American dictator provoked the neighboring countries to put their armies on alert. (bellicose; invincible)

   _____

   _____

5. The reporter provided a _____ summary of the city council meeting. (bellicose; concise)

   _____

   _____

Follow the directions below to write a sentence using a vocabulary word.

6. Describe someone you think is very intelligent and often sees the answer to a problem long before anyone else does. Use the word *incisive*.

   _____

   _____

   _____

7. Write a sentence about a historical event or period. Use the word *genocide*.

   _____

   _____

8. Use *evict* in a sentence about a cruel landlord.

_____

_____

_____

9. Complete the sentence: "Fareed showed his *belligerence* when he

_____."

_____

_____

_____

10. Describe a recent performance by your favorite sports team. Use the word *invincible*.

_____

_____

_____

Bonus Word

kowtow

In ancient China, people showed their deep respect for and obedience to the emperor by kneeling and touching, or knocking, the ground with their head. The Mandarin Chinese word for head was *tou*. The word for knock was *kou*. These words entered the English language as *kowtow*, meaning "to show respect or submission to another." The word is sometimes used in a negative way. Politicians might be accused of kowtowing to some special-interest group.

Write a Paragraph: Do you think people today still kowtow? For example, do they kowtow to television stars or movie stars? Choose something or someone to whom you feel people kowtow, and write a paragraph explaining why you feel that way.

Name _____

How well do you remember the words you studied in Lessons 1 through 3?
Take the following test covering the words from the last three lessons.

Part 1 Antonyms

Each question below includes a word in capital letters, followed by four
words or phrases. Choose the word or phrase that is most nearly <u>opposite</u>
in meaning to the word in capital letters. Consider all choices before deciding on your answer. Write the letter for your answer on the line provided.

Sample

S. GOOD	(A) simple	(B) bad	**S.**	**B**
	(C) able	(D) fast		

1. GLIB	(A) famous	(B) thoughtful	1.	B
	(C) dull	(D) ugly		
2. EVICT	(A) welcome	(B) eject	2.	A
	(C) resist	(D) acknowledge		
3. ELOQUENT	(A) silent	(B) ineffective	3.	C
	(C) ugly	(D) fancy		
4. INDIFFERENT	(A) strange	(B) concerned	4.	B
	(C) same	(D) careless		
5. CONCISE	(A) wordy	(B) concentrated	5.	A
	(C) clever	(D) convincing		
6. INVINCIBLE	(A) unconquered	(B) obvious	6.	D
	(C) transparent	(D) defeated		
7. GARRULOUS	(A) dangerous	(B) talkative	7.	C
	(C) quiet	(D) bright and colorful		
8. TRITE	(A) commonplace	(B) famous	8.	C
	(C) important	(D) stuffy		
9. HISTRIONIC	(A) sincere	(B) historic	9.	D
	(C) cheerful	(D) forgettable		
10. EVINCE	(A) cause	(B) combine	10.	D
	(C) recall	(D) hide		

Go on to next page. ➤

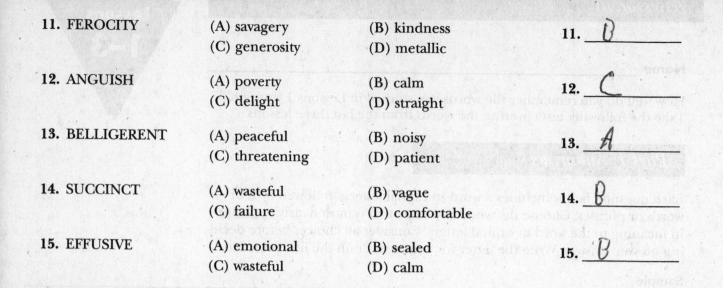

11. FEROCITY   (A) savagery   (B) kindness   11. __B__
               (C) generosity   (D) metallic

12. ANGUISH   (A) poverty   (B) calm   12. __C__
               (C) delight   (D) straight

13. BELLIGERENT   (A) peaceful   (B) noisy   13. __A__
                   (C) threatening   (D) patient

14. SUCCINCT   (A) wasteful   (B) vague   14. __B__
               (C) failure   (D) comfortable

15. EFFUSIVE   (A) emotional   (B) sealed   15. __B__
               (C) wasteful   (D) calm

Part 2   Matching Words and Meanings

Match the definition in Column B with the word in Column A.
Write the letter of the correct definition on the line provided.

Column A   **Column B**

16. incisive   a. a slow, difficult journey   16. __g__

17. verbosity   b. a trick   17. __e__

18. annihilation   c. a false show of courage   18. __d__

19. ruse   d. total destruction   19. __b__

20. bravado   e. wordiness   20. __c__

21. harangue   f. an appeal or request   21. __j__

22. petition   g. sharp and keen   22. __f__

23. laconic   h. the murder of an entire people, race, or cultural group   23. __g i__

24. genocide   i. brief and to the point   24. __h__

25. trek   j. a long, loud speech   25. __a__

Name _____

Lincoln Begins His Second Term

Historians have called the Civil War the defining moment in American history, a time when the issue of whether the states could be truly united would ultimately be answered. More than anyone else, Abraham Lincoln is credited with holding the union of states together.

5   Even though many people now consider Lincoln our greatest president, he was often scorned and ridiculed while he was in office. In fact, just a few short months before the voters cast their ballots in 1864, many felt Lincoln had little chance of winning reelection. People had grown tired of the war, and President Lincoln's popularity was at an all-time low. But
10   Lincoln did win reelection, and on March 4, 1865, the citizens of Washington gathered at the Capitol to witness his second oath of office. The scene has been recorded in numerous diaries and newspaper accounts.

All was quiet. Lincoln was about to **emerge** from the crowd, mount the podium, and raise his right hand to take his second oath of office. The
15   weather was dark and gloomy. Lincoln's tall, **gaunt** appearance seemed in perfect keeping with the dismal gray of the sunless sky. When the assembled crowd saw their president, the **solemnity** of the occasion gave way to applause. It rose to a powerful roar, then just as quickly **subsided.** At that exact moment the sun broke through the gray clouds that had
20   **shrouded** the scene since early morning, and shafts of sunlight shone on the speaker's platform. Many who witnessed the scene and recorded it in their diary saw this as an **omen** of good things to come in Lincoln's second term.

Lincoln had been forced to accept war rather than let the nation
25   **perish.** But now the outcome of the bloodiest conflict in American history seemed clear, and unlike those who sought to punish the South, Lincoln deeply desired that the nation become one again. He moved to the center of the platform and unfolded a single sheet of paper. As he began to speak, it was clear to everyone that his mind was now on peace,
30   not war.

With **malice** toward none; with **charity** for all; with firmness in the right, as God gives us to see the right, let us strive on to finish the work we are in; to bind up the nation's wounds; to care for him who shall have borne the battle, and for his widow, and his
35   orphan—to do all which may achieve and **cherish** a just and lasting peace, among ourselves and with all nations.

With that, Lincoln ended the shortest swearing-in speech since George Washington's inauguration.

Words
charity
cherish
emerge
gaunt
malice
omen
perish
shroud
solemnity
subside

The sentences below are taken from the reading selection. Decide which word or words would best replace the vocabulary word in italic type. Write the letter for that word on the answer line.

1. Lincoln was about to *emerge* from the crowd, mount the podium, and raise his right hand to take his second oath of office.

    (A) escape   (B) turn away

    (C) hide   (D) come forth

    1. ___D___

2. Lincoln's tall, *gaunt* appearance seemed in perfect keeping with the dismal gray of the sunless sky.

    (A) lean   (B) foolish

    (C) humorous   (D) angry

    2. ___A___

3. When the assembled crowd saw their president, the *solemnity* of the occasion gave way to applause.

    (A) boredom   (B) confusion

    (C) ridiculousness   (D) seriousness

    3. ___D___

4. It [the applause] rose to a powerful roar, then just as quickly *subsided*.

    (A) changed   (B) turned away

    (C) declined   (D) became louder

    4. ___B___

5. At that exact moment the sun broke through the gray clouds that had *shrouded* the scene since early morning, and shafts of sunlight shone on the speaker's platform.

    (A) framed   (B) illuminated

    (C) hidden   (D) buried

    5. ___C___

6. Many who witnessed the scene and recorded it in their diary saw this as an *omen* of good things to come in Lincoln's second term.

    (A) example   (B) beginning

    (C) prediction   (D) representation

    6. ___C___

7. Lincoln had been forced to accept war rather than let the nation *perish*.

    (A) die   (B) grow old

    (C) prosper   (D) disappear

    7. ___A___

8. With *malice* toward none; with charity for all. . .

    (A) indifference   (B) kindness

    (C) suspicion   (D) ill will

    8. ___D___

9. With malice toward none; with *charity* for all. . .

    (A) indifference   (B) kindness

    (C) suspicion   (D) ill will

    9. ___B___

10. . . . to do all which may achieve and *cherish* a just and lasting peace, among ourselves and with all nations.

    (A) treasure   (B) ignore

    (C) avoid   (D) steal

    10. ___A___

Applying Meaning

Write the vocabulary word or a form of the vocabulary word that fits each clue below. Then use the word in a sentence.

1. Two synonyms are "kindness" and "generosity."

_____ There _____

_____

2. Breaking a mirror is considered a bad one. Finding a four-leaf clover is considered a good one.

_____

_____

3. Someone who has been ill or hungry might look this way.

_____

_____

4. Clothes for a dead person, or anything that hides or wraps something.

_____

_____

5. To love, to hold dear, to value highly.

_____

_____

6. Flood waters and thunderstorms will eventually do this.

_____

_____

7. Woodchucks do this from their burrows, and facts do this at a trial.

_____

_____

Write each sentence below. In the space write a form of the word in parentheses.

8. If Ted said that I cheated on the examination, he told a _____ lie. (malice)

_____

_____

_____

9. After she was nearly struck by the truck, Sue made a _____ vow never to cross before the light turns green. (solemnity)

_____

_____

_____

10. After the electricity failed, all the _____ food in the refrigerator spoiled. (perish)

_____

_____

_____

Mastering Meaning

Reread Lincoln's short speech on page 15. This speech was given in 1865, when the Civil War was coming to an end. Write a paragraph explaining how you think Lincoln planned to treat the people of the defeated Confederacy. Use some of the words we studied in this lesson.

Name _____

Some real and fictional people and places are so memorable for their characteristics that their name has come to have new meaning. Sometimes the name has so thoroughly taken on this new meaning that it is no longer capitalized, and few people remember that the word once was a name. All the words in this lesson came from proper nouns, but their current meaning has nothing to do with a name anymore.

Unlocking Meaning

Read the brief descriptions of the people and places below. Then choose the word or phrase that correctly completes the sentence. Write the letter for your choice on the answer line.

Charles C. Boycott was an English land agent in Ireland in the 1800s. When he refused to lower his rents, people decided to have nothing to do with him. Nowadays, if you *boycott* certain countries or businesses, you _____.

1. (A) accept them without reservation
   (B) refuse to deal with them
   (C) praise them openly
   (D) ask for a favor

The Hospital of Saint Mary of Bethlehem was an institution for the mentally ill in London. It was a noisy, confusing place. The name of the hospital was commonly shortened to Bedlam. Now *bedlam* has come to mean _____.

2. (A) medicine
   (B) a noisy, confusing place
   (C) religious devotion
   (D) a suburb of London

According to the Bible, Mary Magdalene was a reformed sinner. Artists often pictured her crying uncontrollably for her sins. From her name we get the word *maudlin,* which means _____.

3. (A) a Biblical scholar
   (B) highly religious
   (C) a fool
   (D) tearful and sentimental

According to Greek mythology, the goddess Nemesis avenged all injustices. Her justice was swift and certain. Today, when people meet their *nemesis,* they encounter _____.

4. (A) a beautiful goddess
   (B) a Greek storyteller
   (C) a foe who cannot be beaten
   (D) a heroic fictional character

Words
bedlam
boycott
herculean
maudlin
maverick
mentor
mesmerize
nemesis
procrustean
quixotic

1. _____

2. _____

3. _____

4. _____

Don Quixote, a character in a novel by Miguel de Cervantes, saw himself as a romantic knight. But he frequently rescued women who did not need rescuing and mistook windmills for evil giants. So when we call someone *quixotic*, we mean he or she is _____.

5. (A) sincere, but foolish

   (B) a modern warrior

   (C) the main character in a story

   (D) a person with poor eyesight

5. _____

Franz Mesmer was an 18th-century doctor who used hypnotic techniques to cause sleep-like reactions in his patients. Before long, the term *mesmerize* came to mean _____.

6. (A) to entertain

   (B) to hold spellbound

   (C) to create imaginary people and places

   (D) to prescribe unusual medicine

6. _____

Samuel Maverick was a rancher, but unlike other ranchers, he never branded his cattle. So naturally, when ranchers saw unbranded cattle roaming the range, they called them "mavericks." Today, a *maverick* is also _____.

7. (A) a person who does not follow the rules

   (B) a gambler

   (C) someone who loses his belongings

   (D) an unfenced area

7. _____

Hercules is a character from Greek mythology who gained immortality by performing twelve tasks requiring remarkable strength. Now, when a task is called *herculean*, it is thought to be _____.

8. (A) fascinating

   (B) immortal

   (C) imported from Greece

   (D) unusually difficult

8. _____

According to a popular Greek story, Procrustes invited people to lie in his bed. If they were too short for the bed, he stretched them to fit the bed. If they were too tall for the bed, he cut off their feet. Now someone who is *procrustean* will _____.

9. (A) ignore differences between individuals

   (B) protect innocent people

   (C) sleep on the floor

   (D) respect someone's personal needs

9. _____

Mentor was a trusted friend of the mythical Greek hero Odysseus. He was also the teacher of Odysseus's son and the manager of the house when Odysseus was gone. If a person is called your *mentor*, he or she is _____.

10. (A) a great hero

    (B) a trusted friend or advisor

    (C) someone who loves children

    (D) an identical twin

10. _____

Applying Meaning

Each question below contains at least one vocabulary word from this lesson. Answer each question "yes" or "no" in the space provided.

1. Would a business welcome a *boycott* by the residents of the neighborhood?

1. _____

2. Would you be likely to find a *mentor* at a school or college?

2. _____

3. When you study for an exam, do you try to *mesmerize* certain facts?

3. _____

4. Does running a marathon after school require a *herculean* effort?

4. _____

5. Would a *maudlin* person shed tears while watching a sad movie?

5. _____

6. Would a *procrustean* individual usually agree with a *maverick*?

6. _____

7. Would you expect to find the library in a state of *bedlam*?

7. _____

8. If someone called your pledge to win an Olympic gold medal a *quixotic* dream, would you be flattered?

8. _____

For each question you answered "no," write a sentence using the vocabulary word(s) correctly.

_____

_____

_____

_____

_____

_____

_____

Write a sentence following the directions below.

9. Describe how a sports fan might look as he watches his favorite sport on television. Use a form of the word *mesmerize*.

_____

_____

_____

10. Describe something that you did that required great effort on your part. Use the word *herculean*.

_____

_____

_____

11. Describe a club with very strict rules for its members. Use the word *procrustean*.

_____

_____

_____

12. Describe the behavior of a real or imaginary person. Use the word *maverick*.

_____

_____

_____

Cultural Literacy Note

Pied Piper

According to an old German legend, the town of Hamelin was beset by a plague of rats. One day a man with a musical pipe and dressed in colorful, or "pied," clothing offered to get rid of the rats if the people of the town would pay for the service. The townspeople agreed, so the pied piper played his pipe and the rats followed him to the river and drowned.

When the piper demanded his payment, however, the townspeople refused to pay his fee. When they ignored his warnings, the pied piper began to play his pipe again. This time the children of the town followed him. The pied piper and all the children disappeared into a mountain and were never seen again. As a result of this popular story, a pied piper is thought to be anyone who entices or leads others, often through deceit or delusion.

Write a Paragraph: Are there modern-day pied pipers of our children and young people? Are certain types of music or television kinds of pied pipers? Choose your candidate for the modern pied piper. Explain your choice in a paragraph.

Lesson 6 Part A

Name _____

The Latin word *docere* means "to teach." This word is the source of many English words and often appears as *-doc-* or *-doct-*. You sometimes see *-gno-* and *-dox-* in English words. They are parts of early Greek words and are combined with other affixes or word parts to form English words. The *-gno-* word part, which may appear as *-gnos-* or *-gni-*, means "know." The *-dox-* word part means "belief" or "opinion." All the words in this lesson contain one of these roots or word parts.

Root	Meaning	English Word
-doc-	to teach	doctrine
-dox-	belief, opinion	orthodox
-gno-	know	diagnose
-gni-		incognito

Unlocking Meaning

A vocabulary word appears in italics in each sentence or short passage below. Find the root or word part in the vocabulary word and think about how the word is used in the passage. Then write a definition for the vocabulary word. Compare your definition with the definition on the flash card.

1. Before she boarded the plane, the undercover police officer put on an elaborate disguise. It was important that she travel *incognito*.

_____
_____
_____

2. The candidate found he could not accept his party's *doctrine* on budgets and taxes, so he resigned his office.

_____
_____
_____

3. Before he could *diagnose* the problem with my car's engine, the mechanic had to check the gas tank and look for oil leaks.

_____
_____
_____

4. It seemed a great *paradox* to us, but the protesters claimed that after they were jailed they finally felt truly free. They saw no contradiction in saying this.

_____
_____
_____

Words

agnostic

cognomen

diagnose

docile

doctrinaire

doctrine

incognito

indoctrinate

orthodox

paradox

5. On the bus to the museum, the students were talkative and hard to control, but once we arrived, they became quite *docile*. They followed the guide's instructions and quietly filed into the lobby.

_____

_____

6. Because one of his soldiers said he stood like a "stone wall" when the Union forces attacked, General Jackson's *cognomen* throughout the Civil War was "Stonewall."

_____

_____

7. All of the religious arguments only confused Jamal more. He was not sure anyone knew for certain whether God existed. In the end, he announced that he would continue to be an *agnostic*.

_____

_____

8. Maggie would listen to no one. Her *doctrinaire* attitude simply would not allow her to ask for help. To her, seeking help was a sign of weakness.

_____

_____

9. My grandfather's beliefs on dating are quite *orthodox*. He says that the girl should never ask the boy for a date, and young people should never go out without an adult chaperon.

_____

_____

10. Some parents feared the television program would *indoctrinate* the children against the values being taught at home and school. After all, the children are too young to know that everything they hear is not necessarily true.

_____

_____

Applying Meaning

Read each sentence or short passage below. Write "correct" on the answer line if the vocabulary word has been used correctly. Write "incorrect" on the answer line if the vocabulary word has been used incorrectly.

1. Renata's *docile* personality caused her to challenge every request the teacher made. In the end, everyone simply ignored her.

   1. _____

2. Modern science often presents us with a *paradox*. Passenger planes can travel faster than the speed of sound, but we still have to wait for our luggage.

   2. _____

3. After weeks of worrying about what was going to happen, Juan decided to consult an *agnostic*.

   3. _____

4. New employees were given a short *indoctrination* to the company. They learned about its history, policies, and goals.

   4. _____

5. His company was founded on the simple but important *doctrine* that the customer must come first.

   5. _____

6. After years of hard work and study, my sister was awarded her *doctrinaire* from Columbia University. She plans to continue her studies in Europe.

   6. _____

7. His approach to art was quite *orthodox*. He studied the traditional masters, attended the accepted schools, and followed the standard examples.

   7. _____

8. The issues were complicated and difficult. Only a *cognomen* of experts could possibly arrive at a solution.

   8. _____

9. When it came to cooking, Avi was completely *incognito*. He hardly knew how to turn on a stove.

   9. _____

10. The doctor insisted on running a number of tests on the patient before attempting to *diagnose* the problem.

    10. _____

For each word used incorrectly, write a sentence using the word properly.

_____

_____

_____

_____

_____

_____

_____

_____

_____

_____

_____

_____

_____

_____

_____

Our Living Language

When a new edition of a dictionary is published, it contains thousands of words that have recently been added to the language. Here are three terms that were recently added to the revised edition of one dictionary.

videophile   **sound bite**   **passive smoking**

Cooperative Learning: With a partner, write a definition for each of these words. Then make a list of three words you think might be added to the dictionary in the next few years, and write a definition of each.

Name _____

How well do you remember the words you studied in Lessons 4 through 6?
Take the following test covering the words from the last three lessons.

Part 1 Complete the Sentence

Decide which definition best completes the sentence. Write the letter for
your choice on the answer line.

1. If you see an *omen*, you _____.   1. _____
   (A) get a sign that something   (B) are watching an evil ritual
      is going to happen
   (C) are bewitched   (D) are reading the last words
                          of a prayer

2. A *malicious* smile suggests a _____ attitude.   2. _____
   (A) charming   (B) tasteful
   (C) mean   (D) casual

3. Someone with a *gaunt* appearance would be _____.   3. _____
   (A) short, but husky   (B) thin and bony
   (C) angry   (D) serious

4. If you meet your *nemesis*, you run into someone you _____.   4. _____
   (A) do not remember   (B) dislike
   (C) cannot defeat   (D) enjoy being with

5. If a group of people *boycott* a meeting, they _____.   5. _____
   (A) refuse to attend   (B) take it over
   (C) disrupt it   (D) exclude women

6. A *maudlin* person might often be seen _____.   6. _____
   (A) sleeping peacefully   (B) looking for a fight
   (C) praying   (D) crying

7. A club with *procrustean* rules for membership would _____.   7. _____
   (A) be very expensive   (B) ignore individual differences
   (C) be popular with the   (D) probably be illegal
      wealthy

8. A *docile* pet would be _____.   8. _____
   (A) kept away from children   (B) easily managed
   (C) hard to control   (D) large and muscular

9. If a famous athlete wants to be *incognito* in public, she   9. _____
   desires _____.
   (A) her identity to be   (B) a great deal of attention
      unknown
   (C) to be ignored   (D) to be warm and friendly to her
                          admirers

Go on to next page. ➤

10. If someone states a *paradox*, he _____.

   (A) says something with two meanings   (B) is probably a mathematician

   (C) is guilty of deceit   (D) is making a contradictory statement that seems true

10. _____

11. When a storm *subsides*, it _____.

   (A) moves rapidly away   (B) breaks into parts

   (C) becomes less active   (D) increases in violence

11. _____

12. A *cherished* memory will _____.

   (A) never be forgotten   (B) be held dear

   (C) be the source of grief   (D) be kept secret

12. _____

13. Your *mentor* would be _____.

   (A) a trusted advisor   (B) an unconquered enemy

   (C) a secret admirer   (D) a rival or competitor

13. _____

14. If you found yourself *mesmerized* by something, you would be _____.

   (A) confused   (B) fascinated

   (C) annoyed   (D) fooled

14. _____

15. An *agnostic* is one who _____.

   (A) devotes himself to serving others   (B) lives a life of strict discipline

   (C) is knowledgeable about agriculture   (D) believes we can never know if God exists

15. _____

Part 2 Matching Words and Meanings

Match the definition in Column B with the word in Column A.
Write the letter of the correct definition on the line provided.

Column A	Column B	
16. charity	a. wrapping for a dead person or anything that conceals	**16.** _____
17. perish	b. requiring great strength	**17.** _____
18. bedlam	c. to die or be destroyed	**18.** _____
19. diagnose	d. an independent thinker; nonconformist	**19.** _____
20. indoctrinate	e. noisy confusion	**20.** _____
21. quixotic	f. staying faithful to established beliefs	**21.** _____
22. maverick	g. kindness and love in judging others	**22.** _____
23. shroud	h. idealistic but foolish	**23.** _____
24. orthodox	i. to identify a disease or a condition	**24.** _____
25. herculean	j. to teach a certain set of principles	**25.** _____

Earthquake

The shaking came at dawn, a sudden force they could not escape. The young mother held her children close, trying to protect them. The father covered both his wife and his children with his body, hoping to save them from falling limestone blocks. Their efforts were not enough. Even though
5 the **duration** of the earthquake was short, probably no more than a few minutes, the powerful forces were too much for the walls of their stone house. The family died, huddled together inside. Along with hundreds of others that day, they were victims of an **immense** earthquake that struck southwest Cyprus in the year a.d. 365.

10 For thousands, perhaps millions of years, earthquakes have shaken our planet, causing the fearful destruction and **desolation** that the residents of Cyprus experienced on that fateful day. What conditions produce these powerful events? Can we predict where or when they will occur?

To understand something about earthquakes, you need to understand the
15 **structure** of our planet. The earth's crust is actually broken into huge plates. The continents ride on these plates, which **creep** over the earth's molten core. In some areas the edges of the plates **converge** and grind together, creating one type of earthquake. In other areas one plate may slip beneath another in a process called subduction. In some cases the
20 plates **diverge,** stretching and thinning the crust. This allows molten rock in the earth's core to rise. As this upwelling of extremely hot molten rock occurs, volcanos are created. Some long cracks, or faults, in the earth's surface are visible evidence of where two plates meet. If the plates are moving in different directions, earthquakes will persist in the **vicinity.**

25 Many severe earthquakes have occurred during recorded history, but it was not until the great San Francisco earthquake of 1906 that scientists began to study them. In trying to guess how the earth had moved, scientists built **theoretical** models to show the forces that had been involved. The studies showed that horizontal movement along the San
30 Andreas Fault had caused the Pacific and North American plates to mesh so tightly that no movement had occurred at the fault. Instead the strain along the edge of the Pacific plate had created an S-shaped warp. As the pressure increased, the strain grew, finally **culminating** in the edge of one plate snapping. This caused the two plates to grind along
35 each other, creating a strong vibration that traveled through the earth.

Earthquakes have taught us that the earth is constantly in motion. By using the data collected over hundreds of years, geologists can measure the power of the vibrations and, with the help of computers, map areas of hazardous regions. Although predictions are still very inexact,
40 earthquakes are finally yielding to scientific investigation.

Words
converge
creep
culminate
desolate
diverge
duration
immense
structure
theoretical
vicinity

Each word in this lesson's word list appears in dark type in the selection you just read. Think about how the vocabulary word is used in the selection, then write the letter for the best answer to each question.

1. Which word or words could best replace *duration* in line 5?   1. _____
   (A) length of time   (B) communication
   (C) strength   (D) decline

2. Which word could best replace *immense* in line 9?   2. _____
   (A) enormous   (B) tiny
   (C) moderate   (D) historic

3. Which word could best replace *desolation* in line 11?   3. _____
   (A) crime   (B) plague
   (C) devastation (D) domination

4. Which word could best replace *structure* in line 15?   4. _____
   (A) makeup   (B) warps
   (C) history   (D) substance

5. Which word or words could best replace *creep* in line 16?   5. _____
   (A) move slowly   (B) slip
   (C) linger   (D) rise

6. Which word or words could best replace *converge* in line 17?   6. _____
   (A) confine   (B) separate
   (C) come together (D) convert

7. Which word could best replace *diverge* in line 20?   7. _____
   (A) devise   (B) separate
   (C) travel   (D) revolve

8. Which word could best replace *vicinity* in line 24?   8. _____
   (A) circle   (B) area
   (C) distance   (D) land

9. Which word could best replace *theoretical* in line 28?   9. _____
   (A) pointless   (B) reliable
   (C) actual   (D) imaginary

10. Which word could best replace *culminating* in line 33?   10. _____
    (A) declining   (B) climaxing
    (C) sinking   (D) starting

Applying Meaning

Follow the directions below to write a sentence using a vocabulary word.

1. Describe a series of events in a sport or similar activity. Use any form of the word *culminate*.

   _____

   _____

2. Describe some geographical feature in your city or town or something you saw on a trip or read about. Use the word *immense*.

   _____

   _____

3. Write a sentence telling about a topic you studied in one of your classes. Use any form of the word *structure*.

   _____

   _____

4. Describe a scene from a movie, book, or an event you have seen. Use any form of the word *desolate*.

   _____

   _____

5. Describe the movement of a person, animal, or object using any form of the word *creep*.

   _____

   _____

Read each sentence below. Write "correct" on the answer line if the vocabulary word has been used correctly. Write "incorrect" on the answer line if the vocabulary word has been used incorrectly.

6. The gym was closed for the *duration* of the year because of water damage.   6. _____

7. Allen asked us to *converge* his regrets to our hostess that he would not be able to attend the party.   7. _____

8. Rob and I had *diverging* opinions about how to raise money for the project.   8. _____

9. The Sasaki family was disappointed to find that there was no *vicinity* at the popular resort.   9. _____

10. One hundred years ago, traveling to the moon in a spaceship was only a *theoretical* possibility.

10. _____

11. As she watched the children gather a dandelion bouquet, a soft smile *crept* across her face.

11. _____

12. The Lopez family *culminates* cabbage and tomatoes in its garden.

12. _____

13. For the science fair, the class built a model showing the *structure* of the atom.

13. _____

14. The cake was so *desolate* that we all decided to have a second piece.

14. _____

For each word used incorrectly, write a sentence using the word properly.

_____

_____

_____

_____

_____

_____

_____

_____

_____

_____

Mastering Meaning

Imagine that you are a newspaper reporter in the year 365 A.D. Your assignment is to write a story about the earthquake that recently occurred on the island of Cyprus. Write two paragraphs describing the damage and casualties. Use some of the words you studied in this lesson.

Name _____

The English language has the marvelous ability to borrow words freely from other languages. If no word exists in English for a thought or concept, we simply take a word from another language. After a time the pronunciation of the borrowed word may change to match English pronunciations, but sometimes we even keep the foreign pronunciation. The words in this lesson are all taken from the French language because no English word expresses the idea as well.

Unlocking Meaning

Read the sentences or short passages below. Write the letter for the correct definition of the italicized vocabulary word.

It is very difficult to become a member of the Greenfield Golf Club, but since my older brother is a member, he was my *entrée* to membership.

1. (A) legal advisor
    (B) the means to enter
    (C) obstacle
    (D) admission fee

We were very excited when the plane took off. I pressed my nose to the window and watched the city disappear below. The flight attendants, however, were quite *blasé* about it all. I wondered if they even knew we had taken off.

2. (A) exhilarated and talkative
    (B) worn out from prolonged or difficult work
    (C) distressed and frightened
    (D) bored and uninterested

The craft fair turned out to be a *potpourri* of exhibits. There were holiday ornaments made from cotton balls, cutting boards in the shapes of farm animals, and even a stained-glass wind chime.

3. (A) odd or random collection of things
    (B) elaborate and expensive artwork
    (C) items made from pottery
    (D) old and outdated items

Why must things be as quiet as a mouse or as sly as a fox? Why couldn't they be as quiet as a cemetery or as sly as a riverboat gambler? Why use a *cliché* when a fresh expression will work?

4. (A) animal
    (B) overused expression
    (C) clever figure of speech
    (D) literary classic

Words
blasé
cliché
clientele
entrée
entrepreneur
gauche
naive
nonchalant
potpourri
rendezvous

1. _____

2. _____

3. _____

4. _____

We were free to explore the museums, parks, and stores all afternoon, but it was important that we *rendezvous* in the parking lot at six o'clock to board the bus home.

5. (A) avoid danger
   (B) render or give a report
   (C) meet
   (D) ask for directions

5. _____

Since it was my first trip to New York, I was quite *naive*. I stared up at the tall buildings, failed to tip the waiters, and got lost on the subways.

6. (A) clever and resourceful
   (B) angry
   (C) excessively curious or nosy
   (D) simple or inexperienced

6. _____

The spectators in the gymnasium were applauding and cheering wildly, but the captain of the basketball team acted quite *nonchalant* as he yawned and accepted the trophy.

7. (A) cool and unconcerned
   (B) confused and uncertain
   (C) shy and modest
   (D) embarrassed

7. _____

For months after the restaurant opened the owner lost money, but after a while he built up a *clientele* and his business began to show a good profit.

8. (A) group of regular customers or clients
   (B) debt
   (C) staff of clerks and assistants
   (D) communications system

8. _____

Not only did many people arrive late for the piano concert, they whispered and giggled throughout the performance. Such *gauche* behavior is inexcusable.

9. (A) humorous
   (B) gloomy
   (C) crude and awkward
   (D) informal and friendly

9. _____

After years of working in the factory, Joe Franklin decided to become an *entrepreneur*. So he quit his job, bought a truck, and painted "Joe's Moving Service" on its side.

10. (A) laborer
   (B) one who organizes or runs a business
   (C) foolish or irresponsible person
   (D) one who is unable to make up his mind

10. _____

Applying Meaning

Each question below contains at least one vocabulary word from this lesson. Answer each question "yes" or "no" in the space provided.

1. Would you want a firefighter to be *nonchalant* when coming to your rescue in a burning building?

2. Is it possible to have a quiet *rendezvous* in a restaurant or library?

3. Are *clichés* hard to remember?

4. Does a successful *entrepreneur* usually have a faithful *clientele*?

5. Are people usually *blasé* when taking their first ride on a roller coaster?

6. Could good grades in high school be your *entrée* to college?

1. _____

2. _____

3. _____

4. _____

5. _____

6. _____

For each question you answered "no," write a sentence using the vocabulary word correctly.

_____

_____

_____

_____

_____

_____

_____

_____

_____

_____

_____

_____

_____

_____

_____

Match the description or definition in Column B with the word in
Column A. Write the letter of the correct answer on the answer line.

Column A	Column B	
7. entrepreneur	a. a person who starts a business	7. _____
8. gauche	b. hodgepodge	8. _____
9. naive	c. a child who writes a letter to Santa Claus	9. _____
10. potpourri	d. someone who eats with his fingers at a fancy restaurant	10. _____

Bonus Words

C'est la vie   fait accompli

The French expression *C'est la vie* means "That's life." Its equivalent in English would be something like "What can you do?" It is an expression often used when things go wrong, but you feel powerless to do anything about it.

The French *fait accompli* translates as "accomplished fact." If you sneak into the kitchen and eat the last dessert, there is no point arguing about who should have it because there is little anyone can do about it. It is a fait accompli.

Write a Personal Narrative: Have you ever presented someone with a fait accompli or felt like saying "C'est la vie"? Write a short personal narrative describing something that happened to you or to someone you know that illustrates one of these expressions. Use the expression somewhere in your narrative, and try to use one or more of the vocabulary words as well.

Name _____

In Latin the word *cor* means "heart." This root can be found in a wide variety of English words because the heart is associated with both our physical bodies and our feelings and emotions. It sometimes appears as *-card-* or *-cord-*. The Latin word *currere* means "to run." It, too, appears in a wide range of words because *run* can have so many meanings. It may be spelled *-cur-*, *-cor-*, or *-cour-* in English words.

Root	Meaning	English Word
-cor-	heart	cordial
-card-		cardiac
-cur-	run	incursion
-cour-		recourse

Unlocking Meaning

A vocabulary word appears in italics in each sentence or short passage below. Find the root in each vocabulary word and choose the letter for the correct definition. Write the letter for your choice on the answer line.

1. The manager was very busy, so my application got only a *cursory* look. But the manager promised to study it carefully later.
   (A) thorough   (B) silent
   (C) quick   (D) humorous

2. After long hours of argument and debate over the issues, union and management representatives reached an *accord*. We can expect the strike to end soon.
   (A) destination   (B) impossible obstacle
   (C) victory   (D) harmonious agreement

3. The police officer tried to get the protestors to stop interfering with traffic, but they refused. In the end the only *recourse* was to arrest them.
   (A) source of help or aid   (B) foolish desire
   (C) college training   (D) thought or idea

4. The proposal to build a toxic waste dump was a source of *discord* in the community. Some citizens wanted the jobs that would be created. Others feared that the dump would affect their health.
   (A) affection   (B) rope
   (C) angry disagreement   (D) economic activity

1. _____

2. _____

3. _____

4. _____

5. The dark clouds and high winds were *precursors* of the coming tornado.

   5. _____

   (A) forerunners (B) proof

   (C) cause for swearing (D) enemies

6. The class was being taught to use a *cursive* style of writing instead of printing each letter.

   6. _____

   (A) foreign (B) clever

   (C) impossible (D) having letters run together

7. It is easy to take notes on Ms. Eisner's lectures because her presentation is always very focused and direct. Mr. Todd's lectures, on the other hand, are quite *discursive*. I never know what he will say next.

   7. _____

   (A) disgusting (B) discouraging

   (C) wide-ranging; rambling (D) ordinary

8. Because of Olga's history of *cardiac* problems, the doctor advised her not to overexercise.

   8. _____

   (A) related to the heart (B) financial

   (C) digestive (D) family

9. Josh missed his old neighborhood. Ever since his family moved, he had *recurrent* dreams about the school and the friends he left behind.

   9. _____

   (A) frightening (B) happening repeatedly

   (C) water-related (D) distracting

10. Since we had been such good friends for many years, I was not surprised by her *cordial* welcome.

   10. _____

   (A) hostile (B) insincere

   (C) awkward (D) warm and friendly

Applying Meaning

Read each sentence or short passage below. Write "correct" on the answer line if the vocabulary word has been used correctly. Write "incorrect" on the answer line if the vocabulary word has been used incorrectly.

1. The school offered an American history *recourse* for any student who had failed the previous semester.

   1. _____

2. The master of ceremonies gave a *cursory* introduction; she knew everyone was eager to hear the main speaker.

   2. _____

3. For weeks after the book disappeared, June had one *recurrent* thought: Where could I have put it?

   3. _____

4. His performance in the championship game earned him the *accord* of the spectators and the players.

   4. _____

5. The argument ruined the dinner completely. Everyone left feeling quite *discursive* with the entire evening.

   5. _____

6. The development of the microchip was the *precursor* of a revolution in computer technology.

   6. _____

7. According to this report, *cardiac* patients at City Point Hospital get excellent care.

   7. _____

8. When Andre became angry, his language turned vulgar and *cursive*.

   8. _____

9. The heat had spoiled the fruits and vegetables, so we had to *discord* them.

   9. _____

10. They offered us a cold drink and a comfortable place to sit. We had not expected such a *cordial* welcome from the team we had just defeated.

    10. _____

For each word used incorrectly, write a sentence using the word properly.

_____

_____

_____

_____

_____

_____

_____

_____

_____

_____

_____

_____

_____

Test-Taking Strategies

Some colleges require entering students to take a test of standard English grammar and usage. This test is often used to place students in a freshman English course.

These tests usually ask you to look at four underlined parts of a sentence and decide if one of these parts contains an error. You then write the letter for the underlined part that contains the error. If there is no error, you write E.

Sample

S.	Everybody on the basketball team must take care of their own	S.	D
	A B C D		
	uniform. No Error		
	E		

Always read the entire sentence before deciding on your answer. Look at each choice carefully. If you think you have found the error, ask yourself how you would correct it. There will be no more than one error. Can you tell why D is the correct answer to the sample question?

Practice: Write the letter for the underlined part of the sentence with an error. If there is no error, write E.

1. The teacher's assistant has given the assignment to Frank, Julie,
          A   B   C
   and myself. No Error
       D   E

   1. _____

2. Sam and I love to go to the mall, to look for sea shells, and
   A   B   C
   playing our favorite CDs. No Error
   D   E

   2. _____

3. If you go to the meeting, please give the message to Anne and her.
      A   B   C   D
   No Error
   E

   3. _____

Name _____

How well do you remember the words you studied in Lessons 7 through 9? Take the following test covering the words from the last three lessons.

Part 1 Antonyms

Each question below includes a word in capital letters, followed by four words or phrases. Choose the word or phrase that is most nearly <u>opposite</u> in meaning to the word in capital letters. Consider all choices before deciding on your answer. Write the letter for your answer on the line provided.

Sample

S. GOOD	(A) simple	(B) bad	S. ___**B**___
	(C) able	(D) fast	

1. IMMENSE	(A) great	(B) unimportant	1. _____
	(C) angry	(D) tiny	

2. CURSORY	(A) leisurely	(B) thorough	2. _____
	(C) manual	(D) blessed	

3. NONCHALANT	(A) casual	(B) chalant	3. _____
	(C) concerned	(D) brave	

4. CONVERGE	(A) separate	(B) convert	4. _____
	(C) resist	(D) reverse	

5. THEORETICAL	(A) religious	(B) practical	5. _____
	(C) frequent	(D) immoral	

6. DISCORD	(A) agreement	(B) argument	6. _____
	(C) musical	(D) sensible	

7. CLICHÉ	(A) slander	(B) unique remark	7. _____
	(C) proverb	(D) wisdom	

8. CORDIAL	(A) friendly	(B) dazed	8. _____
	(C) hostile	(D) remarkable	

9. NAIVE	(A) intelligent	(B) nice	9. _____
	(C) simple	(D) experienced	

10. GAUCHE	(A) refined	(B) clumsy	10. _____
	(C) unusual	(D) familiar	

Go on to next page. ➤

11. DESOLATE   (A) solid   (B) prosperous   11. _____

                      (C) foreign   (D) convenient

12. CULMINATE   (A) initiate   (B) destroy   12. _____

                      (C) reward   (D) elevate

13. BLASÉ   (A) extinguished   (B) difficult   13. _____

                (C) injured   (D) excited

14. POTPOURRI   (A) hodgepodge   (B) orderly   14. _____

                                    arrangement

                (C) sober   (D) elaborate

15. DISCURSIVE   (A) direct   (B) repulsive   15. _____

                      (C) appealing   (D) handwritten

Part 2 Matching Words and Meanings

Match the definition in Column B with the word in Column A.
Write the letter of the correct definition on the line provided.

Column A	Column B	
16. vicinity	a. pertaining to the heart	16. _____
17. diverge	b. area or region	17. _____
18. entrepreneur	c. to meet at a certain time and place	18. _____
19. recurrent	d. one's group of customers	19. _____
20. rendezvous	e. to move in different directions	20. _____
21. cardiac	f. occurring again	21. _____
22. duration	g. method of entry	22. _____
23. precursor	h. length of time	23. _____
24. entrée	i. one who runs a business	24. _____
25. clientele	j. forerunner	25. _____

Lesson
10
Part A

Name _____

"Laissez les bons temps rouler!" (*"Let the good times roll!"*)

It's difficult to resist tapping toes, let alone dancing feet, when the hard-driving rhythms and **robust** tones of Cajun music throb and pound. **Indigenous** to the Louisiana bayous where it developed, this unique sound was nourished by the New World. Like jazz, rock, and the blues,
5 Cajun music is a unique **synthesis** of cultural elements. Its lyrics come from French folklore, while its wailing singing style can be traced to the chants of Native Americans. Spanish explorers contributed the guitar, German immigrants supplied the accordion, and African Americans reshaped the fiddle dance tunes with percussion techniques. Lively
10 and infectious, Cajun music **traverses** cultural, generational, and language barriers.

To the Cajuns, however, music is much more than entertainment; it is a link with their treasured but tragic history. The word *Cajun* is an alteration of the word *Acadian,* which refers to the seventeenth-century
15 French colonists who settled in Nova Scotia. Although the Acadians declared neutrality in the rivalry between France and England for **dominion** of North America, the British demanded loyalty when they claimed the area in 1715. In a mass deportation executed with cold **ruthlessness,** British soldiers collected thousands of French Canadians,
20 packed them into boats, and shipped them to widely dispersed areas.

Many of the exiled Acadians settled in remote southwestern Louisiana, where their isolation allowed them to evolve into a distinct, tight-knit ethnic group. When the oil development and road-building programs of World War I brought modern America rushing in, however, the Cajun
25 parishes could no longer resist **acculturation.** In the headlong attempt to become part of the larger society, the language and music were discouraged, **quelled,** and all but forgotten.

In the mid-1970s, many Americans became interested in searching for their roots. As part of this heritage movement, Cajun music was rescued
30 and **validated** as an important folk-music tradition. Today, it is one of the fastest growing regional sounds in the United States. In addition to being played in live concerts, in clubs, and on the radio, Cajun songs appear in movie scores, in the introductions for television situation comedies, and in commercials.

35 Having survived centuries of adversity, isolation, and persecution, the music tells **plaintive** stories about loneliness and lost love. Yet there is nothing depressing about this music. Set against what the Cajuns call a "chanky-chank" beat, the songs urge everyone to sing, dance, laugh, and "let the good times roll."

Words
acculturate
dominion
indigenous
plaintive
quell
robust
ruthless
synthesis
traverse
validate

Unlocking Meaning

Each word in this lesson's word list appears in dark type in the selection you just read. Think about how the vocabulary word is used in the selection, then write the letter for the best answer to each question.

1. Which word could best replace *robust* in line 2?
   (A) confusing   (B) strong
   (C) quiet   (D) childish

   1. _____

2. Which word could best replace *indigenous* in line 3?
   (A) native   (B) baffling
   (C) forgiving   (D) unknown

   2. _____

3. A *synthesis* (line 5) can best be described as a(n) _____.
   (A) denial   (B) lesson
   (C) opinion   (D) combination

   3. _____

4. Which word or words could best replace *traverses* in line 10?
   (A) passes across   (B) signals
   (C) imposes   (D) slows down

   4. _____

5. Which word could best replace *dominion* in line 17?
   (A) exploration   (B) unification
   (C) control   (D) delegation

   5. _____

6. *Ruthlessness* (line 19) can best be described as _____.
   (A) simplicity   (B) cruelty
   (C) sacrifice   (D) courage

   6. _____

7. *Acculturation* (line 25) is a process that involves _____.
   (A) monetary gain   (B) deportation
   (C) government influence (D) adaptation

   7. _____

8. Which word could best replace *quelled* in line 27?
   (A) resisted   (B) honored
   (C) suppressed   (D) tolerated

   8. _____

9. Which word or words could best replace *validated* in line 30?
   (A) confirmed   (B) exported
   (C) reacted to   (D) sickened

   9. _____

10. *Plaintive* (line 36) stories are _____.
    (A) joyous   (B) mournful
    (C) repetitious   (D) unrelated

    10. _____

Applying Meaning

Decide which word in parentheses best completes the sentence.
Then write the sentence, adding the missing word.

1. To report on the conclusions reached by the group, the leader _____
    the opinions and ideas of all the members. (quelled; synthesized)

    _____

    _____

2. In order to prove or disprove hypotheses, scientists must _____ their
    test results. (acculturate; validate)

    _____

    _____

3. Hannibal is credited even today with one of the greatest troop move-
    ments in history because he led an army of 100,000 in _____ the Alps.
    (traversing; validating)

    _____

    _____

4. Sociologists, interested in the way groups or societies come together and
    influence one another, study how they _____. (acculturate; traverse)

    _____

    _____

5. Tantalus, a king in classical mythology, was punished _____ by the
    gods for offending them; every time he reached for a fruit-laden
    branch of the tree that was just above his head, the wind blew it out
    of his reach. (plaintively; ruthlessly)

    _____

    _____

Read each sentence or short passage below. Write "correct" on the answer
line if the vocabulary word has been used correctly. Write "incorrect" on
the answer line if the vocabulary word has been used incorrectly.

6. Homeless people in major cities are *indigenous*. They cannot afford
    to rent or buy homes.

    6. _____

7. Even when perfectly content, the Siamese cat makes a *plaintive* cry
    that gives the impression that it is lonely and miserable.

    7. _____

8. With the exception of a six-year period when it was under the *domin-ion* of Italy, Ethiopia has withstood European attempts at colonization.

8. _____

9. The *robust* tree had a reed-thin trunk that looked as if a light breeze would topple it.

9. _____

10. The owners of the factory *quelled* the effects of the strike by bringing in scabs, or strikebreakers, to maintain production.

10. _____

For each word used incorrectly, write a sentence using the word properly.

_____

_____

_____

_____

_____

_____

_____

_____

_____

_____

_____

_____

Mastering Meaning

Suppose that you are the music critic for your school newspaper. A new Cajun group has just released an album that you want to review. Use your imagination to create a name for the group and for some of its songs. Then write a music review that will introduce your readers to Cajun music and will let them know what they can expect to hear on this album. In your review, use some of the words we studied in this lesson.

Name _____

The process by which people govern themselves is both complex and curious. On the one hand it involves deep philosophical thought; on the other it is as practical as a campaign poster. Our language has spawned numerous words to describe this process and the personalities and philosophies involved in this arena of human experience. In this lesson you will learn ten words that stand for concepts of law and government.

Unlocking Meaning

Words
autonomy
bureaucracy
codify
despot
imperious
reactionary
sedition
sovereign
totalitarian
usurp

Read the sentences or short passages below. Write the letter for the correct definition of the italicized vocabulary word.

It was their fear of *sedition* that prompted the authorities to ban all opposition newspapers and radio stations. In addition, all suspected agitators were confined to jail indefinitely.

1. (A) unfair elections
    (B) conduct likely to incite rebellion
    (C) popular support
    (D) gossip and rumors

The once popular ruler began to ignore the well-being of the citizens, and since no one questioned his authority, he gradually turned into a *despot*.

2. (A) a fair and effective ruler
    (B) democratically elected officeholder
    (C) military officer
    (D) a tyrant with absolute authority

The residents of the island expelled the foreign ministers and proclaimed their *autonomy*. Never again would they bow to another country's flag.

3. (A) freedom and independence
    (B) desire for peace
    (C) dependence on the protection of another nation
    (D) connection with a political party

The president complained that the proposed law would *usurp* his authority as commander-in-chief of the military. The constitution clearly stated that only the president could order an attack.

4. (A) enlarge
    (B) illegally take away
    (C) confuse
    (D) drain or exhaust

1. _____

2. _____

3. _____

4. _____

The government plan to offer tuition assistance to deserving students in poor neighborhoods made sense. But by the time applications worked their way through the *bureaucracy*, many deserving students got tired of waiting and dropped out of the program.

5. (A) local elected officials
   (B) democratic process
   (C) inefficient system of offices and rules
   (D) postal system

5. _____

The proposed reforms in the welfare and health care system had little chance of passing. The expected *reactionary* attitudes began to surface among those quite happy with the way things were.

6. (A) opposed to change
   (B) soft-spoken
   (C) humorous
   (D) medical

6. _____

The candidate's *imperious* manner may have lost him the election. In a democracy, people have a right to expect elected officials to be their servants, and not the other way around.

7. (A) humble and soft spoken
   (B) arrogant and dictatorial
   (C) hard and resistant
   (D) appealing

7. _____

After decades of passing numerous laws and regulations, it was essential that the government attempt to *codify* its work. It had reached the point where judges had difficulty understanding what the law required.

8. (A) translate
   (B) repeal
   (C) arrange and systematize
   (D) legalize

8. _____

Before the United States could come into being, the individual states had to surrender some of their *sovereign* rights.

9. (A) having authority to govern
   (B) financial
   (C) unconstitutional
   (D) illegal

9. _____

After overthrowing the elected officials, the military commander installed a *totalitarian* government. From that time on, even the simplest action required his approval.

10. (A) reformed and improved
    (B) efficient and orderly
    (C) emphasizing personal concern for its citizens
    (D) exercising absolute control

10. _____

Applying Meaning

Decide which word in parentheses best completes the sentence. Then write the sentence, adding the missing word.

1. After the prime minister dissolved parliament, packed the court with his appointees, and cancelled elections, the United States declared it could no longer recognize such a _____ form of government. (bureaucratic; totalitarian)

   _____

   _____

2. By giving the president the right to revise the bill, the senators had allowed their authority to be _____. (codified; usurped)

   _____

   _____

3. The South refused to accept the authority of federal authorities, insisting that _____ lay with the individual states. (bureaucracy; sovereignty)

   _____

   _____

4. Her _____ attitude was predictable. She voted against every bill that would have reformed the election laws. (bureaucratic; reactionary)

   _____

   _____

5. The president declared he would not tolerate acts of terrorism, assassination, or any other _____ acts against the government. (despotic; seditious)

   _____

   _____

Each question below contains a vocabulary word from this lesson. Answer each question "yes" or "no" in the space provided.

6. Was the Revolutionary War fought to make the colonies *autonomous*? 6. _____

7. When the military authorities take over the government, would you expect them to *codify* the former officials? 7. _____

8. Would a despot be found in a *totalitarian* country? 8. _____

9. Should a candidate demonstrate an *imperious* attitude when campaigning for votes?

9. _____

10. Does a ruler welcome the opportunity to have his authority *usurped*?

10. _____

For each question you answered "no," write a sentence using the vocabulary word correctly.

_____

_____

_____

_____

_____

_____

_____

_____

_____

_____

_____

_____

Bonus Word

gerrymander

In 1812, Governor Gerry of Massachusetts and his political allies had the district lines redrawn in ways that gave his party an unfair advantage in future elections. One such district was shaped like a salamander, a long lizard-like animal. It was not long before the newspapers began referring to the senators elected from such districts as gerrymanders, a combination of *salamander* and *Gerry*, the governor whose party was responsible for these strangely shaped districts. In addition, the political strategy of drawing political districts so as to give one party an unfair advantage has been called gerrymandering ever since.

Write a Position Paper: Today, district lines are sometimes drawn to ensure that a minority group will be represented. Write a brief position paper outlining how you feel about such a practice. Use some vocabulary words you have studied.

Name _____

The Latin word *manus* means "hand." Elements of this Latin word appear in many modern English words. For example, work done with the hands is called manual labor. The Latin word *ped,* on the other hand, means foot. A pedestrian is someone traveling on foot. The Greek language had a slightly different word, *pod,* for foot, so it is not unusual to see this root in English words, especially scientific words. It is not always easy to see the "hands" and "feet" meanings in modern English words. For example, the hand is associated with giving, so in a word like *countermand,* the -man- root refers to giving an order.

Root	Meaning	English Word
-man-	hand	manipulate
-ped-	foot	expedite
-pod-		podium

Words

countermand

expedite

impediment

mandate

mandatory

manipulate

pedestal

pedigree

podiatrist

podium

Unlocking Meaning

A vocabulary word appears in italics in each sentence or short passage below. Find the root in each vocabulary word and choose the letter for the correct definition. Write the letter for your answer on the line provided.

1. Lying across the bicycle path, the tree was an *impediment*. We had no choice but to walk around it.
   (A) embarrassment   (B) obstacle
   (C) curiosity   (D) reminder

2. Our mayor has a fascinating *pedigree*. Her grandfather was the first state senator, and her great-grandfather was one of the state's earliest settlers.
   (A) list of ancestors   (B) imagination
   (C) type of political party (D) secret

   1. _____

3. In addition to studying the human anatomy, a surgeon must learn to *manipulate* complicated instruments and machines.
   (A) repair   (B) control with the hands
   (C) explain in detail   (D) move or position

   2. _____

4. The lieutenant's decision to attack meant certain disaster. Fortunately, the captain was able to *countermand* the order and save the regiment.
   (A) understand   (B) analyze and compare
   (C) reverse   (D) write out

   3. _____

   4. _____

5. In order to *expedite* the shipment, the mechanic phoned in the order and asked the supplier to send the parts on the next plane.

5. _____

    (A) check carefully   (B) cancel

    (C) delay   (D) speed up

6. The lecturer stepped to the *podium*, looked straight at the audience, and slowly began to read from his notes.

6. _____

    (A) stand for holding notes   (B) type of speaker

    (C) curtain   (D) someone who introduces a speaker

7. Before anyone can purchase a handgun, there is a *mandatory* five-day waiting period while a background check of the purchaser is conducted.

7. _____

    (A) for men only   (B) required

    (C) prolonged   (D) illegal

8. After the basketball star began seeing the *podiatrist* regularly, the pain began to disappear and his game improved considerably.

8. _____

    (A) foot doctor   (B) type of physical therapist

    (C) fortune teller   (D) sports psychologist

9. The candidate's huge victory in the election was interpreted as a *mandate* for all the new programs she proposed during the campaign.

9. _____

    (A) rejection   (B) symbol

    (C) fascination   (D) authorization

10. The statue was lowered carefully onto the *pedestal*. From this prominent new position, it would now be the main attraction of the museum.

10. _____

    (A) foundation   (B) balcony

    (C) outdoor arena   (D) pedestrian walkway

Applying Meaning

Decide which word in parentheses best completes the sentence. Then write
the sentence, adding the missing word.

1. The project was seriously behind schedule, so the manager hired a
   construction specialist to recommend ways to _____ the work.
   (expedite; impede)

   _____

   _____

   _____

2. Due to a clerical error, the package was dispatched to the wrong location. Before anyone could _____ the order, the contents had
   spoiled. (countermand; mandate)

   _____

   _____

   _____

3. Because the coach was on the league committee, he was able to
   _____ the schedule so his team played only the weaker
   teams. (mandate; manipulate)

   _____

   _____

   _____

4. The Heritage Women's Club was so exclusive, anyone wishing to join
   had to trace her _____ back to the Revolutionary War.
   (pedestal; pedigree)

   _____

   _____

5. The blisters became so infected and painful that I finally had to
   consult a _____. (podiatrist; podium)

   _____

   _____

Read each sentence or short passage below. Write "correct" on the answer line if the vocabulary word has been used correctly. Write "incorrect" on the answer line if the vocabulary word has been used incorrectly.

6. The chemist carefully measured the *podium* before placing it in the solution. Even a slight miscalculation would ruin the experiment.

6. _____

7. In order to be considered for the job, all applicants had to pass a *mandatory* drug test.

7. _____

8. Hawaii's crops include pineapple, avocados, and *mandates*.

8. _____

9. The hikers soon realized they should not have packed so much canned food. The extra weight was a serious *impediment* to their progress.

9. _____

10. The shipment of shoes was stored in a *pedestal* inside the warehouse until the store could be remodeled.

10. _____

For each word used incorrectly, write a sentence using the word properly.

_____

_____

_____

_____

_____

_____

_____

_____

Our Living Language

pedigree

In medieval times, wealth and power often depended on one's ancestry. Great care was taken in charting the family tree. These charts used lines resembling the footprint of a crane, a long-legged bird. In French, these were called *pied de grue*, meaning "foot of a crane." The term came to refer to the chart itself. It entered the English language around 1500 and eventually became *pedigree*, meaning ancestry or the chart of one's family tree.

Use an Unabridged Dictionary: Find the history of these words:

peddle   manacle   maneuver   manuscript

Name _____

How well do you remember the words you studied in Lessons 10 through 12? Take the following test covering the words from the last three lessons.

Part 1 *Choose the Correct Meaning*

Each question below includes a word in capital letters, followed by four words or phrases. Choose the word or phrase that is <u>closest</u> in meaning to the word in capital letters. Write the letter for your answer on the line provided.

Sample

S. FINISH	(A) enjoy	(B) complete	**S.** ___**B**___
	(C) destroy	(D) enlarge	

1. INDIGENOUS	(A) native	(B) careful	**1.** _____
	(C) poor	(D) industrious	
2. SYNTHESIS	(A) illegal act	(B) combination	**2.** _____
	(C) artificial	(D) systematic	
3. DESPOT	(A) railroad station	(B) outlaw	**3.** _____
	(C) tyrant	(D) regulation	
4. MANDATE	(A) authorization	(B) amendment	**4.** _____
	(C) tropical fruit	(D) historic event	
5. USURP	(A) seize illegally	(B) inhale deeply	**5.** _____
	(C) attack	(D) consume	
6. IMPEDIMENT	(A) importance	(B) type of vehicle	**6.** _____
	(C) foundation	(D) obstacle	
7. AUTONOMY	(A) automatic	(B) independence	**7.** _____
	(C) royal decree	(D) dictatorship	
8. RUTHLESS	(A) ancient	(B) benevolent	**8.** _____
	(C) cruel	(D) plain and simple	
9. QUELL	(A) to quiet	(B) writing instrument	**9.** _____
	(C) to overthrow	(D) to confuse	
10. VALIDATE	(A) to value	(B) to prove correct	**10.** _____
	(C) to elect to office	(D) to assist	
11. SEDITION	(A) withdrawal	(B) drugged state	**11.** _____
	(C) negotiation	(D) rebellious behavior	
12. REACTIONARY	(A) very conservative	(B) counterattack	**12.** _____
	(C) progressive	(D) old-fashioned	

Go on to next page. ➤

13. PODIATRIST   (A) architect   (B) foot doctor   13. _____
                 (C) gloomy person   (D) fortune teller

14. ROBUST   (A) sensible   (B) weak   14. _____
                 (C) punctured   (D) vigorous

15. COUNTERMAND   (A) cancel   (B) government clerk   15. _____
                 (C) conceal   (D) official document

Part 2 Complete the Sentence

Decide which definition best completes the sentence. Write the letter for your choice on the answer line.

16. If a department store promised to *expedite* your order, you would expect it _____.   16. _____
    (A) to be replaced   (B) to arrive quickly
    (C) to be damaged   (D) to be delayed

17. A school with a *mandatory* entrance examination would _____.   17. _____
    (A) be open to men only   (B) test physical coordination
    (C) require applicants to pass a test   (D) probably be very strict

18. A country with a *totalitarian* form of government would probably _____.   18. _____
    (A) hold regular elections   (B) regulate the press
    (C) enjoy popular support   (D) be run by religious leaders

19. When listening to a *plaintive* song, the audience might _____.   19. _____
    (A) cry   (B) laugh
    (C) suddenly stand up   (D) feel embarrassed

20. In which of these would you be most likely to encounter a *bureaucracy*?   20. _____
    (A) a small family   (B) a bedroom
    (C) the school playground   (D) a large government agency

21. A *sovereign* nation is one that _____.   21. _____
    (A) is free and independent   (B) has a king or queen
    (C) is occupied by a foreign power   (D) invades another nation

22. If a bookkeeper tries to *manipulate* the numbers in a company's records, he or she is attempting to _____ them.   22. _____
    (A) alter or change   (B) double check
    (C) destroy   (D) erase

23. If you *traverse* a soccer field, you _____ it.   23. _____
    (A) measure   (B) inspect
    (C) change   (D) walk across

24. If one country has *dominion* of another, it _____ it.   24. _____
    (A) borders on   (B) rules
    (C) has a low opinion of   (D) fears

25. Someone who brags about his or her *pedigree* might _____.   25. _____
    (A) claim to have met the president   (B) say his dog just won a blue ribbon
    (C) claim his grandfather was royalty   (D) be arrested

Name _____

"I Have a Dream"—*Dr. Martin Luther King Jr.*

Our Constitution guarantees certain civil rights to all citizens of the United States. However, not long ago these rights were often **abridged** by local or state laws. These laws created segregated schools and limited voting rights by requiring so-called literacy tests or imposing poll taxes
5　designed to keep African Americans from voting.

For decades, a number of civil rights groups fought these restrictions, but progress was painfully slow. It took the words and actions of Dr. Martin Luther King Jr. to renew and **galvanize** the movement.

This articulate and **charismatic** African American minister inspired an
10　entire generation that had grown impatient for change. Dr. King had for many years been an **indefatigable** worker for civil rights. His frequent, nonviolent efforts on behalf of equality often landed him in jail.

On August 28, 1963, King spoke to the more than 250,000 people assembled in the nation's capital and to millions of Americans on live television.
15　This remarkable speech gave the civil rights movement new strength.

　　I say to you today, my friends, that in spite of the difficulties and **frustrations** of the moment, I still have a dream. It is a dream deeply rooted in the American dream.

　　I have a dream that one day this nation will rise up and live out
20　the true meaning of its **creed:** "We hold these truths to be self-evident, that all men are created equal . . . ."

　　I have a dream that my four little children will one day live in a nation where they will not be judged by the color of their skin, but by the content of their **character** . . . .

25　So let freedom ring from the prodigious hilltops of New Hampshire . . . .

　　Let freedom ring from the curvaceous peaks of California . . . .

　　When we let freedom ring, when we let it ring from every village and every hamlet, from every state and every city, we will be able
30　to speed up that day when all of God's children — black men and white men, Jews and Gentiles, Protestants and Catholics — will be able to join hands and sing in the words of the old Negro spiritual, "Free at last! Free at last! Thank God Almighty, we are free at last!"

Delivered before the Lincoln Memorial, these words are among the most
35　**renowned** and often quoted in American history. They had an immediate and **immeasurable** impact upon the nation and upon the civil rights movement in the years that followed. A series of civil rights acts were **eventually** passed, and the long road to Dr. King's dream become a little shorter.

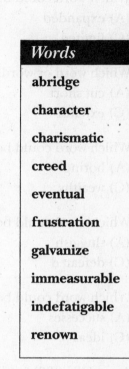

Words

abridge

character

charismatic

creed

eventual

frustration

galvanize

immeasurable

indefatigable

renown

Each word in this lesson's word list appears in dark type in the selection you just read. Think about how the vocabulary word is used in the selection, then write the letter for the best answer to each question.

1. Which word could best replace *abridged* in line 2?   1. _____
   (A) expanded   (B) improved
   (C) limited   (D) transferred

2. Which word or words could best replace *galvanize* in line 8?   2. _____
   (A) cut short   (B) reduce
   (C) exhaust   (D) energize

3. Which word could best replace *charismatic* in line 9?   3. _____
   (A) boring   (B) simple
   (C) wealthy   (D) magnetic

4. Which word could best replace *indefatigable* in line 11?   4. _____
   (A) sluggish   (B) tireless
   (C) defeated   (D) ineffective

5. Which word could best replace *frustrations* in line 17?   5. _____
   (A) successes   (B) disappointments
   (C) ideas   (D) anger

6. A *creed* (line 20) is a(n) _____.   6. _____
   (A) anthem   (B) arrangement
   (C) belief   (D) proud boast

7. *Character* (line 24) is a person's _____.   7. _____
   (A) appearance   (B) ideas
   (C) religious beliefs   (D) good and bad qualities

8. Which word could best replace *renowned* in line 35?   8. _____
   (A) ignored   (B) ridiculed
   (C) famous   (D) unusual

9. Which word could best replace *immeasurable* in line 36?   9. _____
   (A) enormous   (B) immediate
   (C) uncertain   (D) small

10. Which word could best replace *eventually* in line 37?   10. _____
   (A) finally   (B) never
   (C) rudely   (D) foolishly

Applying Meaning

Follow the directions below to write a sentence using a vocabulary word.

1. Describe an experience you have had in school, on a job, or at home. Use a form of the word *frustrate*.

   _____

   _____

   _____

2. Describe the effect of some historic event using any form of the word *immeasurable*.

   _____

   _____

   _____

3. Complete the following: The Peace Corps is looking for young men and women of good *character*. All applicants must . . . .

   _____

   _____

   _____

4. Use any form of the word *renown* to describe an athlete, movie star, or musical group.

   _____

   _____

   _____

5. Describe a real or imaginary person you feel has worked hard on behalf of an important cause such as the environment or a political candidate. Use a form of the word *indefatigable*.

   _____

   _____

   _____

Read each sentence or short passage below. Write "correct" on the answer line if the vocabulary word has been used correctly. Write "incorrect" on the answer line if the vocabulary word has been used incorrectly.

6. The mayor's demand that the newspaper stop publishing critical editorials was met with numerous protests. Most citizens felt this was an *abridgement* of the freedom of the press.

6. _____

7. The police investigation proved conclusively that the professor was really a *charisma*. He had fooled everyone into thinking he was a famous scientist.

7. _____

8. Until the accident, residents had shown little interest in the traffic problems. But seeing one of their neighbors lying injured on the street *galvanized* their efforts to reduce the speed limit.

8. _____

9. If we practice hard every day after school and follow the coach's directions, the *eventual* victory will be ours.

9. _____

10. The rusty hinges on the door made an eerie *creed* as it swung back and forth in the evening breeze.

10. _____

For each word used incorrectly, write a sentence using the word properly.

_____

_____

_____

_____

_____

_____

_____

_____

_____

Mastering Meaning

Martin Luther King's speech had a strong impact on his audience. In addition to his powerful use of words, he had a remarkable talent for stating things in memorable ways. In his August 1963 speech he repeated the phrase "I have a dream . . ." several times, building slowly to the climactic "Free at last!" Write a series of statements stating your dream for the future of our nation. Begin each statement with "I have a dream . . ." Use some words you studied in this lesson.

Lesson
14
Part A

Name _____

You may not agree with the old saying, "Money makes the world go 'round," but it is hard to deny that money and business play an important part in everyone's life. It is no surprise then that our language has so many words to describe our interactions in the areas of money and business. In this lesson you will learn ten words frequently used in the world of business and money.

Unlocking Meaning

Read the sentences or short passages below. Write the letter for the correct definition of the italicized vocabulary word.

At the annual meeting of the nation's popcorn growers, the growers decided to form a *cartel* to set the prices charged by all the producers.

1. (A) an association of producers in a particular industry that works to improve the industry's image
   (B) an association of producers in a particular industry that buys out the smaller producers
   (C) an association of producers in a particular industry that works to control the market
   (D) an association of producers in a particular industry that works to influence public officials and legislators

An advantage of keeping your money in a savings account is that your money will *accrue* interest.

2. (A) invest
   (B) accumulate over time
   (C) discount
   (D) keep track of

The drug company printed long warnings on packages of its new drug in an attempt to *indemnify* itself from legal action in case the medicine had some unexpected side effects.

3. (A) insure or protect against loss, damage, or injury
   (B) safeguard the reputation of a person or business
   (C) use the media to inform the public about a product
   (D) cause a movement to gain strength or vigor

The United States was able to industrialize because it had workers and natural resources. Perhaps most important, it had the *capital* and the confidence to spend it building factories and railroads, knowing such investments would pay for themselves in the long run.

4. (A) the most important kind of wealth a person possesses
   (B) money loaned to a company by others
   (C) wealth that comes from land
   (D) wealth that is used to produce more wealth

Words

accrue

audit

capital

cartel

collateral

indemnify

liquidate

lucrative

pecuniary

usury

1. _____

2. _____

3. _____

4. _____

No one could understand how Inez Santos could leave a *lucrative* job on Wall Street to go back to art school. Inez said she didn't mind giving up a few luxuries for a more personal challenge.

5. (A) temporary
   (B) profitable
   (C) difficult
   (D) illegal

5. _____

When businesses hire an accounting firm to *audit* their financial records, they hope the accountants will not find big mistakes.

6. (A) examine and verify the accounts of a business
   (B) listen carefully to the complaints of employees
   (C) copy and store the records of a business
   (D) conceal from competitors

6. _____

After some banks began charging interest rates of 20 percent and more, the legislature considered several laws to prevent such *usury*.

7. (A) excessive rates of interest
   (B) illegal business practices
   (C) generosity
   (D) confusion

7. _____

To get her new business started, Mavina Gates borrowed money from the bank, putting up her house as *collateral*.

8. (A) proof of success
   (B) a major source of customers for a business
   (C) a temporary turnover of property
   (D) property pledged as security for the repayment of a loan

8. _____

Before Lee applied for a mortgage, he used his inheritance from Aunt Molly to *liquidate* his college loans so that he would have a clean financial slate.

9. (A) combine into a more fluid state
   (B) refinance
   (C) pay off
   (D) get rid of by force or violence

9. _____

When Senator Dobbs announced that he would not run for a third term, he reminded his listeners that the *pecuniary* rewards of public service are few and that he had children to send to college.

10. (A) personal
    (B) financial
    (C) intangible
    (D) usable

10. _____

Applying Meaning

Read each sentence or short passage below. Write "correct" on the answer line if the vocabulary word has been used correctly. Write "incorrect" on the answer line if the vocabulary word has been used incorrectly.

1. Although you had to give the landlord a month's rent for security, at least it *accrued* interest while you lived in the apartment.

1. _____

2. Henry Bell knew something was wrong at the factory when he heard the garbled *audit* on his answering machine.

2. _____

3. Before you decide to invest in a company, you must decide if you like the location and design of its *capital.*

3. _____

4. By limiting the number of cattle offered to the meat packing companies, the *cartel* of ranchers hoped to be able to raise the prices they charged.

4. _____

5. My brother-in-law asked me to put up my land in Maine as *collateral* for a loan so he could finish school.

5. _____

6. The actress said that she was going to sue the sleazy newspaper that *indemnified* her reputation by printing bogus pictures of her.

6. _____

7. In order to *liquidate* the deceased man's debts, his survivors auctioned his estate.

7. _____

8. John told me that he passed up the Raymond account. He said it might have been *lucrative*, but the Raymond people were just too hard to work with.

8. _____

9. I like all of the candidate's ideas on foreign affairs. However, I think his *pecuniary* policies would destroy this country's economy.

9. _____

10. After years of *usury*, the car was rusted and badly in need of repair.

10. _____

For each word used incorrectly, write a sentence using the word properly.

_____

_____

_____

_____

_____

_____

Our Living Language

pecuniary

In many early societies, one's wealth was measured by the number of cattle the person owned. This was especially true in times and places where there was no standard currency. The Latin word for cattle was *pecus*, and it naturally became associated with wealth and money. It eventually entered the English language as *pecuniary*, meaning "having to do with money."

Cooperative Learning: Money is a word that inspires numerous slang expressions such as "bread" and "dough." Work with a partner to list as many slang expressions as you can think of for money and wealth.

Name _____

In Latin the word for good or well is *bene*. We often find it at the beginning of English words like *benefit* or similar words with "good" as part of their meaning. The Latin word *malus,* on the other hand, means "bad." It, too, is found at the beginning of many English words like *malcontent*, words with "bad" as part of their meaning. The vocabulary words in this lesson all have one of these "good" or "bad" roots.

Root	Meaning	English Word
-ben- -bene-	good, well	benign benefactor
-mal-	bad	malignant

Unlocking Meaning

Write the vocabulary word that fits each clue below. Then say the word and write a short definition. Compare your definition and pronunciation with those given on the flash card.

1. This noun came into English through the French word *malade,* meaning "sick" or "in a bad condition."

_____

_____

_____

2. This verb is derived from the Middle English word *malignen,* which meant "to attack." The modern word is more narrow, with its "slanderous" connotation.

_____

_____

_____

3. In this adjective, you can see the Latin word *velle*, meaning "to wish." It now suggests doing good.

_____

_____

_____

Words

- **benediction**
- **benefactor**
- **benevolent**
- **benign**
- **malady**
- **malaise**
- **malevolence**
- **malicious**
- **malign**
- **malignant**

4. This adjective is a form of the answer to number 2, but it is usually used in a medical context.

_____

_____

_____

5. The literal meaning of the roots in this noun are "bad ease." You can see the French word *aise* meaning "ease" in this word.

_____

_____

_____

6. This noun might name someone who gives a big donation to a school or hospital.

_____

_____

_____

7. This word is the adjective form of *malice*. It can be used to describe gossip or someone's intentions.

_____

_____

_____

8. This noun is a combination of two Latin words. One is the Latin word *dicere*, meaning "to say." This word literally means "saying good."

_____

_____

_____

9. This word is related to *benevolent,* but the word is a noun and has a "bad" meaning.

_____

_____

_____

10. If a tumor or similar growth is not cancerous, or if a smile is pleasant and friendly, we refer to it with this "good" adjective.

_____

_____

_____

Applying Meaning

Follow the directions below to write a sentence using a vocabulary word.

1. Complete this sentence: With the help of a *benevolent* wind, the
   sailboat _____.”

   _____

   _____

   _____

2. Describe the way grandparents might look at their grandchildren. Use
   a form of the word *benign*.

   _____

   _____

   _____

3. Use the word *benediction* in a sentence about a wedding or a funeral.

   _____

   _____

   _____

4. Write a sentence describing what a *benefactor* might do for the school
   she attended.

   _____

   _____

   _____

5. Write a sentence about how someone might feel after being alone and
   a long way from home for months. Use the word *malaise*.

   _____

   _____

   _____

Decide which word in parentheses best completes the sentence. Then write
the sentence, adding the missing word.

6. His jealousy of his brother's success ate at Nick like a _____
   tumor. (benevolent; malignant)

   _____

   _____

7. During the campaign, Anita Schneider attempted to _____ Mike Halligan's character by suggesting he cheated on his taxes. (benign; malign)

_____

_____

8. The mysterious _____ were apparently transmitted throughout the hotel through the heating system. (benedictions; maladies)

_____

_____

9. The _____ of the evil queen toward Snow White was dramatically portrayed in the film. (malady; malevolence)

_____

_____

10. The vandalism at the school was no small joke; it was a _____ attempt to destroy property. (malicious; malign)

_____

_____

Bonus Word

malaria

The word *malaria,* a disease carried by mosquitoes, got its name from an early belief about how this disease was transmitted. Initially, it was thought that the fever and chills associated with the illness were the result of breathing unwholesome air. Consequently, it was named for the Italian words for bad air, *mal aria.*

Use Your Dictionary: Find additional words beginning with the *-mal-* or *-ben-* root. Write a sentence that demonstrates the meaning of each word you find.

Name _____

How well do you remember the words you studied in Lessons 13 through 15? Take the following test covering the words from the last three lessons.

Part 1 Choose the Correct Meaning

Each question below includes a word in capital letters, followed by four words or phrases. Choose the word or phrase that is <u>closest</u> in meaning to the word in capital letters. Write the letter for your answer on the line provided.

Sample

S. FINISH	(A) enjoy	(B) complete	**S.** _____**B**_____
	(C) destroy	(D) send	

1. ABRIDGE	(A) restrict	(B) prolong	**1.** _____
	(C) join	(D) cancel	
2. MALADY	(A) tune	(B) quiet	**2.** _____
	(C) evil intent	(D) illness	
3. LUCRATIVE	(A) foolish	(B) ridiculous	**3.** _____
	(C) profitable	(D) easily disposed of	
4. ACCRUE	(A) trim	(B) grow	**4.** _____
	(C) accuse	(D) watch closely	
5. BENIGN	(A) kind	(B) generous	**5.** _____
	(C) simple	(D) enlarged	
6. CREED	(A) belief	(B) give up	**6.** _____
	(C) credit	(D) money	
7. INDEFATIGABLE	(A) undefeated	(B) tireless	**7.** _____
	(C) slender	(D) cheerful	
8. BENEDICTION	(A) addiction	(B) proverb	**8.** _____
	(C) blessing	(D) inheritance	
9. LIQUIDATE	(A) melt	(B) settle accounts	**9.** _____
	(C) appear in court	(D) seal	
10. CHARACTER	(A) personal qualities	(B) opinion	**10.** _____
	(C) type of myth	(D) facial expression	

Go on to next page. ➤

11. MALAISE (A) suggestion (B) violence 11. _____
(C) type of food (D) uneasiness

12. COLLATERAL (A) throw back (B) gigantic 12. _____
(C) security for a loan (D) high rate of interest

13. MALIGNANT (A) harmful or evil (B) easily bent 13. _____
(C) believable (D) remorseful

14. GALVANIZE (A) harden (B) move to action 14. _____
(C) decay (D) measure

15. PECUNIARY (A) financial (B) small 15. _____
(C) place where birds are kept (D) risky

Part 2 Matching Words and Meanings

Match the definition in Column B with the word in Column A.
Write the letter of the correct answer on the line provided.

Column A	Column B	
16. usury	a. a group that tries to control the price of a product	16. _____
17. benevolent	b. to examine and verify	17. _____
18. indemnify	c. a quality that attracts followers	18. _____
19. audit	d. excessive interest on a loan	19. _____
20. malign	e. desiring to do good	20. _____
21. charisma	f. to protect from loss or damage	21. _____
22. renown	g. to prevent from achieving a goal	22. _____
23. frustrate	h. to slander	23. _____
24. cartel	i. honor or fame	24. _____
25. benefactor	j. a person who has given money or help	25. _____

Name _____

Lightning

Spectacular, searing, explosive, and *fiery* are words used in attempts to **depict** the image of a bolt of lightning. Even fireworks, with their color and noise, cannot **surpass** the drama of lightning in the summer sky. The cause for these mysterious **exhibitions** of light patterns has always
5 fascinated the curious who seek to explain such things.

The Earth, like an enormous battery, leaks electricity. Electrons bleed from negatively charged areas of the Earth to the **atmosphere.** In time, clouds may build up an electrical charge 100 million times more powerful than the charge contained on the Earth below. When this charge becomes
10 stronger than the insulating air, it returns to Earth in the form of lightning.

Another source of lightning is thunderheads. These clouds are filled with moisture in the form of ice crystals. As some of the ice crystals grow larger, becoming hail, they start to fall. Within the billowing thunderhead, the falling hail **collides** with rising ice crystals and strips electrons off the
15 crystals. The result is that the upper section of the cloud becomes positively charged, while the bottom is negatively charged, This **induces** an area of positive charge on the Earth below. Eventually, it forces the electrons from the sky to the Earth. Just as a spark leaps between the points of a spark plug, electrons jump the gap. The result is lightning.

20 Lightning strikes the earth as many as 100 times every second. A single bolt of lightning may develop 3,750 million kilowatts of power, but its energy lasts only a fraction of a second. Much of the **inherent** energy in a lightning bolt is lost as heat. The peak temperature in a channel (the path a bolt of lightning travels) may be as high as 55,000 degrees
25 Fahrenheit. However, it lasts for only a few millionths of a second. Even more **impressive** is the speed at which lightning bolts can travel—as fast as 100,000 miles per second.

One of the hot spots for lightning in the United States is central Florida. Why is lightning so **prevalent** in this area? Central Florida has two of the
30 main **ingredients** for electrical storms—moist air and heat. By contrast, the state of Washington, which also has plenty of moisture, has almost no lightning storms. The reason is simply that temperatures are much lower than the tropical heat of the Sunshine State.

As fascinating as such storms are to watch, one should always seek shel-
35 ter in an electrical storm. Standing out in the open or under a tree can be very dangerous. Lightning is attracted to both tall trees and open areas. Golf courses, parks, and beaches are excellent targets for bolts from the blue. As many as one hundred Americans are killed by light-ning every year. So, no matter how much one enjoys watching nature's
40 fireworks, electrical storms should always be treated with respect.

Words
atmosphere
collide
depict
exhibition
impressive
induce
ingredient
inherent
prevalent
surpass

Unlocking Meaning

Each word in this lesson's word list appears in dark type in the selection you just read. Think about how the vocabulary word is used in the selection, then write the letter for the best answer to each question.

1. Which word could best replace *depict* in line 2?
   (A) portray   (B) distort
   (C) deceive   (D) deny

   1. _____

2. Which word could best replace *surpass* in line 3?
   (A) surprise   (B) lack
   (C) limit   (D) exceed

   2. _____

3. In line 4, *exhibitions* means _____.
   (A) arrangements   (B) displays
   (C) disguises   (D) jumbles

   3. _____

4. Which word could best replace *atmosphere* in line 7?
   (A) wind   (B) air mass
   (C) tides   (D) pressure

   4. _____

5. Which word could best replace *collides* in line 14?
   (A) brushes   (B) falls
   (C) slips   (D) bumps

   5. _____

6. In line 16, the word *induces* means _____.
   (A) causes   (B) defines
   (C) determines   (D) leads

   6. _____

7. Which word could best replace *inherent* in line 22?
   (A) inherited   (B) exact
   (C) built-in   (D) irregular

   7. _____

8. Which word could best replace *impressive* in line 26?
   (A) dramatic   (B) influential
   (C) expectant   (D) ineffective

   8. _____

9. Which word could best replace *prevalent* in line 29?
   (A) unusual   (B) mild
   (C) widespread   (D) uncommon

   9. _____

10. In line 30, the word *ingredients* means _____.
    (A) opinions   (B) arguments
    (C) elements   (D) predictions

    10. _____

Applying Meaning

Follow the directions below to write a sentence using a vocabulary word.

1. Describe the weather in the desert. Use the word *atmosphere* in your description.

_____

_____

2. Tell about a close call on the basketball court. Use any form of the word *collide* in your answer.

_____

_____

3. Think of a painting or poster you have seen and tell about it. Use the word *depict* in your sentence.

_____

_____

4. Tell about a museum display you have seen. Use any form of the word *exhibition*.

_____

_____

_____

5. Describe an important day in your life. Use any form of the word *impressive*.

_____

_____

_____

6. Complete the following sentence: To induce an electric current, . . .

_____

_____

7. Tell about someone you know who has a natural ability or talent. Use the word *inherent* in your answer.

_____

_____

8. Tell about plants or animals that are found only in certain areas of the world. Use the word *prevalent* in your answer.

_____

_____

9. Describe an athletic record that was broken. Use a form of the word *surpass*.

_____

_____

10. Describe how to prepare one of your favorite foods. Use a form of the word *ingredient*.

_____

_____

Read each sentence or short passage below. Write "correct" on the answer line if the vocabulary word has been used correctly. Write "incorrect" on the answer line if the vocabulary word has been used incorrectly.

11. It was sad to see that family *depicted* from their apartment.

11. _____

12. The young women put on an amazing *exhibition* of tap dancing.

12. _____

13. Billowing thunderheads extend high into the *atmosphere*.

13. _____

14. Thick vegetation was *prevalent* in the rain forest.

14. _____

15. Janet's blond hair was *inherent* from her mother.

15. _____

For each word used incorrectly, write a sentence using the word properly.

_____

_____

_____

_____

_____

_____

_____

Mastering Meaning

As a TV weather forecaster, you must give a brief explanation of lightning storms. Write two or three paragraphs explaining the dangers of lightning and precautions to take if you are caught in a storm. Use some of the words you have studied in this lesson.

Lesson 17 Part A

Name _____

Having a command of a large vocabulary allows you to make clear and exact distinctions. A large vocabulary also enables you to know the difference between words that look and sound very much alike, but have important differences in their meanings. In this lesson, you will learn five pairs of words that can be easily confused because they look and sound very much alike but have different meanings.

Unlocking Meaning

Read the sentences or short passages below. Write the letter for the correct definition of the italicized vocabulary word.

The workers made *continual* complaints to the manager about the conditions in the mill. It seemed as though there was an angry letter on his desk every other day.

1. (A) repeated frequently
(B) going on without interruption

The *continuous* sound of the waves lapping at the side of the boat caused everyone to feel relaxed. At night everyone went to sleep immediately.

2. (A) repeated frequently
(B) going on without interruption

He said he knew nothing about the disappearance of the last piece of cake, but his smile *implied* that he ate it himself.

3. (A) to conclude or reason out from evidence
(B) to hint or suggest without stating directly

Since she kept looking at her watch and reaching for the door latch, I was forced to *infer* that she was eager to leave.

4. (A) to conclude or reason out from evidence
(B) to hint or suggest without stating directly

The heavy rains will *affect* the wheat crops. We can expect the price of bread to go up in the next few months.

5. (A) to influence or change
(B) result

The high price of bread is just one *effect* of the flood. Insurance rates are certain to go up as well.

6. (A) to influence or change
(B) result

Words
affect
effect
avenge
revenge
continual
continuous
disinterested
uninterested
imply
infer

1. _____

2. _____

3. _____

4. _____

5. _____

6. _____

The Northside basketball team swore they would *avenge* their humiliating defeat at the hands of their crosstown rivals at Southside. They would meet again at the end of the season, and they planned to be ready.

7. (A) to get satisfaction for a wrong
   (B) a desire to inflict an injury in return for an insult or injury

7. _____

When the final buzzer sounded, the scoreboard showed Northside had won by 24 points. Their *revenge* was complete.

8. (A) to get satisfaction for a wrong
   (B) a desire to inflict an injury in return for an insult or injury

8. _____

For the game to be fair, we need a *disinterested* referee. I do not think Mr. Clark is a good choice. His daughter plays for one of the teams.

9. (A) without interest
   (B) free from bias; impartial

9. _____

David begged me to play golf with him this weekend, but I declined. I am simply *uninterested* in hitting a ball and then chasing after it.

10. (A) without interest
    (B) free from bias; impartial

10. _____

Applying Meaning

Decide which word in parentheses best completes the sentence. Then write
the sentence, adding the missing word.

1. Seeing him drive by in that expensive car and wearing his fancy
   leather jacket, one might easily _____ that he had won the
   lottery. (imply; infer)

   _____

   _____

   _____

2. The teacher promised that the absence caused by my illness would
   not _____ my grade. (affect; effect)

   _____

   _____

   _____

3. Instead of going to the concert with my sister, I stayed home and
   watched the football game. Perhaps when I understand it better, I will
   enjoy classical music, but right now I am simply _____.
   (disinterested; uninterested)

   _____

   _____

   _____

4. When the telephone rang for the fourth time, we decided to discon-
   nect the phone. None of us could stand these _____ inter-
   ruptions during dinner. (continual; continuous)

   _____

   _____

   _____

5. The sheriff feared that the citizens of the town might seek _____,
   so they kept the man accused of the crime under close guard.
   (avenge; revenge)

   _____

   _____

   _____

Read each sentence or short passage below. Write "correct" on the answer line if the vocabulary word has been used correctly. Write "incorrect" on the answer line if the vocabulary word has been used incorrectly.

6. The baby cried *continuously* for two hours before the babysitter realized the child's shoe was tied too tightly.

6. _____

7. I tried to finish the book you gave me, but after two chapters I became completely *disinterested*.

7. _____

8. The weather is certain to *effect* attendance at the picnic. Why would anyone want to be outside in a thunderstorm?

8. _____

9. Unless we speak up in opposition to that proposal, we will be *implying* that we agree with the plan.

9. _____

10. Instead of trying to get *avenge* ourselves, it is better to let the police handle things.

10. _____

For each word used incorrectly, write a sentence using the word properly.

_____

_____

_____

_____

_____

_____

_____

_____

_____

_____

Bonus Word

malapropism

The Rivals, an 18th-century comedy by Richard Sheridan, featured a character named Mrs. Malaprop, who confuses words with similar sounds but quite dissimilar meanings. For example, at one point she exclaims, "She's as headstrong as an allegory on the banks of the Nile." The word *malapropism* has entered the language as a common noun meaning "the comical confusion of two similar words."

Work with a Partner: Write a list of malapropisms. You might try to include in a sentence some vocabulary words you have studied, such as "I asked the band to play my favorite malady."

Name _____

The Greek word *pathos* meant suffering. The *-path-* word part has entered the English language in a variety of ways. It has been added to the ends of some words to mean a type of disorder, as in *psychopath*, meaning one who suffers from an extreme emotional or mental disorder. It can also mean a particular type of medical study, such as *pathology*, the study of the origins and causes of disease.

The Greek word *phobos* meant fear. In English the *-phobia-* word part usually adds the "fear" meaning to another word part or root, as in *hydrophobia*, hydro (water) + phobia (fear) = fear of water. Each vocabulary word in this lesson has one of these word parts.

Root	Meaning	English Word
-path-	suffer strong feelings	psychopath
-phobia-	fear	hydrophobia

Words
acrophobia
apathy
claustrophobia
empathy
hydrophobia
pathetic
pathology
pathos
psychopath
xenophobia

Unlocking Meaning

Write the vocabulary word that fits each clue below. Then say the word and write a short definition. Compare your definition and pronunciation with those given on the flash card.

1. This noun is often used to describe a quality of literature or art that evokes certain feelings. It was taken without change from a Greek word.

   _____

   _____

   _____

2. This noun combines the word part *-path-* with the Greek word *psyche* meaning "soul" or "spirit."

   _____

   _____

   _____

3. In this noun, you can see the Greek word *xenos*, meaning "foreign" or "strange."

   _____

   _____

   _____

4. This noun begins with the Greek word part -*a*- meaning "without." It is combined with the word part meaning "strong feelings."

_____

_____

5. This word for a type of fear comes in part from the Latin word *claustrum* meaning "an enclosed place."

_____

_____

6. This adjective is derived from *pathos* and is a synonym for "pitiful."

_____

_____

7. This word combines the Greek prefix *en-*, which is sometimes spelled *em-*, and means "with" or "within," and the word part for "strong feelings."

_____

_____

8. This word includes the familiar -*ology* ending found in the words for various studies such as geology and biology.

_____

_____

_____

9. In addition to meaning "an unnatural fear of water," this is another word for rabies, perhaps because one symptom of rabies is a watery mouth.

_____

_____

_____

10. This word begins with the same Greek word part as *acropolis,* meaning "the highest part of an ancient Greek city."

_____

_____

_____

Applying Meaning

Each question below contains a vocabulary word from this lesson. Answer each question "yes" or "no" in the space provided.

1. Would a coach want his team to be *apathetic* before a big game?   1. _____

2. Would a *claustrophobic* person prefer working on a ranch over working in a coal mine?   2. _____

3. Does a *pathologist* study ancient trails and migration patterns?   3. _____

4. Would you expect a social worker to *empathize* with those he is trying to help?   4. _____

5. Should a person with *hydrophobic* tendencies consider enlisting in the navy?   5. _____

For each question you answered "no," write a sentence using the vocabulary word correctly.

_____

_____

_____

_____

_____

_____

Read each sentence or short passage below. Write "correct" on the answer line if the vocabulary word has been used correctly. Write "incorrect" on the answer line if the vocabulary word has been used incorrectly.

6. Some historians claim that opposition to immigration at the turn of the century was a *xenophobic* reaction to the cultural differences of the Europeans.   6. _____

7. The magician demonstrated her *psychopathic* powers by reading the mind of several people in the audience.   7. _____

8. The visitor declined the invitation to climb to the top of the Eiffel Tower, claiming he was *acrophobic*.   8. _____

9. After waiting for several hours for the rain to stop, the umpires ran out of *pathos* and called the game off.   9. _____

10. When the dog began to whimper *pathetically* at the door, Maxine took him for a walk.   10. _____

For each word used incorrectly, write a sentence using the word properly.

_____

_____

_____

_____

_____

Test-Taking Strategies

Tests of vocabulary sometimes ask you to choose a synonym for the word being tested. A synonym has the same or nearly the same meaning. For example, *inspect* is a synonym for *examine*. Sometimes the word being tested is given in a sentence. You are given four or five choices from which to select the correct synonym.

Sample

S. We already had milk in the refrigerator, so it was *deleted* from the shopping list.	**S.** _____ **A** _____
(A) removed (B) missing (C) chosen (D) read	

When taking this type of test, you should look at each choice and eliminate any answers that are clearly wrong. Test makers may also try to confuse you by including words with sounds or spellings similar to the correct word's or by including antonyms, words with opposite meanings, among the choices.

Practice: Choose the <u>synonym</u> for the italicized word in each sentence. Write your choice on the answer line.

1. His *obnoxious* behavior in public caused him to lose most of his friends.
     (A) obscure   (B) pleasant
     (C) disagreeable   (D) ordinary
                                     1. _____

2. At the end of the meeting, the recorder provided a *recapitulation* of the discussion.
     (A) opinion   (B) contradiction
     (C) summary   (D) reminder
                                     2. _____

3. When the clock began to strike midnight, everyone knew it was time to *terminate* the discussion.
     (A) finish   (B) frighten
     (C) begin   (D) remove
                                     3. _____

Name _____

How well do you remember the words you studied in Lessons 16 through 18? Take the following test covering the words from the last three lessons.

Part 1 Choose the Correct Meaning

Each question below includes a word in capital letters, followed by four words or phrases. Choose the word or phrase that is <u>closest</u> in meaning to the word in capital letters. Write the letter for your answer on the line provided.

| **S. FINISH** | (A) enjoy | (B) complete | **S.** ___**B**___ |
| | (C) destroy | (D) send | |

1. INDUCE   (A) tempt   (B) require   **1.** _____
             (C) persuade   (D) enter

2. APATHY   (A) indifference   (B) fear of heights   **2.** _____
             (C) pity   (D) type of medicine

3. INGREDIENT   (A) argument   (B) element   **3.** _____
             (C) poison   (D) investigation

4. INHERENT   (A) natural   (B) receive through   **4.** _____
                                        a will
             (C) false   (D) dangerous

5. AVENGE   (A) ambush   (B) flee   **5.** _____
             (C) arrange   (D) repay

6. XENOPHOBIA   (A) fear of strangers   (B) fear of machinery   **6.** _____
             (C) suffering   (D) emotional distress

7. COLLIDE   (A) put in order   (B) hit   **7.** _____
             (C) collect   (D) cooperate

8. AFFECT   (A) flaw   (B) love   **8.** _____
             (C) influence   (D) cleanse

9. PATHOS   (A) landscape   (B) pity   **9.** _____
             (C) anger   (D) fear

10. IMPRESSIVE   (A) forceful   (B) flattened   **10.** _____
             (C) producing awe   (D) simple

Go on to next page. ➤

11. PREVALENT   (A) common   (B) preventable   11. _____
                (C) silly   (D) one who pretends

12. PATHOLOGY   (A) mental disorder   (B) logical argument   12. _____
                (C) branch of medicine (D) the study of
                                          migration

13. DEPICT   (A) tool for digging (B) deposit   13. _____
                (C) trust   (D) show

14. PATHETIC   (A) pitiful   (B) surprising   14. _____
                (C) charitable   (D) famous

15. DISINTERESTED (A) bored   (B) impartial   15. _____
                   (C) impoverished   (D) disorderly

Part 2 Matching Words and Meanings

Match the definition in Column B with the word in Column A.
Write the letter of the correct definition on the answer line.

Column A	Column B	
16. empathy	a. a person with a severe mental disorder	16. _____
17. claustrophobia	b. sharing another's feelings	17. _____
18. continuous	c. to conclude from an examination of evidence	18. _____
19. continual	d. fear of enclosed places	19. _____
20. acrophobia	e. without interruption	20. _____
21. surpass	f. a display	21. _____
22. infer	g. repeated frequently	22. _____
23. imply	h. fear of high places	23. _____
24. psychopath	i. to go beyond	24. _____
25. exhibition	j. to hint or suggest	25. _____

Name _____

In Search of a Common Language

For centuries, **legions** of clever linguists have attempted to create a world language. With this universal language, they hoped to **foster** good-will as well as serve the causes of international commerce and learning. None of these languages has been as successful as Esperanto. Although
5   people assume that it was an experiment that failed, Esperantists, estimated to number between eight million and sixteen million, are found throughout the world.

In 1887 Lazarus Ludwig Zamenhof published *Lingvo Internacia de la Doktoro Esperanto (International Language by Doctor Hopeful)*. Bialystok, Rus-
10 sia (now part of Poland), where Zamenhof grew up, was a place where numerous languages were spoken. As a result, Russians, Poles, Germans, Estonians, and Latvians **profoundly** mistrusted and misunderstood each other. Zamenhof's dream was to fashion a new language through which his neighbors could learn to coexist. His initial goals for the **nascent** lan-
15 guage were for it to be so simple and logical that anyone could learn it, and to be so neutral in political and cultural connotations that it could become everyone's second language.

Zamenhof succeeded in at least one way. The central **tenets** of Esperanto are its elegant simplicity and its **relentless** logic. In contrast to English,
20 with its sometimes bewildering spelling and pronunciation, Esperanto is strictly phonetic. Every word is pronounced exactly as it is spelled. Furthermore, grammar and **syntax** have been reduced to sixteen rules that have no exceptions. For example, every noun ends in *-o*, every adjective in *-a*, and every adverb in *-e*. Experts claim that even a **novice** can learn
25 the language in one hundred hours or less.

Furthermore, in keeping with his **prosaic** approach to language, Zamenhof searched dictionaries of the Western world, choosing from each the most common roots on which to graft his new language. From only 2,000 roots, plus a variety of prefixes and suffixes, Esperantists have
30 access to a 10,000-word vocabulary.

Zamenhof's dream of establishing Esperanto as a universal second language never completely caught on. By the end of World War II, English had become the language of business, diplomacy, and science. On a smaller scale, however, Esperanto is doing the work its creator intended.
35 Countries like Japan and China use it to **facilitate** discussions between speakers of different dialects. In this way, Esperanto helps to expand communication among people who might otherwise never communicate at all.

Words

facilitate

foster

legion

nascent

novice

profound

prosaic

relentless

syntax

tenet

Unlocking Meaning

Each word in this lesson's word list appears in dark type in the selection you just read. Think about how the vocabulary word is used in the selection, then write the letter for the best answer to each question.

1. Which words could best replace *legions* in line 1?   1. _____
   (A) reduced quantities   (B) secret organizations
   (C) limited groups   (D) large numbers

2. Which word could best replace *foster* in line 2?   2. _____
   (A) promote   (B) conquer
   (C) transfer   (D) communicate

3. Which word could best replace *profoundly* in line 12?   3. _____
   (A) remarkably   (B) deeply
   (C) rarely   (D) selectively

4. A *nascent* language (line 14) can best be described as one that is _____.   4. _____
   (A) expressive   (B) coming into being
   (C) rejected as too difficult (D) imposed on speakers

5. The word *tenets* (line 18) can best be explained as _____.   5. _____
   (A) speculations   (B) followers
   (C) strange twists   (D) principles

6. Which word could best replace *relentless* in line 19?   6. _____
   (A) inadequate   (B) amusing
   (C) steady   (D) mandatory

7. *Syntax* (line 22) can best be explained as a _____.   7. _____
   (A) way words are put   (B) complicated theory
       together to form sentences
   (C) system for translating   (D) demonstration of how
       foreign languages   something works

8. Which word or words could best replace *novice* in line 24?   8. _____
   (A) expert   (B) participant
   (C) teacher   (D) beginner

9. Which word could best replace *prosaic* in line 26?   9. _____
   (A) fictional   (B) straightforward
   (C) obscure   (D) gentle

10. Which word or words could best replace *facilitate* in line 35?   10. _____
    (A) complicate   (B) record
    (C) make easier   (D) confuse

Applying Meaning

Follow the directions below to write a sentence using a vocabulary word.

1. Describe how a visitor to Washington, D.C., might react to seeing a historical monument for the first time. Use any form of the word *profound*.

   _____

   _____

   _____

2. Describe the weather on a typically bleak November day. Use any form of the word *relentless*.

   _____

   _____

   _____

3. Describe a crowd of people at a sporting event or concert. Use any form of the word *legion*.

   _____

   _____

   _____

4. Explain how you learned a new task or pursued a new interest. Use any form of the word *novice*.

   _____

   _____

   _____

5. Write a sentence describing how a gardener might help his plants grow. Use any form of the word *foster*.

   _____

   _____

   _____

Each question below contains a vocabulary word from this lesson. Answer each question "yes" or "no" in the space provided.

6. Would a professional writer be familiar with grammar and *syntax*?   6. _____

7. Is television regarded as *nascent* technology?

   7. _____

8. Would a *prosaic* speech move its audience to take action because of its imaginative and persuasive power?

8. _____

9. Do mnemonic devices *facilitate* memorization of difficult material?

9. _____

10. Are *tenets* something that you can acquire at a store or through catalogue shopping?

10. _____

For each question you answered "no," write a sentence using the vocabulary word correctly.

_____

_____

_____

_____

_____

_____

_____

_____

_____

_____

_____

_____

_____

_____

Mastering Meaning

Suppose a proposal has been made to add Esperanto to the school curriculum. Write a persuasive letter to your school board, urging the members to support your stand on the proposal. Use some of the words you studied in this lesson.

Name _____

Language is made up of words, and literature is written by people who are interested in the way words work. It is not surprising, then, that we have many special words associated with language and literature. This lesson presents ten of them.

Unlocking Meaning

Read the sentences or short passages below. Write the letter for the correct definition of the italicized vocabulary word.

Jay put on a blond wig and bright red lipstick and walked around the room with a smug look on his face. His *parody* of the movie star brought roars of laughter from the audience.

1. (A) love
   (B) exaggerated imitation
   (C) detailed description
   (D) theft of another person's ideas

Real estate salespeople hardly ever try to sell you a "house." They always use the word "home" because that word has *connotations* of warmth, coziness, and family.

2. (A) all the meanings of a word
   (B) misleading meanings
   (C) ideas and emotions associated with a word
   (D) unusual or seldom-used meanings

Some crafty politicians purposely use slang or poor grammar in their speeches. They think such *solecisms* make them appear more "folksy."

3. (A) unusual behavior
   (B) humorous speech
   (C) political slogans
   (D) errors in grammar or usage

Playwrights today rarely include *soliloquies* for their characters, perhaps because in real life people do not talk to themselves very much.

4. (A) long, boring speeches
   (B) moments of decision for the main characters in a play
   (C) talking to oneself as if thinking aloud
   (D) lines spoken directly to the audience

Words

allegory

allusion

connotation

idiom

jargon

metaphor

parody

patois

solecism

soliloquy

1. _____

2. _____

3. _____

4. _____

Although she spoke excellent French, Henriette was not comfortable with the *patois* of Quebec. It was not the same as the French she had studied.

5. (A) dialect other than the standard or literary dialect   5. _____
   (B) slang
   (C) rapid and mechanical style of speech
   (D) place names and landmarks of a locality

On the surface John Bunyan's *allegory* titled *Pilgrim's Progress* is about a pilgrim's journey to a place called the Celestial City. In reality, however, the book is about a soul's journey to heaven.

6. (A) story in which animals act like humans   6. _____
   (B) story in which characters stand for abstract ideas
   (C) any story about pilgrims
   (D) long narrative about a hero

William Shakespeare is famous for his *metaphors*. Perhaps his most famous one is "All the world's a stage, and all the men and women merely players."

7. (A) figures of speech   7. _____
   (B) songs
   (C) words having more than one meaning
   (D) long speeches

Most people trying to learn English have difficulty understanding *idioms* such as "put up with" and "giving way."

8. (A) expressions in which words have different or unusual meanings   8. _____
   (B) foolish remarks
   (C) thoughtless comments
   (D) types of speech used by uneducated people

When the speaker called the candidate a modern-day Benedict Arnold, he was making an *allusion* to the infamous Revolutionary War traitor.

9. (A) vague term   9. _____
   (B) accusation or threat
   (C) word that has recently entered the language
   (D) indirect reference or suggestion

One of the hardest things about learning computers is getting familiar with the *jargon*. Words like "byte," "download," and "mouse" come up all the time.

10. (A) titles and duties of certain people.   10. _____
    (B) specialized vocabulary
    (C) code or system for communicating
    (D) humor unique to a particular group

Applying Meaning

Decide which word in parentheses best completes the sentence. Then write the sentence, adding the missing word.

1. My grandmother lives in rural Louisiana, and it's sometimes hard to understand her _____ when she gets excited. (patois; soliloquy)

   _____

   _____

   _____

2. When the minister began his remarks with the overused _____ "Life is a journey," I knew we were in for a long, boring talk. (idiom; metaphor)

   _____

   _____

   _____

3. Because our foreign visitors did not understand the _____, when I asked them to carry out my orders they picked up the papers and went outside. (idiom; parody)

   _____

   _____

   _____

4. In Hamlet's famous "To be or not to be" _____, he thinks aloud about committing suicide. (allegory; soliloquy)

   _____

   _____

   _____

5. It was no accident that the candidate made numerous _____ to his military service, since his opponent had no such experience. (allusions; connotations)

   _____

   _____

   _____

6. When Steve rehearsed his speech before the school administrators, he shocked them by using numerous _____. (connotations; solecisms)

   _____

   _____

   _____

7. There is nothing as frustrating as having a doctor explain your illness using _____ you do not understand. (jargon; parodies)

_____

_____

_____

8. To many Americans, the word *politician* _____ smoke-filled rooms and shady deals. (alludes; connotes)

_____

_____

_____

9. In the medieval _____ *Everyman*, the title character must meet Death. All his friends, including Five Wits, Beauty, and Knowledge, desert him, but Good Deeds stays with him to the end. (allegory; parody)

_____

_____

_____

10. For my senior drama project, I am going to write and produce a _____ of *The Phantom of the Opera* called *The Fantom of the Auditorium*. (parody; patois)

_____

_____

_____

●	**Bonus Word**
	shibboleth
	According to the Bible, when the soldiers of Gilead captured an important crossing point over the Jordan River, they devised an unusual way to keep the enemy from using the crossing. Anyone seeking to cross the river was asked to say the word *shibboleth*, the Hebrew word for stream. Being unfamiliar with the *sh* sound in Hebrew, their enemies would pronounce it *sibboleth*, and thereby reveal their true identity. In English *shibboleth* now means a kind of password or way of using language that distinguishes one group or profession from another.
	Write a List: Make a list of other shibboleths you recognize. Music, movies, and the computer fields are good sources.

Name _____

When medieval monks wanted to write, they retired to the scriptorium, a room set aside for writing and copying. The word *scriptorium,* like many other English words having to do with writing, comes from the Latin word *scribere* meaning "to write."

Words containing the Latin root *-tract-* come from the verb *trahere,* meaning "to draw" or "to pull." You see this word in *tractor* and *distraction.* The vocabulary words in this lesson all have one of these roots

Root	Meaning	English Word
-scrib-	write	ascribe
-script-		scripture
-tract-	draw, pull	extract

Unlocking Meaning

Write a vocabulary word for each of these definitions or clues. Then rewrite the definition in your own words. Use the flash card to check your answer.

1. to force or order into military service through a written notice; to draft

_____
_____
_____

2. a note or a series of notes written at the end of a letter; it has the prefix *post-,* meaning "after"

_____
_____
_____

3. not easily handled or moved; stubborn

_____
_____
_____

4. to assign or attribute to a cause

_____
_____
_____

Words

ascribe

conscript

detract

extract

intractable

nondescript

postscript

proscribe

protract

scripture

5. without distinctive qualities and therefore difficult to describe

_____

_____

_____

6. to draw or pull out; it has the *ex-* prefix, meaning "out"

_____

_____

_____

7. a sacred writing or book

_____

_____

_____

8. to draw out or lengthen in time

_____

_____

_____

9. to take away a desirable part; to lessen in value or importance

_____

_____

_____

10. to condemn or prohibit

_____

_____

_____

Applying Meaning

Write the vocabulary word that fits each clue below. Then write a sentence using any form of the vocabulary word correctly. You may want to use the information in the clue.

1. The Bible and the Koran are examples.

_____

_____

_____

2. The abbreviation for this word in a letter is P.S.

_____

_____

_____

3. Dentists do it to teeth. You might do it to the juice in an orange.

_____

_____

_____

4. This word could describe a house in a neighborhood of identical houses.

_____

_____

Each question below contains a vocabulary word from this lesson.
Answer each question "yes" or "no" in the space provided.

5. If a discussion of a problem becomes *protracted,* does it last longer?   5. _____

6. If you *ascribe* to a magazine, does it arrive in the mail?   6. _____

7. Is a volunteer army made up of *conscripts?*   7. _____

8. If a donkey is stubborn, might you call him *intractable?*   8. _____

9. If an activity is against the law, can you say it is a *proscribed* activity?   9. _____

10. Is *detraction* a synonym for subtraction?   10. _____

For each question you answered "no," write a sentence using the vocabulary word correctly.

_____

_____

_____

_____

_____

_____

_____

_____

_____

_____

_____

Our Living Language

Long ago only a few well-educated people could read and write. Consequently, the task of keeping public records and accounts was assigned to someone with these special skills. This person was called a scribe, from the Latin word *scribere*. This term was taken into English virtually unchanged around the 13th century. Like most workers, scribes occasionally hurried through their work and sometimes did not do a very good job. When this happened they were said to have "scribbled." Hence, a new word was born.

Check the Dictionary: Look up the following words in an unabridged dictionary. Try to find how the *-script-* or *-scrib-* root figures in their meaning.

scrip	scriptwriter	scrivener

Name _____

How well do you remember the words you studied in Lessons 19 through 21? Take the following test covering the words from the last three lessons.

Part 1 Complete the Sentence

Decide which definition best completes the sentence. Write the letter for your choice on the answer line.

1. If you tell a computer expert to explain something without using a lot of *jargon,* you want her to _____.

    (A) be brief and to the point
    (B) avoid technical or highly specialized words
    (C) use humor
    (D) tell her thoughts without interruption

    1. _____

2. A *nondescript* suit would _____.

    (A) look very much like every other suit
    (B) lend itself to a detailed description
    (C) probably be very expensive
    (D) have a special pocket for pencils and pens

    2. _____

3. A *prosaic* task would probably _____.

    (A) be lively and interesting
    (B) require great strength
    (C) take several days
    (D) be dull and practical

    3. _____

4. If a new law had a *profound* effect on crime, its impact was _____.

    (A) hardly noticeable
    (B) thorough and far-reaching
    (C) impossible to determine
    (D) unusual

    4. _____

5. An actor who recites a *soliloquy* would _____.

    (A) reveal his thoughts in a long speech
    (B) probably provoke laughter
    (C) speak to another character
    (D) make fun of someone or something

    5. _____

6. If an old manuscript is *ascribed* to Mark Twain, it _____.

    (A) was signed by Mark Twain
    (B) may have been stolen from Mark Twain
    (C) is assumed that Mark Twain wrote it
    (D) was addressed to Mark Twain

    6. _____

Go on to next page. ➤

7. A *novice* mechanic _____.

    (A) is an expert on new machinery

    (B) is an inexperienced beginner

    (C) refuses to learn new techniques

    (D) is an experienced expert

7. _____

8. When the teacher *proscribed* chewing gum in class, she _____.

    (A) allowed it

    (B) outlawed it

    (C) restricted it to certain areas

    (D) encouraged it

8. _____

9. When a speaker *alludes* to a historic event, he _____.

    (A) discredits it

    (B) describes it in detail

    (C) takes credit for it

    (D) makes an indirect reference to it

9. _____

10. Someone holding an *intractable* opinion on an issue _____.

    (A) stubbornly refuses to change

    (B) is uncertain about his or her position

    (C) tends to change his or her mind frequently

    (D) knows little about the issue

10. _____

Part 2 Matching Words and Meanings

Match the definition in Column B with the word in Column A.
Write the letter of the correct definition on the line provided.

Column A	Column B	
11. syntax	a. prolong	11. _____
12. facilitate	b. advance	12. _____
13. conscript	c. belief	13. _____
14. parody	d. way of putting words together in sentences	14. _____
15. nascent	e. written afterthought	15. _____
16. relentless	f. to force into service	16. _____
17. tenet	g. sacred writing	17. _____
18. protract	h. coming into being	18. _____
19. scripture	i. make easier	19. _____
20. connotation	j. implied comparison	20. _____
21. metaphor	k. steady	21. _____
22. extract	l. local form of a language	22. _____
23. patois	m. humorous imitation	23. _____
24. foster	n. implied meaning of a word	24. _____
25. postscript	o. take out by pulling	25. _____

Name _____

The Delany Sisters

The oldest living members of a **preeminent** African American family are also the oldest living authors in this country. Annie Elizabeth (Bessie) and Sarah (Sadie) Delany were 102 and 104 when they wrote *Having Our Say: The Delany Sisters' First Hundred Years.* The **annals** of their life together
5   comprise a best-selling book that offers remarkable insight into what it means to live for over a century.

Bessie and Sadie are the daughters of a man born into slavery and a woman of mixed racial parentage who was born free. Two of ten children, they lived on the campus of St. Augustine's School in Raleigh,
10 North Carolina, where their father was principal and the first elected African American bishop of the Episcopal Church. Coming from a large, racially mixed family, the Delany children thought little about color. So they were **confounded** by the racial prejudices they encountered as they ventured into the outside world. During the era of Jim
15 Crow, when segregation was enforced by legal **sanctions,** it was a shock to be **relegated** to the back of the trolley and to drinking fountains labeled "colored."

After graduating from St. Augustine's, Bessie and Sadie worked as teachers to earn money for college tuition. By 1916 they had moved to New
20 York, where Sadie enrolled at Pratt Institute and Bessie was accepted into Columbia University's School of Dentistry. At a time when few Americans, black or white, ever went beyond high school, Sadie transferred to Columbia and earned her bachelor's and master's degrees, and Bessie became the second black woman licensed to practice dentistry in New York City.

25 Each sister developed her own way of coping with the racism she encountered. Bessie, **feisty** and outspoken, believed in confrontation at any cost. As a female black dentist, she was on the front lines of double battles for equal rights. At first she refused to join her friends at sit-ins at the lunch counters of white restaurants in Harlem; however, after being
30 threatened by the Ku Klux Klan on Long Island, she became more **militant.** Sadie, more **serene** and easygoing than her sister, learned to navigate through the system. When a principal of a white school refused to hire her because he thought her southern accent would be damaging to the children, Sadie went to a speech coach. Eventually she became
35 the first African American in New York to teach domestic science on the high school level.

Still **hale** and fiercely independent, the Delany sisters handle their own finances, prepare their meals, and look after the home that they have always shared. They attribute their **longevity** to a routine of morning yoga,
40 a concoction of chopped garlic and cod liver oil, and a diet dominated by vegetables and boiled tap water.

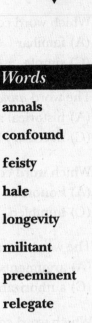

Words

- **annals**
- **confound**
- **feisty**
- **hale**
- **longevity**
- **militant**
- **preeminent**
- **relegate**
- **sanction**
- **serene**

Each word in this lesson's word list appears in dark type in the selection you just read. Think about how the vocabulary word is used in the selection, then write the letter for the best answer to each question.

1. Which word could best replace *preeminent* in line 1?
   (A) familiar   (B) outstanding
   (C) simple   (D) exclusive

   1. _____

2. The word *annals* (line 4) could best be explained as _____.
   (A) historical accounts   (B) rumors
   (C) necessary lessons   (D) predictions

   2. _____

3. Which word could best replace *confounded* in line 13?
   (A) honored   (B) escaped
   (C) humbled   (D) confused

   3. _____

4. The word *sanctions* (line 15) could best be explained as _____.
   (A) arguments   (B) unexpected entanglements
   (C) authorizations   (D) announcements

   4. _____

5. Which word could best replace *relegated* in line 16?
   (A) assisted   (B) promoted
   (C) banished   (D) discarded

   5. _____

6. Which word could best replace *feisty* in line 26?
   (A) foolish   (B) quiet
   (C) clumsy   (D) quarrelsome

   6. _____

7. A *militant* (line 31) person could best be described as someone who _____.
   (A) fights for a cause   (B) avoids conflict
   (C) ignores tradition   (D) follows a leader

   7. _____

8. Which word could best replace *serene* in line 31?
   (A) spellbound   (B) calm
   (C) charitable   (D) opposite

   8. _____

9. Which word could best replace *hale* in line 37?
   (A) available   (B) vague
   (C) vigorous   (D) obedient

   9. _____

10. *Longevity* (line 39) could best be described as _____.
    (A) adaptability   (B) a quest for equal rights
    (C) standard behavior   (D) length of life

    10. _____

Applying Meaning

Decide which word in parentheses best completes the sentence. Then
write the sentence, adding the missing word.

1. George Washington Carver was the first African American to take his
   place in the _____ of science because of his contributions to agriculture and the economy. (annals; sanctions)

   _____

   _____

   _____

2. As the moon rose over our lonely campsite, only the sound of crickets and
   the babbling of the stream broke the _____ night air. (hale; serene)

   _____

   _____

   _____

3. The more doctors learn about how the human body ages, the better health
   care they can provide to increase _____. (longevity; preeminence)

   _____

   _____

   _____

4. The intricate plots of some English mysteries can _____ even the
   most experienced and careful readers. (confound; relegate)

   _____

   _____

   _____

5. In foreign affairs, _____ are economic penalties imposed by one
   or more nations on another nation. (militants; sanctions)

   _____

   _____

   _____

Follow the directions below to write a sentence using a vocabulary word.

6. Describe the behavior of an animal that is difficult to train. Use any
   form of the word *feisty*.

   _____

   _____

   _____

7. Explain the fate of a favorite childhood possession. Use any form of the word *relegate*.

_____

_____

_____

8. Explain the circumstances that led to a protest. Use any form of the word *militant*.

_____

_____

_____

9. Describe the condition of someone who has been sick or injured. Use any form of the word *hale*.

_____

_____

_____

10. Describe a person's or a group's accomplishments or reputation. Use any form of the word *preeminent*.

_____

_____

_____

_____

Mastering Meaning

Biographies and autobiographies are extremely popular because they provide fascinating insights into events, times, places, and people that we would otherwise not have known. Write a sketch about yourself, a person you know well, or a historical figure in which you reveal something special or curious. Use some of the words you studied in this lesson.

Lesson 23

Part A

Name _____

Samuel Johnson wrote "Whereso'er I turn my view,/All is strange, yet nothing new." Our language supports Johnson's statement; it is full of words that refer to various degrees of strangeness. In this lesson you will learn ten words that deal with the strange and unusual.

Unlocking Meaning

Read the sentences or short passages below. Write the letter for the correct definition of the italicized vocabulary word.

1. Beatrice is a brilliant musician, but her habits are so *erratic* that she may never have the discipline for a professional career.

   (A) strictly uniform
   (B) wrong or sinful
   (C) reliable
   (D) lacking consistency and regularity

2. That performer is known for her *outlandish* costumes and elaborate hairdos. In her last performance she wore her jacket backward.

   (A) conspicuously unconventional
   (B) plain or simple
   (C) offensive to decency and morality
   (D) from the wilderness or hinterland

3. When our family plays the game, we *deviate* from the instructions and give each player more turns than the rules state.

   (A) separate into parts, sections, groups, or branches
   (B) depart from a set course
   (C) misuse, break, or destroy
   (D) hide

4. The ugly characters, twisted scenery, and pointless actions in the *bizarre* movie haunted us for weeks.

   (A) foreign, imported
   (B) wicked, evil, sinister
   (C) odd, grotesque
   (D) painful

5. Emily Dickinson displayed a number of *eccentricities*. For years she wore only white dresses and rarely left her house.

   (A) odd or peculiar characteristics
   (B) childlike actions
   (C) lively personality traits
   (D) costumes

Words

aberrant

anomaly

bizarre

deviate

eccentricity

errant

erratic

idiosyncratic

incongruous

outlandish

1. _____

2. _____

3. _____

4. _____

5. _____

6. I will keep Aunt Sophie's big, overstuffed chair even though it may look a little *incongruous* with the rest of my sleek, modern furniture.

    (A) unreliable

    (B) wild, out of control

    (C) simple

    (D) inconsistent or inappropriate

6. _____

7. Isabella Stewart Gardner liked to shock the proper society of Boston with *idiosyncratic* habits such as walking a tame leopard on a leash.

    (A) illegal

    (B) irritating

    (C) peculiar

    (D) dangerous

7. _____

8. *Aberrant* behavior is often the first noticeable symptom of a mental illness.

    (A) unique

    (B) differing from the normal

    (C) attractive

    (D) humorous or witty

8. _____

9. The veterinarian said that our cat, who has one green eye and one blue eye, is something of an *anomaly*.

    (A) something different from the usual or expected

    (B) eerie stranger

    (C) something not acceptable

    (D) ghostly shape

9. _____

10. Sir Gawain was an *errant* knight who was almost killed by the tricky Green Knight. If you look for trouble, you usually find it.

    (A) invisible

    (B) out of control

    (C) lost

    (D) wandering in search of an adventure

10. _____

Applying Meaning

Read each sentence or short passage below. Write "correct" on the answer line if the vocabulary word has been used correctly. Write "incorrect" on the answer line if the vocabulary word has been used incorrectly.

1. Members of the English upper class are known for their many *eccentrics*. They must feel their wealth entitles them to do anything.

    1. _____

2. My lab results *deviated* from those of every other member of my class, so the teacher made me do the whole experiment over.

    2. _____

3. When you take a standardized test you must fill in all the *incongruous* blanks on the page.

    3. _____

4. It is easier to forgive the *idiosyncrasies* of a genius if he or she accomplishes things for society.

    4. _____

5. The outbreaks of the disease were so *erratic*, it was easy to predict and prepare for the next outbreak.

    5. _____

6. The church held a crafts *bizarre* to raise money for the trip.

    6. _____

7. "My children are *anomalies*," laughed Mrs. DiGeorgio. "They love vegetables and they don't like sweets at all."

    7. _____

8. The judge decided that the child's *aberrant* behavior called for a psychiatric evaluation.

    8. _____

9. The flames in the fireplace made *errant* shadows on the castle wall.

    9. _____

10. Candidates for president of the United States usually do *outlandish* things to make them seem like normal citizens.

    10. _____

For each word used incorrectly, write a sentence using the word properly.

_____

_____

_____

_____

_____

_____

_____

_____

_____

_____

_____

Cultural Literacy Note

The Weird Sisters

According to Greek and Roman mythology, a person's fortunes or misfortunes were determined by the Fates—three women sometimes called the Weird Sisters, who arbitrarily wove and cut the fabric of a person's life. The Middle English *werde* meant "fate," the control of a person's life and death. The modern word *weird* retains part of the original suggestion of "strange" or "odd."

Do Some Research: Check the mythologies of various cultures, such as the Native American and Scandinavian, to see how they explained the concept of fate.

Name _____

The Latin word *jacere* means "to throw." This word survives as the *-ject-* root in numerous English words that still retain a suggestion of "throwing." For example, if you "reject" something, you are in a sense throwing it out. Another Latin word, *tangere*, means "to touch." It too survives in many English words in slightly different forms, such as *-tang-* in *tangent* and *-tact-* in *contact*.

Root	Meaning	English Word
-ject-	to throw	conjecture
-jac-		adjacent
-tang-	to touch	tangible
-tact-		tact
-tig-		contiguous
-tin-		contingent

Words

- **abject**
- **adjacent**
- **conjecture**
- **contiguous**
- **contingent**
- **intact**
- **subjective**
- **tact**
- **tangent**
- **tangible**

Unlocking Meaning

A vocabulary word appears in italics in each sentence or short passage below. Find the root in the vocabulary word and think about how it is used in the passage. Then write a definition for the vocabulary word. Compare your definition with the definition on the flash card.

1. We had no way of knowing for certain how the experiment would turn out. Jason's belief that the liquid would change color was only a *conjecture*.

   _____
   _____
   _____

2. The fierce tornado uprooted trees, destroyed homes, and closed down the power plant. It seemed miraculous that the school was left *intact*.

   _____
   _____
   _____

3. She thought she knew poverty in her own city. But the cardboard shacks and open sewage canals she surveyed on her mission to Bangladesh were the most *abject* forms of poverty she had ever seen.

   _____
   _____
   _____

4. In a marathon or similar contest, the winner is easy to pick; it is the person who crosses the finish line first. Deciding the winner in figure skating or diving is much more *subjective*. Judges may differ in their opinions.

_____

_____

5. Because the merchandise had been damaged, Sarah could not give the customer a refund. Giving him this news would require great *tact*. He was, after all, one of the store's best customers.

_____

_____

6. The picnic is planned for Saturday at Memorial Park, but everything is *contingent* on the weather. If it rains, we will reschedule the picnic for next week.

_____

_____

7. The ice-skating rink will be easy to find. Everyone knows how to get to Springside School, and the skating rink is *adjacent* to the school.

_____

_____

8. The principal was not satisfied by assurances that the class was doing much better work. She wanted to see some test scores or other *tangible* results.

_____

_____

9. The weather report did not include the forecasts for Alaska and Hawaii. It mentioned only the *contiguous* forty-eight states.

_____

_____

10. As the sun slowly dropped in the western sky, its outline momentarily was *tangent* with the horizon.

_____

_____

Applying Meaning

Read each sentence or short passage below. Write "correct" on the answer line if the vocabulary word has been used correctly. Write "incorrect" on the answer line if the vocabulary word has been used incorrectly.

1. The city council *abjects* to the mayor's plan to raise taxes.

   1. _____

2. Everyone seemed confident that the club could keep expenses within the budget, but the president insisted that we have a *contingency* plan in case we run out of money.

   2. _____

3. It was little wonder that Ellen would not speak to him. He showed no *tact* in talking about her brother's difficulty finding a job.

   3. _____

4. The police worked in close *conjecture* with the FBI to solve the kidnapping.

   4. _____

5. The water dripped *contiguously* from the broken pipe and kept us awake all night.

   5. _____

6. The circular driveway in front of her house was *tangent* to the street, so we were able to squeeze into traffic.

   6. _____

For each word used incorrectly, write a sentence using the word properly.

_____

_____

_____

_____

_____

_____

_____

Follow the directions below to write a sentence using a vocabulary word.

7. Describe the location of your school or home. Use the word *adjacent*.

_____

_____

_____

8. Tell about something you or someone you know has managed to preserve or protect from harm. Use the word *intact*.

_____

_____

_____

9. State an opinion or belief you hold or someone you know holds on an issue. Use the word *subjective*.

_____

_____

_____

10. Describe a prize or award you or someone you know received. Use the word *tangible*.

_____

_____

_____

Cultural Literacy Note

Achilles' Heel

Achilles is one of the most famous warriors in Greek mythology, but he had one weakness. When he was born, his mother dipped him into the River Styx, so that the sacred water would make him invulnerable. Unfortunately, she held him by his heel and therefore left him with one vulnerable spot. In the final year of the Trojan War, Achilles received a mortal wound in his heel.

Today if you refer to someone's Achilles' heel you are talking about his or her one weakness. Mathematics might be one student's Achilles' heel. Pitching may be a baseball team's Achilles' heel.

Write a Paragraph: In a short paragraph identify and explain someone's or something's Achilles' heel.

Name _____

How well do you remember the words you studied in Lessons 22 through 24? Take the following test covering the words from the last three lessons.

Choose the Correct Meaning

Each question below includes a word in capital letters, followed by four words or phrases. Choose the word or phrase that is <u>closest</u> in meaning to the word in capital letters. Write the letter for your answer on the line provided.

Sample

S. FINISH	(A) enjoy	(B) complete	**S.** _____**B**_____
	(C) destroy	(D) send	

1. LONGEVITY	(A) lengthy illness	(B) scientific theory	**1.** _____
	(C) long life	(D) easily stretched	
2. OUTLANDISH	(A) normal	(B) foreign	**2.** _____
	(C) silly	(D) outstanding	
3. ERRANT	(A) wandering	(B) characterized by many errors	**3.** _____
	(C) peculiar	(D) elderly	
4. CONFOUND	(A) confuse	(B) mix together	**4.** _____
	(C) discover	(D) arrange	
5. INTACT	(A) careful	(B) fastened firmly	**5.** _____
	(C) interesting	(D) undamaged	
6. SUBJECTIVE	(A) main topic	(B) personal	**6.** _____
	(C) underwater object	(D) illegal	
7. ANOMALY	(A) something not normal	(B) related to the body	**7.** _____
	(C) misnamed	(D) liveliness	
8. INCONGRUOUS	(A) grooved	(B) related to Congress	**8.** _____
	(C) unsuited	(D) appropriate	
9. HALE	(A) frozen rain	(B) vigorous	**9.** _____
	(C) ill-tempered	(D) spiritual or saintly	
10. SANCTION	(A) holy place	(B) to restrain	**10.** _____
	(C) to calm or relax	(D) to authorize	
11. MILITANT	(A) aggressive in defending a cause	(B) member of the armed service	**11.** _____
	(C) very small portion	(D) one who studies military strategy	

Go on to next page. ➤

12. **DEVIATE** (A) to consume (B) to devise 12. _____
  (C) to guard against (D) to depart from the expected

13. **CONJECTURE** (A) a guess (B) an overcrowded condition 13. _____
  (C) rejection (D) a combination or association

14. **TACT** (A) type of fastener (B) vulgarity 14. _____
  (C) grace and diplomacy (D) unharmed

15. **TANGIBLE** (A) real and concrete (B) unusual 15. _____
  (C) vague and abstract (D) tasty

16. **ADJACENT** (A) thoroughly hopeless (B) near 16. _____
  (C) far removed (D) adjustable

17. **ERRATIC** (A) a wanderer (B) predictable 17. _____
  (C) inconsistent (D) mistaken

18. **RELEGATE** (A) a representative (B) to banish 18. _____
  (C) related to current interests (D) to narrate

19. **SERENE** (A) calm and peaceful (B) shrill and piercing 19. _____
  (C) heavenly (D) nervous and agitated

20. **CONTINGENT** (A) repeated regularly and frequently (B) depending on certain conditions 20. _____
  (C) side by side (D) satisfied and content

21. **PREEMINENT** (A) church official (B) preferred 21. _____
  (C) someone claiming knowledge of the future (D) superior to all others

22. **ABERRANT** (A) disgusting and repulsive (B) simple 22. _____
  (C) not normal (D) abandoned

23. **FEISTY** (A) lazy (B) easily fooled 23. _____
  (C) frisky and full of spirit (D) young

24. **CONTIGUOUS** (A) joined (B) constant 24. _____
  (C) slippery (D) contradictory

25. **ANNALS** (A) books published once a year (B) chronological record of events 25. _____
  (C) to cancel (D) place to deposit items

Name _____

Typhoon!

The year was 1281. A giant naval force of 4,400 ships commanded by the Mongol emperor Kublai Khan, grandson of Genghis Khan, had quietly set sail from China and Korea. Their destination: Japan. The 4,400 commanders of these ships had no doubt about the purpose of this voyage.
5 Each had been given very **specific** orders—they were to attack and conquer Japan. Each commander had a part to play in this grand **conspiracy.** Even so, this huge gathering of military strength and careful planning was doomed, not by the Japanese, but by nature, which chose to **intervene.**

Strong winds and storms were not uncommon in these seas, especially in
10 August. But on this particular August day a storm struck with winds so **abnormally** strong that nearly all the Mongol ships were sunk, over 100,000 lives were lost, and the Japanese were saved from foreign conquerors. Such a powerful and fortunate occurrence was deemed by the Japanese to be the result of divine will. In gratitude, they named the
15 typhoon *kamikaze,* from *kami* (divine) and *kaze* (wind).

Few typhoons are considered to be fortunate events. Most cause great damage and destruction as they build in strength over the ocean before moving across land. What exactly is a typhoon? Typhoons and their **kindred** storms, called hurricanes when they occur in the Atlantic
20 Ocean, are the most powerful storms on earth. It is common for hurricanes to **sustain** winds of over 100 miles per hour for days. In 1992, Hurricane Andrew had winds that reached 200 miles per hour.

Typhoons and hurricanes are regularly **generated** at certain times of the year by the warm waters of the ocean. These storms begin when evapo-
25 rated sea water is drawn into the clouds and begins dropping as rain. Energy in the form of heat is released by this rain, which in turn provokes strong winds. The rotation of the earth causes the wind to travel in a large, circular pattern. The warm, moist air travels toward the center or eye of the storm, where the air pressure is low. Because the air is
30 warm, it rises, creating updrafts so fierce that they can tear the roof off a house, snap trees, and lift boats and automobiles. As if this were not enough, such strong storms often **spawn** tornadoes and torrential rains.

Hurricanes are classified by the Saffir-Simpson scale. On this scale a storm rated 1.0 is considered **minimal,** while a storm that is rated 5.0 could be
35 **catastrophic.** Before Hurricane Andrew, only three storms had been rated as level 5.0. On Labor Day, 1935, a hurricane hit the Florida Keys and caused great damage. Hurricane Camille, in 1969, was another level 5.0 hurricane, as was Hurricane Allen in 1980. But, in one way, Hurricane Andrew should probably be placed in a category by itself. Causing $30 billion
40 in damage, it was more destructive than the other three storms combined.

Words

abnormal

catastrophic

conspiracy

generate

intervene

kindred

minimal

spawn

specific

sustain

Each word in this lesson's word list appears in dark type in the selection you just read. Think about how the vocabulary word is used in the selection, then write the letter for the best answer to each question.

1. Which word could best replace *specific* in line 5?   1. _____
   (A) unusual   (B) impossible
   (C) exact   (D) peculiar

2. The word *conspiracy* in line 6 means _____.   2. _____
   (A) plot   (B) group
   (C) agreement   (D) naval campaign

3. Which word or words could best replace *intervene* in line 8?   3. _____
   (A) stand aside   (B) appear
   (C) disappear   (D) interfere

4. The word *abnormally* in line 11 means _____.   4. _____
   (A) commonly   (B) unusually
   (C) ridiculously   (D) typically

5. Which word could best replace *kindred* in line 19?   5. _____
   (A) related   (B) kind
   (C) childlike   (D) identical

6. Which word could best replace *sustain* in line 21?   6. _____
   (A) stop   (B) destroy
   (C) relieve   (D) support

7. The word *generated* in line 23 means _____.   7. _____
   (A) overlooked   (B) produced
   (C) studied   (D) changed

8. Which word or words could best replace *spawn* in line 32?   8. _____
   (A) spurn   (B) expand
   (C) bring forth   (D) spray

9. The word *minimal* in line 34 means _____.   9. _____
   (A) pleasant   (B) least amount
   (C) large   (D) unimportant

10. Which word could best replace *catastrophic* in line 35?   10. _____
    (A) beneficial   (B) adventurous
    (C) disastrous   (D) casual

Applying Meaning

Follow the directions below to write a sentence using a vocabulary word.

1. Describe a secret plan. Use the word *conspiracy*.

_____

_____

_____

2. Use any form of the word *abnormal* to describe the weather you had last winter.

_____

_____

_____

3. Use any form of the word *generate* to tell how you might raise money for a class project.

_____

_____

_____

4. Tell how a fight was stopped. Use any form of the word *intervene*.

_____

_____

_____

5. Use the word *kindred* in a sentence about someone you feel close to.

_____

_____

_____

6. Use any form of the word *catastrophic* to describe an event in history.

_____

_____

_____

Read each sentence below. Write "correct" on the answer line if the vocabulary word has been used correctly. Write "incorrect" on the answer line if the vocabulary word has been used incorrectly.

7. The recipe gave *specific* instructions on how to prepare the pizza crust.

7. _____

8. A new bridge is being planned to *spawn* the river at its narrowest point.

8. _____

9. Ralph tried to *sustain* his dog from attacking the letter carrier.

9. _____

10. Through most of the year, the desert regions of the Southwest get a *minimal* amount of rain.

10. _____

For each word used incorrectly, write a sentence using the word properly.

_____

_____

_____

_____

_____

_____

_____

_____

_____

_____

_____

Mastering Meaning

In a weather emergency, a warning and instructions for evacuating the area are usually given over a local radio station. Write a radio script warning of such a weather emergency in your town or city. Use some of the words you studied in this lesson.

Lesson 26 Part A

Name _____

Suppose you suddenly get a chance to visit a foreign country. You leave almost immediately, and you know nothing of the language. What are the absolute basic phrases you would want to learn on the plane? "Please" and "thank you," surely. Most tourists also need to learn the phrase "How much?" The question "How much?" can be answered in many ways, as you will learn in this lesson on words that tell quantity and amount.

Words
accretion
appreciable
copious
fathomless
finite
insatiable
iota
paltry
pittance
plethora

Unlocking Meaning

Read the sentences or short passages below. Write the letter for the correct definition of the italicized vocabulary word.

As Mr. Almirez wheeled his overflowing shopping cart to the grocery store checkout counter, he marveled at the *insatiable* appetites of his growing children.

1. (A) simple
   (B) not subject to suffering or pain
   (C) impossible to satisfy
   (D) characterized by sudden energy, impulsive

Peter hotly denied Irma's charge against him. "There's not even an *iota* of truth in what she says," he cried. "I never cheated."

2. (A) tiny amount
   (B) kind word
   (C) atom or group of atoms
   (D) refund

The Mississippi River continuously deposits sediment as it enters the Gulf of Mexico. This *accretion* of deposits causes the river to form fan-like deltas.

3. (A) acceleration
   (B) problem
   (C) provision of what is needed or desired
   (D) growth or enlargement through accumulation

A well-furnished parlor in Victorian times had a *plethora* of decorative items. Sometimes there were so many vases, pictures, pillows, doilies, scarves, and small trinkets that one could hardly see the furniture.

4. (A) matching sets
   (B) excess
   (C) shortage
   (D) deficiency

1. _____

2. _____

3. _____

4. _____

Like the ocean depths, outer space holds *fathomless* mysteries.

5. (A) incapable of being measured or understood   5. _____
   (B) inconsequential
   (C) easily explained
   (D) without foundation

Even though Woodstock is only thirty or so miles from Plymouth, its higher elevation gives the village *appreciably* cooler temperatures.

6. (A) dangerously   6. _____
   (B) noticeably
   (C) impossibly
   (D) immeasurably

Michele tried to prove to her parents that her allowance is only a *pittance* compared to the amounts her classmates receive every week.

7. (A) fair amount   7. _____
   (B) insult
   (C) small amount of money
   (D) foreign currency

Joan took such *copious* notes in history class that she did not have time to review them all before the exam.

8. (A) simple   8. _____
   (B) poorly organized
   (C) repetitious
   (D) abundant

Ms. Fazon had hoped that Polk's Antique Shop would make a substantial donation to the charity auction. Instead, Polk's gave some *paltry* bits of china.

9. (A) meager; insignificant   9. _____
   (B) new
   (C) excellent; outstanding
   (D) foul smelling

There is a *finite* number of combinations to the safe. It may take thousands of attempts, but we will eventually find the numbers that work.

10. (A) unending; eternal   10. _____
    (B) limited
    (C) constantly changing
    (D) incalculable; uncertain

Applying Meaning

Follow the directions below to write a sentence using a vocabulary word.

1. Describe a conversation in which many people give someone advice.
   Use the word *plethora* in your description.

   _____

   _____

   _____

2. Describe a birthday present. Use any form of the word *paltry* in your
   description.

   _____

   _____

   _____

3. Complete the sentence: Even though no one knows exactly how many,
   there is a *finite* number of ...

   _____

   _____

   _____

4. Write a short weather forecast. Use the word *copious*.

   _____

   _____

   _____

5. Write a sentence describing a person's salary. Use the word *pittance*.

   _____

   _____

   _____

Decide which word in parentheses best completes the sentence. Then
write the sentence, adding the missing word.

6. The Roman Empire grew by _____ until it controlled most of the
   lands around the Mediterranean Sea. (accretion; iota)

   _____

   _____

   _____

7. I have seen no _____ difference in the skaters' performances since they began using a choreographer. (appreciable; finite)

_____

_____

_____

8. In the melodramatic story, the heroine gazed into the hero's _____ dark eyes. (copious; fathomless)

_____

_____

_____

9. My boss has a(n) _____ need to control every situation, no matter how trivial. (paltry; insatiable)

_____

_____

_____

10. There was not one _____ of fear in his voice as he calmly guided the rescuer. (iota; pittance)

_____

_____

_____

Our Living Language

humongous

The slang term *humongous,* meaning extremely large or gigantic, was probably formed by combining *huge* and *monstrous* or *tremendous.* Although *humongous* has not as yet been accepted as a standard English word, many commonly accepted words have been formed by combining two existing words.

motor + hotel = motel

breakfast + lunch = brunch

Cooperative Learning: Work with a partner to see how many words you can think of that are a blend of two other words, then check their history in an unabridged dictionary. Here are two hints.

smoke + fog =   **blot + botch =**

Name _____

A surprising variety of English words have their root in the Latin word *portare,* which means "to carry." Perhaps the variety is less surprising when you consider how many ways we use the word *carry.* Trucks carry loads, we carry ourselves in various ways, mammals carry their young before birth, words carry meaning. All the words in this lesson contain the root -*port-*.

Root	Meaning	English Word
-port-	carry	portage
	harbor	opportune

Words

- **comport**
- **deportment**
- **opportune**
- **portable**
- **portage**
- **portfolio**
- **portly**
- **purport**
- **rapport**
- **sportive**

Unlocking Meaning

Write the vocabulary word that fits each clue below. Then say the word and write a short definition. Compare your definition and pronunciation with those given on the flash card.

1. This adjective could describe a small television with a handle, or a cordless telephone.

   _____

   _____

   _____

2. This word comes from the Latin word *comportare,* which combines the prefix *com-,* meaning "together," with the root -*port-*. The Latin word means "to bring together, to support." Now it refers to how individuals "carry" themselves.

   _____

   _____

   _____

3. This adjective might describe a person who enjoys soccer, rugby, swimming, or any kind of playful activity.

   _____

   _____

   _____

4. In this word you can see the word *folio,* meaning "leaves" or "pages."

   _____

   _____

   _____

5. This word refers to one's behavior or how a person carries himself or herself. It has the prefix *de-* meaning "out" or "away."

_____

_____

6. This word came to English through the Latin word *opportunus,* which described a wind that blew sailors toward port. Naturally, this word is used to describe something good.

_____

_____

_____

7. The spelling of this word might lead you to think it means "to carry one's age." However, it has more to do with carrying boats than with carrying years.

_____

_____

_____

8. This adjective can be used to describe a person with a stately bearing, but it more often is a reference to one's size.

_____

_____

9. This word for a pleasant relationship comes to us through the French *rapporter,* which means "to bring back" or "to bring together."

_____

_____

_____

10. This word came to English through the French word *porporter,* meaning "to contain."

_____

_____

_____

Applying Meaning

Follow the directions below to write a sentence using a vocabulary word.

1. Tell how someone should act at a funeral. Use any form of the verb *comport*.

_____

_____

_____

2. Describe the relationship between a coach and the members of a team. Use the word *rapport*.

_____

_____

_____

3. Use any form of the word *portage* in a sentence about a camping trip.

_____

_____

_____

4. Describe a telephone that does not need a cord. Use the word *portable*.

_____

_____

_____

5. Write a sentence about an artist's work. Use the word *portfolio*.

_____

_____

_____

Decide which word in parentheses best completes the sentence. Then write the sentence, adding the missing word.

6. The editor changed Manny's description of the famous opera singer from "fat" to "_____." (portly; sportive)

_____

_____

7. The new doctor on the staff _____ to have experience in five or six highly specialized fields. (comports; purports)

_____

_____

8. I am waiting for a(n) _____ moment to tell my mother about my grade on the test. (opportune; portable)

_____

_____

9. Today report cards contain comments on children's social skills. Your grandparents may have been graded on their _____ . (deportment; opportunism)

_____

_____

10. The soft drink industry often produces commercials in which _____ young people work up a thirst playing volleyball or football. (sportive, portly)

_____

_____

Test-Taking Strategies

Some college entrance examinations contain antonym questions. These questions ask you to choose the word that means the <u>opposite</u> of a word in capital letters.

Sample

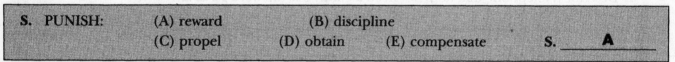

S. PUNISH:	(A) reward	(B) discipline				
	(C) propel	(D) obtain	(E) compensate	S. ____ **A** ____

Always read all of the choices before deciding on your answer. Think of the definition of the given word and then think of the opposite of that definition. Often tests will include a synonym as one of the answers. Do not allow this to confuse you.

Remember that words often have multiple meanings. If you do not find an opposite for the first meaning you think of, consider other meanings. Can you tell why A is the correct answer in the sample?

Practice: On the blank write the letter for the word most nearly opposite in meaning to the underlined word.

1. HALCYON: (A) foul   (B) hearty   1. _____
   (C) impoverished   (D) calm   (E) foolish

2. MORTIFY: (A) embarrass   (B) degrade   2. _____
   (C) disperse   (D) glorify   (E) indulge

3. INCUMBENT: (A) delegate   (B) challenger   3. _____
   (C) criminal   (D) adherence   (E) officer

Name _____

How well do you remember the words you studied in Lessons 25 through 27? Take the following test covering the words from the last three lessons.

Part 1 Antonyms

Each question below includes a word in capital letters, followed by four words or phrases. Choose the word or phrase that is most nearly <u>opposite</u> in meaning to the word in capital letters. Consider all choices before deciding on your answer. Write the letter for your answer on the line provided.

Sample

S. GOOD	(A) simple	(B) bad	**S.**	**B**
	(C) able	(D) fast		

1. COPIOUS	(A) limited	(B) remarkable	**1.** _____
	(C) generous	(D) visible	
2. SUSTAIN	(A) spoil	(B) hinder	**2.** _____
	(C) clean	(D) hold dear	
3. ABNORMAL	(A) weird	(B) rowdy	**3.** _____
	(C) calm	(D) typical	
4. OPPORTUNE	(A) strange sounds	(B) unfortunate	**4.** _____
	(C) of poor quality	(D) imaginary	
5. PORTABLE	(A) imported	(B) careless	**5.** _____
	(C) immovable	(D) heavy	
6. RAPPORT	(A) quiet	(B) requirement	**6.** _____
	(C) stately manner	(D) incompatibility	
7. INTERVENE	(A) ignore	(B) entangle	**7.** _____
	(C) release	(D) interrupt	
8. GENERATE	(A) imagine	(B) arouse	**8.** _____
	(C) simplify	(D) halt	
9. INSATIABLE	(A) easily satisfied	(B) inflated	**9.** _____
	(C) greedy	(D) insane	
10. PALTRY	(A) trivial	(B) important	**10.** _____
	(C) attractive	(D) unpaved	

Go on to next page. ➤

11. SPECIFIC   (A) vague   (B) exact   11. _____

                    (C) special   (D) narrow

12. MINIMAL   (A) remarkable   (B) complex   12. _____

                    (C) maximum   (D) foreign

13. PORTLY   (A) protected   (B) exposed   13. _____

                  (C) hidden   (D) lean

14. PLETHORA   (A) abundance   (B) prehistoric   14. _____

                   (C) modern   (D) shortage

15. SPORTIVE   (A) lifeless   (B) athletic   15. _____

                   (C) tendency to cheat   (D) humble

Part 2 Matching Words and Meanings

Match the definition in Column B with the word in Column A.
Write the letter of the correct definition on the line provided.

Column A	Column B	
16. finite	a. immeasurable	16 _____
17. deportment	b. carrying case	17. _____
18. conspiracy	c. noticeable	18. _____
19. kindred	d. limited	19. _____
20. spawn	e. related	20. _____
21. pittance	f. to claim	21. _____
22. fathomless	g. conduct	22. _____
23. appreciable	h. to produce	23. _____
24. portfolio	i. plot	24. _____
25. purport	j. tiny amount	25. _____

Name _____

Street Art

With the rapid spread of industry and the **ensuing** transformation of the urban landscape, city dwellers have found themselves living in increasingly bleak surroundings. Graffiti writers, in their attempts to adorn the bare walls of their environment, have become the **scourge** of politicians
5 and police. Under the **aegis** of neighborhood planning boards and even some mayors, however, what was once vandalism is now being converted into community art.

Many wall-writers, tired of **wielding** spray-paint cans and dodging police, have, on their own, branched into safer and more **remunerative** forms
10 of art. Some have redirected their efforts from buildings, bridges, and fences to tee shirts, theatrical stage sets, and compact disc covers. Others have adapted their messages to advertising, gracing the walls of commercial establishments with graffiti-style signs.

It is the **amnesty** programs for graffiti writers that have been most suc-
15 cessful at turning eyesores into art. In many large cities, former scrawlers now work to beautify the walls they once **ravaged.** Part government agency, part social service organization, and part art workshop, each group paints its town in rich **hues** while learning discipline, responsibility, and cooperation.

20 The street artists begin by obtaining the necessary permission to use unsightly fences, abandoned buildings, and blank walls as the canvases for astonishing murals. They seek ideas from local residents so that the paintings will reflect neighborhood heritage and values. Hours of effort are required to turn a vision into reality. Once the design conception is
25 **refined,** graffiti writers and neighborhood volunteers erect a scaffold, scrape and whitewash the surface, and create a grid for the sketch. Professional artists may be hired to transfer the design to the larger surface, but it is the ex–wall writers and members of the community who add the color and the detail to exotic tropical gardens, portraits of **illustrious**
30 sports stars, and memorable scenes from history.

Each of the murals is a treasured asset and a source of pride for its neighborhood. Like giant postcards or living museum walls, these murals carry a message that everyone can understand. By channeling the talents of graffiti artists into community art, color triumphs over
35 drabness in constructive self-expression.

Words

aegis

amnesty

ensue

hue

illustrious

ravage

refine

remunerative

scourge

wield

Unlocking Meaning

Each word in this lesson's word list appears in dark type in the selection you just read. Think about how the vocabulary word is used in the selection, then write the letter for the best answer to each question.

1. Which word or words could best replace *ensuing* in line 1?   **1.** _____
   (A) resulting   (B) spiritual
   (C) inspiring   (D) fully disclosed

2. Which word or words could best replace *scourge* in line 4?   **2.** _____
   (A) political cause   (B) inspiration
   (C) legal setback   (D) cause of widespread distress

3. *Aegis* (line 5) could best be replaced by _____.   **3.** _____
   (A) objections   (B) sponsorship
   (C) guarantee   (D) proposal

4. Which word or words could best replace *wielding* in line 8?   **4.** _____
   (A) handling with skill (B) succeeding with
   (C) admiring   (D) dispensing illegally

5. *Remunerative* (line 9) forms of art could best be explained as _____.   **5.** _____
   (A) tiresome   (B) ridiculous
   (C) profitable   (D) repetitive

6. *Amnesty* programs (line 14) could best be explained as those that _____.   **6.** _____
   (A) look foolish   (B) are forgetful
   (C) seem pointless   (D) pardon offenders

7. Which word could best replace *ravaged* in line 16?   **7.** _____
   (A) ignored   (B) eliminated
   (C) ruined   (D) discovered

8. *Hues* (line 18) could best be described as _____.   **8.** _____
   (A) energy waves   (B) shades of color
   (C) intentional errors (D) excuses

9. Which word could best replace *refined* in line 25?   **9.** _____
   (A) polished   (B) substituted
   (C) limited   (D) destroyed

10. Which word could best replace *illustrious* in line 29?   **10.** _____
    (A) angry   (B) dangerous
    (C) famous   (D) retired

Applying Meaning

Read each sentence below. Write "correct" on the answer line if the vocabulary word has been used correctly. Write "incorrect" on the answer line if the vocabulary word has been used incorrectly.

1. In an *amnesty* program, people with parking violations will be arrested unless they pay their fines with interest.

   1. _____

2. The music of *illustrious* composers like George Gershwin and Aaron Copland continues to have universal appeal.

   2. _____

3. Under the *aegis* of the United Nations, food and medicine were sent to the earthquake victims.

   3. _____

4. People with *refined* behavior might improve their poor manners with some simple instruction in etiquette.

   4. _____

5. Elijah was offended by several of the speaker's *remunerative* statements.

   5. _____

For each word used incorrectly, write a sentence using the word properly.

_____

_____

_____

_____

_____

_____

_____

_____

_____

_____

_____

Follow the directions below to write a sentence using a vocabulary word.

6. Describe a disease that has caused serious problems for people or animals. Use any form of the word *scourge*.

   _____

   _____

   _____

7. Describe how artists or musicians use the tools of their trade. Use any form of the word *wield*.

_____

_____

_____

8. Tell about a flood or similar natural disaster. Use any form of the word *ravage*.

_____

_____

_____

9. Describe a cause and its effect. Use any form of the word *ensue*.

_____

_____

_____

10. Describe a famous painting or a beautiful scene. Use the word *hue*.

_____

_____

_____

_____

Mastering Meaning

Choose a social issue, such as child labor or civil rights, or the theme of an administration, such as the New Frontier of John F. Kennedy or the Great Society of Lyndon Johnson. Then write a report about the success or failure of the program. Use some of the words we studied in this lesson.

Name _____

Throughout history, civilizations have been troubled by crime and criminals. From pirates and highway robbers to carjackers and computer hackers, there have always been people who, for many reasons, defy the law. In this lesson, you will learn ten words that describe crimes and the people who commit them.

Unlocking Meaning

Read the short passages below. Write the letter for the correct definition of the italicized vocabulary word.

One of the greatest fortunes in the United States was begun by a *charlatan*. With no medical background, William Rockefeller worked as a traveling medicine man, selling fake remedies for any illness.

1. (A) spokesperson
   (B) respected scientist
   (C) politician
   (D) someone falsely claiming to be an expert

The judge showed *clemency* during sentencing. Instead of sending the defendant to jail, she imposed a fine and community service.

2. (A) mercy
   (B) hostility
   (C) uprightness
   (D) self-interest

John Brown, who sought to free the slaves by military force, was found *culpable* for the crime of treason. He and a band of his followers took over an arsenal in Harpers Ferry, Virginia.

3. (A) unprepared
   (B) at fault
   (C) searching
   (D) unqualified

The *culprit* responsible for the neighborhood graffiti was led away by the police. He was arrested as he tried to dispose of three cans of neon-colored spray paint.

4. (A) person least likely to be suspected
   (B) respectable citizen
   (C) candidate for office
   (D) person accused or found guilty of an offense

Words
charlatan
clemency
culpable
culprit
exonerate
extort
felony
incorrigible
pilfer
reprobate

1. _____

2. _____

3. _____

4. _____

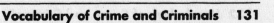

Although some historians have theorized that Ethel and Julius Rosenberg were innocent victims of hysteria against Communists, the couple has never been *exonerated*. They were executed in 1953 as convicted spies for the Soviet Union.

5. (A) thrust aside
   (B) assured of fame
   (C) proven blameless
   (D) dismissed as unworthy

5. _____

One technique that the gang used to build its power was to *extort* money from shopkeepers. Even though tradespeople found it difficult to afford the weekly payments, it was cheaper to pay for protection than to risk the destruction of their stores by the gang.

6. (A) obtain something through force or threats
   (B) encourage voluntary donation
   (C) misinterpret the need for
   (D) cleverly coax

6. _____

Although its worth has never actually been determined, the *Mona Lisa* is probably the most valuable object ever stolen. It disappeared from the Louvre museum in Paris on August 21, 1911, and was recovered in Italy in 1913. Vincenzo Perruggia was convicted of the *felony*.

7. (A) amusing blunder
   (B) source of the trouble
   (C) serious crime
   (D) minor violation

7. _____

The writers Zelda and F. Scott Fitzgerald were *incorrigible* pranksters. From splashing in public fountains to turning cartwheels and somersaults down crowded city streets, there seemed to be no end to their bad habits and zany behavior.

8. (A) capable of being misinterpreted
   (B) serious-minded
   (C) incapable of being reformed
   (D) easily reformed

8. _____

It made sense to Mark that many embezzlers, who steal huge amounts of money entrusted to their care, probably started small. He imagined that they might begin by *pilfering* from their mother's purse or a sister's piggy bank.

9. (A) borrowing
   (B) stealing small sums
   (C) acquiring in major installments
   (D) suffering a loss

9. _____

The ease with which Griffin lies and cheats indicates that he is a *reprobate*. Even his own family cannot trust him to know the difference between right and wrong.

10. (A) morally unprincipled or wicked person
    (B) one who possesses large amounts of property
    (C) person who excels at games of chance
    (D) discourteous individual

10. _____

Applying Meaning

Read each sentence or short passage below. Write "correct" on the answer line if the vocabulary word has been used correctly. Write "incorrect" on the answer line if the vocabulary word has been used incorrectly.

1. Receiving a minimum sentence of ten years, the jewel thief was *exonerated* for the robbery.

   1. _____

2. Mother couldn't figure out where all the socks had gone. She was amazed to learn that the *culprit* was the family dog.

   2. _____

3. The famous doctor, praised as an important *charlatan,* received an award for her contributions to medicine.

   3. _____

4. Even though the defense attorney pleaded for *clemency* for the seventy-year-old grandmother, the judge decided to make an example of her and issued the maximum penalty.

   4. _____

5. Having devoted her entire life to helping the poor and the sick, Mother Teresa has proven herself to be a devoted *reprobate.*

   5. _____

For each word used incorrectly, write a sentence using the word properly.

_____

_____

_____

_____

_____

_____

_____

_____

_____

_____

_____

Decide which word in parentheses best completes the sentence. Then write the sentence, adding the missing word.

6. The class officers finally discovered the year-long _____ of the graduation gift fund. (extortion; pilferage)

_____

_____

_____

7. The _____ of those involved in selling secrets to the enemy is undeniable. (clemency; culpability)

_____

_____

_____

8. "Obedience school will change your pup's _____ behavior," the trainer argued persuasively. (culpable; incorrigible)

_____

_____

_____

9. By demanding part of his classmates' lunches in return for his promise not to hurt them, the bully had begun a campaign of _____. (extortion; pilferage)

_____

_____

_____

10. Although never arrested or imprisoned for their _____ activities, the gangsters were believed to be responsible for several murders. (felonious; incorrigible)

_____

_____

_____

Bonus Word

abet

Abet, meaning "to instigate or encourage someone to act, often wrongfully," comes from the sport of bearbaiting that was popular in fourteenth- and fifteenth-century England. In bearbaiting, a bear, starved to ensure its viciousness, was chained to a stake or placed in a pit. A pack of dogs was set loose on it in a fight usually to the death. Spectators who urged the dogs on were said to abet them, *abet* being a form of the Old French word *abeter,* meaning "to bait or to hound on."

Cooperative Learning: Like *abet,* many other words and expressions from sports have taken on larger meanings and usage. With a group of your classmates, brainstorm a list of these terms and expressions, such as *playing hardball* (baseball) and *sidestep* (boxing).

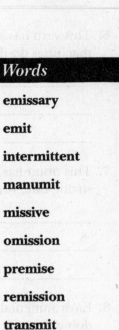

Lesson 30

Part A

Name _____

The roots *-mit-* and *-mis-* come from the Latin word *mittere,* meaning "to send." When combined with different prefixes and suffixes, these roots give us a number of words like the ones in this lesson. Each word has something to do with sending.

Root	Meaning	English Word
-mit-	to send	emit, intermittent
-mis-		missive, premise

Words

- **emissary**
- **emit**
- **intermittent**
- **manumit**
- **missive**
- **omission**
- **premise**
- **remission**
- **transmit**
- **unremitting**

Unlocking Meaning

Write the vocabulary word that fits each clue below. Then say the word and write a short definition. Compare your definition and pronunciation with those given on the flash card.

1. This word is always a noun. An ambassador to another country may play this role. It begins with the prefix *e-,* meaning "out."

_____

_____

2. This adjective has a prefix that means "at intervals." The telephone might provide this kind of interruption to your work.

_____

_____

_____

3. President Lincoln did this to slaves following the Civil War. It contains the Latin root *-manu-,* meaning "hand."

_____

_____

_____

4. This noun has a prefix that means "back." If the symptoms of a disease subside, a person might be described as being in this condition.

_____

_____

_____

5. It might take time to read one of these from a friend. It came into English through the Latin *missivus,* meaning "sent."

_____

_____

6. This verb has a prefix that means "across." Telegraph and facsimile machines do this to messages.

_____

_____

7. This noun has a prefix that means "before." If this concept is not a strong one, you may want to rethink your conclusion.

_____

_____

8. Environmental clean-air laws try to prevent factories and vehicles from doing this with harmful fumes. It begins with a prefix meaning "out."

_____

_____

9. This word has two prefixes; one means "not" and the other "back." The sound of crickets on a summer night could be described with this adjective.

_____

_____

10. If there are too many of these, your story will not be complete. It begins with a form of the Latin prefix *ob-,* meaning "against."

_____

_____

Applying Meaning

Follow the directions below to write a sentence using a vocabulary word.

1. Describe a problem with a machine or electrical device. Use any form of the word *intermittent*.

_____

_____

_____

2. Explain how someone might convey a message without using words. Use any form of the word *transmit*.

_____

_____

_____

3. Write a sentence about nuclear energy. Use any form of the word *emit*.

_____

_____

_____

4. Write to someone who has not met your expectations in doing a job. Use any form of the word *omission*.

_____

_____

_____

5. Describe a debate on a controversial issue. Use the word *premise*.

_____

_____

_____

Each question below contains a vocabulary word from this lesson.
Answer each question "yes" or "no" in the space provided.

6. Do *unremitting* hunger and thirst continue without relief? **6.** _____

7. Can a *missive* be launched at an enemy on a battlefield? **7.** _____

8. Is *manumission* a synonym for "emancipation"? **8.** _____

9. If a mission fails and a second attempt is made, is it a *remission*?   9. _____

10. Are all emigrants foreign *emissaries*?   10. _____

For each question you answered "no," write a sentence using the vocabulary word correctly.

_____

_____

_____

_____

_____

_____

_____

_____

_____

_____

Our Living Language

Acronyms, words formed by combining the initial letters or parts of a series of words, are one way in which new words enter the language. Several well-known scientific acronyms have to do with sending out signals. *Radar* was coined from **ra**dio **d**etecting **a**nd **r**anging, *laser* comes from **l**ight **a**mplification by **s**timulated **e**mission of **r**adiation, and *quasar* was developed from **quas**i-stell**ar** objects that are powerful emitters of radio waves.

Cooperative Learning: With a partner, brainstorm a list of possible new acronyms. For example, if someone you don't like keeps smiling at you, you might tell that person to *sysel*, or **s**end **y**our **s**miles **el**sewhere. Create an acronym for several of your best ideas, and define each new word. Then present your acronyms to the class.

Name _____

How well do you remember the words you studied in Lessons 28 through 30? Take the following test covering the words from the last three lessons.

Part 1 *Choose the Correct Meaning*

Each question below includes a word in capital letters, followed by four words or phrases. Choose the word or phrase that is <u>closest</u> in meaning to the word in capital letters. Write the letter for your answer on the line provided.

Sample

S. FINISH	(A) enjoy	(B) complete	**S.**	**B**
	(C) destroy	(D) send		

1. AMNESTY	(A) accusation	(B) forgiveness	**1.** _____
	(C) decoration	(D) agreement	
2. CULPRIT	(A) fake	(B) enemy	**2.** _____
	(C) murderer	(D) lawbreaker	
3. OMISSION	(A) something left out	(B) religious trip	**3.** _____
	(C) message	(D) representative	
4. FELONY	(A) legal document	(B) serious crime	**4.** _____
	(C) argument	(D) companion	
5. CHARLATAN	(A) faker	(B) court officer	**5.** _____
	(C) healer	(D) diplomat	
6. WIELD	(A) drive	(B) join together	**6.** _____
	(C) handle	(D) destroy	
7. ILLUSTRIOUS	(A) sensible	(B) illustrated	**7.** _____
	(C) unknown	(D) famous	
8. EMIT	(A) discard	(B) give off	**8.** _____
	(C) catch	(D) explain	
9. MANUMIT	(A) legal document	(B) small crime	**9.** _____
	(C) clever trick	(D) release	
10. REFINE	(A) perfect	(B) punish	**10.** _____
	(C) ruin	(D) refer	

Go on to next page. ➤

11. REPROBATE   (A) refund   (B) threat   11. _____
                      (C) scoundrel   (D) court officer

12. AEGIS   (A) label   (B) sponsorship   12. _____
                      (C) quarrel   (D) exit

13. CULPABLE   (A) deserving blame (B) portable   13. _____
                      (C) rare   (D) unable to be
                                              reformed

14. INTERMITTENT (A) broken   (B) starting and   14. _____
                                              stopping
                      (C) seldom used   (D) secret message

15. RAVAGE   (A) uncivilized person (B) compliment   15. _____
                      (C) remarkable   (D) ruin

Part 2 Matching Words and Meanings

Match the definition in Column B with the word in Column A.
Write the letter of the correct definition on the line provided.

Column A	Column B	
16. emissary	a. steal a small amount	16. _____
17. scourge	b. shade of color	17. _____
18. hue	c. constant	18. _____
19. clemency	d. send	19. _____
20. missive	e. representative	20. _____
21. pilfer	f. take by force	21. _____
22. extort	g. cause of suffering	22. _____
23. transmit	h. declare innocent	23. _____
24. unremitting	i. letter	24. _____
25. exonerate	j. mercy	25. _____

Name _____

Jeanealogy

If you are like many people your age, the major **sartorial** decision you make each morning is which pair of jeans to wear. Well over 600 million pairs were sold in 1992 alone, making jeans the best-selling pants in the world. Denim is one of the last **legitimate** connections to our past.
5   Throughout their **hallowed** history, jeans have never gone out of style.

Blue jeans got their name long before they reached their current popularity. In the late sixteenth century, the cotton cloth used to make them was called *Genoa Fustian* after Genoa, Italy, where the material was first woven. *Genoa* was changed to *Gene* and then to *Jean* by the English, *Fustian*
10   was dropped, and the work pants made from the material were called blue jeans for their color.

The first pair of jeans were waist overalls (as opposed to bib overalls) made by Levi Strauss, a Bavarian immigrant to the United States. In 1850, Strauss went to California with bolts of brown canvas that he
15   hoped to sell as tenting to gold miners. When he realized how quickly miners' work clothes wore out, he decided to use the canvas to make **staunch** pants. After he exhausted his canvas stock, he ordered the heavy, more **versatile** fabric called *denim* from a textile company in New Hampshire.

20   Strauss's pants were enormously popular with the miners, with one exception: the pockets tore off too easily when the men filled them with lumps of ore. In 1873, he added the copper rivets that strengthen the pocket seams. Some **extrinsic** modifications followed, such as the "bird in flight" stitching on the back pockets.

25   Although we take them for granted now, jeans were not widely accepted until the late 1970s, when John Travolta wore them in *Urban Cowboy*. Designer jeans were the rage in the 1980s, when stonewashed and faded denim were introduced for those who had no time to let their jeans age gracefully. More **gratuitous** innovations were inaugurated, such as zip-
30   pers up and down the pants legs, fashionable patches in **strategic** places, and carefully designed machine rips and tears.

In spite of all the fine-tuning, basic blue jeans not only have survived, but they have triumphed. People from around the world **covet** jeans as pieces of Americana that rank with Mickey Mouse and fast food. Re-
35   cycled jeans are a hot **commodity,** often selling overseas at five times their original price. Little did Levi Strauss realize that one day his creation would clothe the world.

Words
commodity
covet
extrinsic
gratuitous
hallowed
legitimate
sartorial
staunch
strategic
versatile

Unlocking Meaning

Each word in this lesson's word list appears in dark type in the selection you just read. Think about how the vocabulary word is used in the selection, then write the letter for the best answer to each question.

1. Which word or words could best replace *sartorial* in line 1?
   (A) relating to orderliness   (B) intellectual
   (C) relating to clothing   (D) quick

   1. _____

2. *Legitimate* (line 4) connections could best be explained as _____.
   (A) confused   (B) genuine
   (C) current   (D) happy

   2. _____

3. Which word or words could best replace *hallowed* in line 5?
   (A) highly respected   (B) perfectly conceived
   (C) suppressed   (D) remote

   3. _____

4. Which word or words could best replace *staunch* in line 17?
   (A) abbreviated   (B) having delicate lines
   (C) having strong construction   (D) comfortable

   4. _____

5. *Versatile* (line 18) could best be explained as _____.
   (A) conforming   (B) having distinct patterns
   (C) unusual   (D) having many uses

   5. _____

6. *Extrinsic* (line 23) could best be explained as _____.
   (A) vital   (B) not essential
   (C) witty   (D) not precise

   6. _____

7. Which word could best replace *gratuitous* in line 29?
   (A) unnecessary   (B) elaborate
   (C) sensitive   (D) satisfying

   7. _____

8. *Strategic* (line 30) could best be explained as _____.
   (A) sensitive   (B) permissive
   (C) nearly all   (D) well-planned

   8. _____

9. Which word or words could best replace *covet* in line 33?
   (A) acknowledge   (B) longingly wish for
   (C) completely refuse to accept   (D) tolerate

   9. _____

10. A *commodity* (line 35) could best be explained as _____.
    (A) a lavish compliment   (B) an awkward situation
    (C) something bought and sold   (D) anything seen as new and improved

    10. _____

Applying Meaning

Decide which word in parentheses best completes the sentence. Then write
the sentence, adding the missing word.

1. Michael's sarcastic tone and his _____ remarks about the quality of the
   food would have hurt the feelings of our hostess. (gratuitous; sartorial)

   _____

   _____

   _____

2. Hattie McDaniel, the first African American to win an Academy Award
   for her performance in *Gone with the Wind,* was a _____ performer
   who could sing as well as act. (staunch; versatile)

   _____

   _____

   _____

3. Beau Brummell, known for his _____ elegance, refused to tip his
   hat to the ladies out of fear that he might mess up his wig.
   (hallowed; sartorial)

   _____

   _____

   _____

4. Although never the _____ leader of Argentina, Eva Perón had
   immense influence over her husband and achieved enormous popularity among her people. (extrinsic; legitimate)

   _____

   _____

   _____

5. Copies of designer merchandise, such as watches and handbags, have
   become important _____ to street vendors and to shoppers looking for a bargain. (commodities; strategies)

   _____

   _____

   _____

Each question below contains a vocabulary word from this lesson. Answer each question "yes" or "no" in the space provided.

6. Does a *covetous* person experience jealousy and envy?　　6. _____

7. Is a *staunchly* built house apt to collapse during a storm?　　7. _____

8. Are tires and seats considered to be *extrinsic* features of a car?　　8. _____

9. Is devising a *strategy* one type of problem solving?　　9. _____

10. Is *hallowed* ground deeply indented or full of empty spaces?　　10. _____

For each question you answered "no," write a sentence using the vocabulary word properly.

_____

_____

_____

_____

_____

_____

_____

_____

_____

_____

_____

Mastering Meaning

You have decided to enter an essay contest on the greatest invention of the twentieth century. Select an invention that is important to you, such as the personal stereo, the computer, or the zipper. Then write an essay discussing why people would find it difficult to live without this invention. Use some of the words you studied in this lesson.

Although we tend to think of discord as a situation in which hostile feelings are expressed, disagreement can often have a positive result. Differences of opinion can lead to better understanding or changed attitudes. In this lesson, you will learn ten words that deal with forms of discord and their effects.

Unlocking Meaning

Read the sentences or short passages below. Write the letter for the correct definition of the italicized vocabulary word.

The hiring of an outsider as a supervisor caused *dissension* between workers and management and interfered with productivity.

1. (A) a dramatic action or gesture
   (B) a mixture of elements
   (C) a difference of opinion
   (D) a systematic method for obtaining obedience

Two hockey players spent several crucial minutes in the penalty box as a result of their *altercation* with the referee.

2. (A) angry or heated argument
   (B) lengthy discussion
   (C) something believed or accepted as true
   (D) devastating collision

As *retribution* for offending Zeus, Sisyphus was forced to roll an enormous boulder to the top of a steep hill. Every time the boulder neared the top, it would roll back down, and Sisyphus would have to start over.

3. (A) a return to a previous state or position
   (B) a loss of freedom
   (C) the ability to remember
   (D) something demanded in payment, especially punishment

Although he never provided sufficient evidence to support the charges, Senator McCarthy managed to ruin the lives of the people he accused of being Communists. For example, many talented writers, directors, and actors found themselves *ostracized* by Hollywood and unable to find work.

4. (A) lied to and deceived
   (B) treated in a friendly manner
   (C) banished or excluded from a group
   (D) admired for patriotic actions

Words

acerbity

affront

altercation

antagonism

contentious

dissension

ostracize

pugnacious

rancor

retribution

1. _____

2. _____

3. _____

4. _____

Realizing that their *antagonism* has led to the tragic death of their children Romeo and Juliet, the Montague and Capulet families declare a tardy, sorrowful truce at the end of the play.

5. (A) regretful acknowledgment of a fault or offense
    (B) opposition or hostility
    (C) dishonest behavior
    (D) disastrous defeat

5. _____

In *Gulliver's Travels,* Jonathan Swift's *acerbity* was directed against the stupidity of people. The novel contains his bitterest denunciation of human beings.

6. (A) sharpness of mood or expression
    (B) trivial or petty thoughts
    (C) sudden, overpowering terror
    (D) powerful emotion or appetite

6. _____

Rancor was maintained by generations of Hatfields and McCoys, even though only a few members of each family could remember the original cause of the feud.

7. (A) offensive remark
    (B) bitter, long-lasting resentment
    (C) a poorly hidden feeling
    (D) something that signifies authority

7. _____

When Jack is in a *contentious* mood, he contradicts everything we say.

8. (A) free from guilt
    (B) quarrelsome
    (C) tolerant in judging others
    (D) vividly expressive

8. _____

Carmen was so defensive that she took her painting instructor's comments as an *affront* rather than as constructive criticism.

9. (A) violation of a confidence
    (B) example of an old-fashioned belief
    (C) vigorous enjoyment
    (D) intentional insult

9. _____

With his *pugnacious* temperament and his nasty attitude, Peter makes an enemy of everyone he cares about.

10. (A) independent
    (B) beyond what is normal or reasonable
    (C) ready and eager to fight
    (D) excessively dramatic

10. _____

Applying Meaning

Decide which word in parentheses best completes the sentence. Then write
the sentence, adding the missing word.

1. Joseph Smith, the founder of the Mormon religion, was killed
   because of the _____ of a mob that wanted to see his church
   destroyed. (acerbity; antagonism)

   _____

   _____

   _____

2. Although she denied that she was bitter, we could hear the _____
   in Denise's voice when she talked about not being invited to the
   banquet. (dissension; rancor)

   _____

   _____

   _____

3. The minor accident on the parkway resulted in an _____ between
   the two drivers, both of whom jumped out of their cars shouting and
   waving their fists. (affront; altercation)

   _____

   _____

   _____

4. Because he had reported the students who had vandalized the computer lab, Dwight was _____ by some of his classmates.
   (affronted; ostracized)

   _____

   _____

   _____

5. Many who caused _____ in the Soviet Union were sent to Siberia
   as their punishment. (dissension; retribution)

   _____

   _____

   _____

Write each sentence below. In the space write a form of the word in parentheses. The form of the word in parentheses may be correct.

6. Tomás de Torquemada, the first inquisitor-general of the Spanish Inquisition, was feared for the severity of his punishments as well as his _____ personality. (acerbity)

_____

_____

7. The _____ between Caligula and the Roman senators came to a head when he appointed his horse to the senate in order to humiliate them. (contentious)

_____

_____

8. Mr. Kusack sued the tabloid newspaper as _____ for the damage done to his reputation. (retribution)

_____

_____

9. The mother grizzly bear, disturbed during feeding, rose on her hind legs and roared _____. (pugnacious)

_____

_____

10. The diners _____ the waiter by leaving a tiny tip. (affront)

_____

_____

Our Living Language

The word *ostracize*, meaning "to banish or exclude from a group," comes from *ostrakon*, the Greek word for oyster shell. A vote to banish someone was a serious matter. Given that paper was scarce, the banishment ballot was written on oyster shells or pieces of tile that resembled them. It followed that the Greek word *ostrakismos* became the name of the act itself.

Write an Advice Column: Ostracism is still used today as a more subtle form of peer or social pressure. Write an advice column for teenagers in which you explain other, more effective methods for achieving unity within a group. Use some of the words you studied in this lesson.

Name _____

The roots *-pos-* and *-pon-* and the variant form *-pou-* come from the Latin word *ponere,* meaning "to put" or "to place." When combined with prefixes and suffixes, these roots give us a number of words that share a single idea. For example, both *component* and *composite* have prefixes that mean "together." Although both words share the literal idea of "putting together," they are actually very different. Whereas a *component* is a part of a whole, a *composite* is a whole made up of parts. In this lesson, you will learn ten words whose meanings have something to do with putting or placing.

Root	Meaning	English Word
-pos-	to put or place	composite
-pon-		component
-pou-		expound

Words

component

composite

disposition

exponent

expound

impostor

juxtaposition

propound

repository

supposition

Unlocking Meaning

Write the vocabulary word that fits each clue below. Then say the word and write a short definition. Compare your definition and pronunciation with those given on the flash card.

1. This word is the noun form of *dispose,* meaning "to put in order" or "to get rid of." You could think of it as putting your mood in order.

_____

_____

_____

2. It begins with the prefix *com-,* meaning "with" or "together." Its root meaning is "put together."

_____

_____

_____

3. You see the word *position* in this longer word. It is more difficult to see the Latin word *iuxta,* meaning "close by" in it.

_____

_____

4. Since the verb form of this noun means "to lay oneself down," it stands to reason that this is the place where it occurs.

_____

_____

_____

5. This "phony" individual literally puts on a misleading or improper name. If you claimed to be a famous movie star, you would be one.

_____

_____

_____

6. This word came into English through the Latin *componere*, meaning "to put together." Some stereo systems are made up of these.

_____

_____

_____

7. This word begins with the prefix *ex-* meaning "out." In its literal, root sense it means someone who puts or places something out. In reality it has more to do with speaking out.

_____

_____

_____

8. It is the noun form of *suppose*, meaning "to assume to be true or accurate."

_____

_____

_____

9. This word is a synonym for *propose*. Both begin with the prefix *pro-* meaning "forward."

_____

_____

_____

10. Change the prefix to your answer to number 9 to make this word. The new prefix changes "forward" to "out" or "out of."

_____

_____

_____

Applying Meaning

Read each sentence or short passage below. Write "correct" on the answer line if the vocabulary word has been used correctly. Write "incorrect" on the answer line if the vocabulary word has been used incorrectly.

1. A collage is an artistic *composite* of materials and objects pasted over a surface.

   1. _____

2. A person who *propounds* a theory dismisses it as irrelevant on the basis of its age.

   2. _____

3. A bus or train station locker seems to be the favorite *repository* of shady characters intent upon stashing illegal articles.

   3. _____

4. The police had to *expound* the stolen automobile until the trial could be held.

   4. _____

5. As a devoted *exponent* of method acting, DeVona believes the approach to be artificial and haphazard.

   5. _____

6. Buster Keaton, the slapstick comedian, was famous for his expression-less face and his gentle *disposition.*

   6. _____

7. Anna Anderson, who claimed to be the youngest daughter of Czar Nicholas II of Russia, could not be entirely dismissed as an *impostor.* In 1957 a German court decided that it could neither confirm nor deny her identity.

   7. _____

8. "The *juxtaposition* of the vase on top of the pedestal should allow you to fit everything into your camera frame," advised the photography instructor.

   8. _____

9. According to an early *supposition,* milk in combination with any other food was considered poisonous. Obviously, this misconception was proven false long ago.

   9. _____

10. Plastic, glass, and paper must be placed in separate *components* before the recycling center will accept them.

    10. _____

11. Before the *disposition* of the financier's estate can take place, the will must go to a probate court to establish its validity.

    11. _____

12. Alan is the company's *repository* of trademark and patent data.

    12. _____

For each word used incorrectly, write a sentence using the word properly.

_____

_____

_____

_____

_____

_____

_____

_____

_____

_____

_____

_____

_____

_____

_____

_____

_____

Cultural Literacy Note

Idiomatic expressions, which are common phrases or traditional ways of saying something, rarely make sense if taken literally. For example, if you "put on the dog," you make a show of wealth or elegance. If you "put your foot in your mouth," you make an embarrassing or tactless blunder when speaking. Many of these expressions have interesting histories. For example, "putting one's best foot forward" probably originated with the ancient belief that it was unlucky to begin any journey or enterprise with the left foot. Therefore, the best foot was the right foot.

Cooperative Learning: With a partner, brainstorm a list of idiomatic expressions that begin with _put_, such as "put in a good word for someone," "put up your dukes," and "put on the spot." Write a brief explanation of the meaning for each expression. Then use an etymological dictionary of word and phrase origins to investigate the sources of the expressions.

Name _____

How well do you remember the words you studied in Lessons 31 through 33? Take the following test covering the words from the last three lessons.

Part 1 Antonyms

Each question below includes a word in capital letters, followed by four words or phrases. Choose the word or phrase that is most nearly <u>opposite</u> in meaning to the word in capital letters. Consider all choices before deciding on your answer. Write the letter for your answer on the line provided.

Sample

S. GOOD	(A) simple	(B) bad	S. ___**B**___
	(C) able	(D) fast	

1. COVET	(A) expose	(B) hide	1. _____
	(C) dislike	(D) crave	
2. DISSENSION	(A) cooperation	(B) arrangement	2. _____
	(C) declaration	(D) confrontation	
3. COMPOSITE	(A) without parts	(B) compound	3. _____
	(C) decomposed	(D) argument	
4. EXTRINSIC	(A) additional	(B) relaxed	4. _____
	(C) imported	(D) essential	
5. OSTRACIZE	(A) ignore	(B) care for	5. _____
	(C) include	(D) crush violently	
6. SUPPOSITION	(A) invitation	(B) proven fact	6. _____
	(C) interruption	(D) assumption	
7. PROPOUND	(A) withdraw	(B) release	7. _____
	(C) vigorously defend	(D) lighten	
8. VERSATILE	(A) uninformed	(B) useful	8. _____
	(C) rigid	(D) imaginary	
9. PUGNACIOUS	(A) generous	(B) smooth	9. _____
	(C) logical	(D) peaceful	
10. ANTAGONISM	(A) hostility	(B) faith	10. _____
	(C) harmony	(D) strong desire	
11. LEGITIMATE	(A) not valid	(B) despised	11. _____
	(C) theoretical	(D) ordinary	

Go on to next page. ➤

12. AFFRONT (A) background (B) escape 12. _____
(C) compliment (D) diminish

13. STAUNCH (A) firm (B) frail 13. _____
(C) starched (D) humorous

14. HALLOWED (A) completely filled (B) silent 14. _____
(C) blessed (D) condemned

15. GRATUITOUS (A) ungrateful (B) essential 15. _____
(C) alarming (D) lovable

Part 2 Matching Words and Meanings

Match the definition in Column B with the word in Column A.
Write the letter of the correct definition on the line provided.

Column A	Column B	
16. commodity	a. relating to clothes	16. _____
17. sartorial	b. something bought or sold	17. _____
18. altercation	c. mood or attitude	18. _____
19. juxtaposition	d. well-planned	19. _____
20. exponent	e. a fight	20. _____
21. component	f. explain and clarify	21. _____
22. disposition	g. side-by-side placement	22. _____
23. expound	h. one who explains and defends	23. _____
24. strategic	i. quarrelsome	24. _____
25. contentious	j. part of a larger system	25. _____

Name _____

An Early Voice for the Environment

In the 1930s, long before most people were concerned about the environment, a conservationist named Aldo Leopold sought to change America's attitude toward the natural world. From the time European settlers first set foot on the North American continent, nature had been
5 viewed as something to be tamed and used. Buffalo hides brought profit, and buffalo stood in the way of ranchers and cattle, so millions of buffalo were slaughtered. Eventually, houses were built. Land was plowed. Oil and other resources were used up. For two hundred years, decisions about the land were primarily **economic** decisions.

10 Leopold was one of the first to express **anxiety** over that kind of thinking. He knew that modern civilization had its price. Expanded highways and railroads could connect all parts of the country, but they also meant that forests had to be cut and open space destroyed. The factories and mills that provided steel and other materials for the automobile and the sky-
15 scraper also released clouds of smoke and gas and often dumped waste into rivers. Leopold was **appalled** by this devastation of the natural environment, and he worried that future generations of Americans might not have the wonder and beauty of an undisturbed land to enjoy. Once the peaceful **serenity** of open space was disturbed, he feared, it would be dif-
20 ficult if not impossible to regain.

Leopold made an important observation: As people became more and more distanced from the land, they began to lose sight of how much they depended on it. Then, he reasoned, the **converse** must also be true: If people could be brought in closer contact with the land, they would begin
25 to understand the **interdependence** between the land and its inhabitants.

Leopold was convinced that if people were brought closer with the land, they would regain an **appreciation** for the need to respect and preserve it. They could see firsthand the **myriad** interactions that exist in nature— how the quality of the soil affects the sugar maple, how the snow serves
30 to hide the meadow mouse from the birds that prey on it. In planting and harvesting a vegetable garden, they could relearn the **intricate** pattern formed by the soil-plant-animal food chain. In short, people would gain a new view of the nature around them and choose to **nurture** it rather than exploit and destroy it.

35 In his 1949 book titled *A Sand County Almanac*, Leopold recorded his experiences reclaiming a parcel of land in Sand County, Wisconsin. This book strongly influenced the nation's attitude toward the environment. While we now have many individuals and organizations concerned with the environment, this was not always the case. During his lifetime, Aldo
40 Leopold stood virtually alone in his fight to preserve nature's gifts.

Words

anxiety

appall

appreciate

converse

economic

interdependence

intricate

myriad

nurture

serenity

Each word in this lesson's word list appears in dark type in the selection you just read. Think about how the vocabulary word is used in the selection, then write the letter for the best answer to each question.

1. Which word or words could best replace *economic* in line 9?   1. _____
   (A) educational   (B) difficult
   (C) related to money   (D) careful

2. Which word could best replace *anxiety* in line 10?   2. _____
   (A) interest   (B) delight
   (C) joy   (D) concern

3. Which word could best replace *appalled* in line 16?   3. _____
   (A) impressed   (B) shocked
   (C) confused   (D) amused

4. Which word could best replace *serenity* in line 19?   4. _____
   (A) boredom   (B) calm
   (C) loneliness   (D) confusion

5. *Converse* in line 23 means _____.   5. _____
   (A) opposite   (B) theory
   (C) logical arguments   (D) facts

6. Which word or words could best replace *interdependence* in line 25?   6. _____
   (A) suspicion   (B) reliance on each other
   (C) independence   (D) hostility

7. Which word could best replace *appreciation* in line 27?   7. _____
   (A) ignorance   (B) dislike
   (C) enjoyment   (D) understanding

8. Which word could best replace *myriad* in line 28?   8. _____
   (A) rare   (B) senseless
   (C) numerous   (D) limited

9. Which word could best replace *intricate* in line 31?   9. _____
   (A) confusing   (B) simple
   (C) orderly   (D) complex

10. Which word could best replace *nurture* in line 33?   10. _____
    (A) support   (B) rearrange
    (C) neglect   (D) betray

Applying Meaning

Follow the directions below to write a sentence using a vocabulary word.

1. Tell about a time when you had to take an important test that you were not prepared to take. Use any form of the word *anxiety*.

_____

_____

_____

2. Describe your reaction to a surprising event that you witnessed. Use any form of the word *appall*.

_____

_____

_____

3. Describe the relationship between two countries or people. Use any form of the word *interdependence*.

_____

_____

_____

4. Describe the appearance of a city or a landscape. Use the word *myriad*.

_____

_____

_____

5. Describe a gardener caring for plants. Use any form of the word *nurture*.

_____

_____

_____

6. Tell about a surprise party or similar event you might plan. Use any form of the word *intricate*.

_____

_____

_____

Read each sentence below. Write "correct" on the answer line if the vocabulary word has been used correctly. Write "incorrect" on the answer line if the vocabulary word has been used incorrectly.

7. Where people choose to live is often a matter of *economics*.

7. _____

8. My father plans to *converse* our garage into an extra bedroom.

8. _____

9. The *serene* patient tossed and turned in her bed, called for the nurse, and finally threw a pitcher of water on the floor.

9. _____

10. After the power failure, I had a better *appreciation* of how much we depend on electricity.

10. _____

11. Teasing that huge dog the way he did showed an *appalling* lack of good sense.

11. _____

12. Hiking and fishing are good ways of getting close to *nurture*.

12. _____

For each word used incorrectly, write a sentence using the word properly.

_____

_____

_____

_____

_____

_____

_____

_____

_____

_____

Mastering Meaning

Write a series of advertising slogans aimed at educating people about the need to preserve our environment. Each slogan should be no more than one sentence long. Make a poster for the one you feel is the best. Use some of the words you studied in this lesson.

Lesson
35

Part A

Name _____

You have no doubt heard the expression "Actions speak louder than words." This lesson focuses on ten words related to strength and action. Adding these words to your vocabulary will help your words speak as loudly as your actions.

Unlocking Meaning

Read the sentences or short passages below. Write the letter for the correct definition of the italicized vocabulary word.

I have never liked high places very much. Just the thought of taking a plane trip makes my heart begin to *palpitate*.

1. (A) relax
   (B) beat rapidly
   (C) swell with pride
   (D) leap with joy

After the coach gives another rousing halftime speech, the inspired team will again *sally* onto the football field eager to take on their opponents.

2. (A) walk leisurely
   (B) ride ceremoniously
   (C) slide carelessly
   (D) rush forth

Only the most *dexterous* performer could juggle four balls while walking a tightrope.

3. (A) physically skillful
   (B) expensive
   (C) demanding
   (D) unusual

The plan to build a huge shopping center near the elementary school encountered *vehement* opposition. Parents demanded that the city council consider the danger that increased traffic would pose for their children.

4. (A) uncertain
   (B) intense and passionate
   (C) banished or excluded from a group
   (D) senseless and foolish

Words

- **brazen**
- **dexterous**
- **incursion**
- **palpitate**
- **redoubtable**
- **resolute**
- **sally**
- **stalwart**
- **stamina**
- **vehement**

1. _____

2. _____

3. _____

4. _____

As the election results came in, it was clear that Senator Sloan was hopelessly behind. Except for a few *stalwart* supporters, his campaign staff quickly departed.

5. (A) exhausted
   (B) uninformed
   (C) strong; loyal
   (D) weak; simple

5. _____

The Yorktown Eagles were a *redoubtable* opponent. They were taller, stronger, and more experienced. It was little wonder that they had not lost a game in three years.

6. (A) arousing fear
   (B) hated
   (C) weird
   (D) timid

6. _____

The company's threat to move its factory to another state was nothing less than a *brazen* attempt to avoid obeying environmental rules.

7. (A) clever
   (B) successful
   (C) admirable
   (D) shameless

7. _____

After three overtime periods, it was clear that the team with the most *stamina* would eventually win.

8. (A) training
   (B) endurance
   (C) loyal supporters
   (D) caution

8. _____

The mission had had numerous setbacks. Supplies had been lost or misplaced, and the workers were demoralized. Only the *resolute* courage of the leader kept hope alive.

9. (A) determined
   (B) meager
   (C) foolish
   (D) generous

9. _____

The Confederate *incursion* into the North during the Civil War was repelled at Gettysburg, Pennsylvania.

10. (A) invitation
    (B) accidental movement
    (C) retreat
    (D) invasion

10. _____

Applying Meaning

Each question below contains a vocabulary word from this lesson. Answer
each question "yes" or "no" in the space provided.

1. Would someone who has a habit of making *brazen* remarks be considered polite?

1. _____

2. Is the star player on a basketball team likely to be highly *dexterous*?

2. _____

3. Does daily exercise usually increase one's *stamina*?

3. _____

4. If someone constantly changes his opinion on an issue, is he *redoubtable*?

4. _____

5. Would a *stalwart* supporter of a presidential candidate be likely to forget to vote in the election?

5. _____

6. Would bringing a loud radio into the library be considered an *incursion* by students doing their homework?

6. _____

For each question you answered "no," write a sentence using the vocabulary word correctly.

_____

_____

_____

_____

_____

_____

_____

_____

_____

_____

_____

_____

_____

_____

_____

_____

Decide which word in parentheses best completes the sentence. Then write the sentence, adding the missing word.

7. As the convicted robber was led from the courtroom, he _____ denied his guilt to the judge and jury. (dexterously; vehemently)

_____

_____

_____

8. At a given signal, the troops _____ forth to meet the enemy. (palpitated; sallied)

_____

_____

_____

9. "We will put an end to government waste!" With those _____ words the senator opened the committee meeting. (dexterous; resolute)

_____

_____

_____

10. The doctor warned her that the medication might cause heart _____ . (incursions; palpitations)

_____

_____

_____

Cultural Literacy Note

Cutting the Gordian Knot

King Gordius of Phrygia is supposed to have tied a tight, complicated knot. It was predicted that whoever untied this knot would rule all of Asia. However, rather than attempt to untie it, Alexander the Great impatiently cut it with a single swing of his sword. Nowadays when we refer to "cutting the Gordian knot," we mean solving a difficult problem quickly and boldly.

Present a Report: Look through some newspapers or news magazines for an example of a proposal or decision you consider to be an attempt to "cut a Gordian knot." Report on it to the class.

Name _____

The concept of time or timing is a vital part of how we see things. The Greek word for time was *khronos*. When it began appearing in English words, the spelling was changed to *-chron-*. The word *tempus* in Latin means "time." In English it usually appears as the root *-tempor-*. Each vocabulary word in this lesson has one of these "time" roots or word parts.

Root	Meaning	English Word
-chron-	time	chronological
-tempor-		contemporary

Unlocking Meaning

A vocabulary word appears in italics in each sentence or short passage below. Find the root or word part in the vocabulary word and think about how the word is used in the passage. Then write a definition for the vocabulary word. Compare your definition with the definition on the flash card.

1. After hearing him recite his daily list of problems and criticisms, I am forced to believe Roger is just a *chronic* complainer.

   _____

   _____

   _____

2. The election could not be held for several months. In the meantime, the governor appointed Ann Kamazi to serve *pro tempore* on the commission.

   _____

   _____

   _____

3. For the rescue attempt to be a success, the helicopter and the ground crew would need to *synchronize* their efforts. If the helicopter arrived too soon, its whirling propellers would interfere with the work.

   _____

   _____

   _____

4. After photocopiers became available, carbon paper quickly became an *anachronism* in most offices.

   _____

   _____

   _____

Words

anachronism

chronic

chronicle

chronological

contemporary

extemporaneous

pro tempore

synchronize

temporal

temporize

5. The biography of Abraham Lincoln gave a *chronological* account of his life, beginning with his early years in Kentucky and ending with his assassination in Washington, D.C.

_____

_____

_____

6. Alicia was not looking forward to taking the makeup test, so she began to *temporize* with the teacher. If she could do it long enough, perhaps the final bell would ring and the test would need to be rescheduled.

_____

_____

_____

7. The church leaders urged their congregations to worry less about such *temporal* concerns as money and social status. All of these things are left behind at the end of one's life.

_____

_____

_____

8. We learned a great deal about the daily life of ordinary soldiers in the Civil War from the detailed *chronicles* many of them kept.

_____

_____

_____

9. I am not very good at making *extemporaneous* remarks. I prefer to plan my speech and answer only questions that have been submitted a day in advance.

_____

_____

_____

10. Today Van Gogh is considered one of the great postimpressionist painters. However, most of his *contemporaries* thought his art was strange and worthless.

_____

_____

_____

Lesson
36
Part B

Applying Meaning

Rewrite each sentence or short passage below. Replace the underlined word or words with a vocabulary word or a form of a vocabulary word.

1. I was so worried about Hilary's <u>habitual</u> headaches that I advised her to see a doctor.

   _____

   _____

2. Sometimes the best picnics are the ones that are <u>unplanned</u>. Planning makes everyone expect too much.

   _____

   _____

3. The investigator asked the witness to describe the events <u>in the order in which they happened</u>.

   _____

   _____

4. The raising of the bridge was <u>coordinated</u> with the passing of the large boat.

   _____

   _____

5. The vice-chair presided <u>temporarily</u> over the discussion while the chair conferred with the senate.

   _____

   _____

Follow the directions below to write a sentence using a vocabulary word.

6. Use any form of the word *anachronism* to describe something you noticed in a picture or movie.

   _____

   _____

   _____

7. Tell how you might get out of doing an unpleasant task. Use any form of the word *temporize*.

   _____

   _____

   _____

8. Make a New Year's resolution. Use any form of the word *temporal.*

_____

_____

_____

9. Use any form of the word *chronicle* in a sentence to describe a diary.

_____

_____

_____

10. Complete the following sentence: In history class we studied the life of Thomas Jefferson and his *contemporaries,* especially . . . .

_____

_____

_____

Test-Taking Strategies

The verbal section of the PSAT and SAT tests requires you to choose a pair of words with the same relationship as another pair of words. Called analogy tests, they require you to think carefully about how two words are related and then find the word pair that <u>best</u> expresses a similar relationship.

S. FISH:WATER::	**S.** _____ **C** _____
(A) leaves:tree (B) salt:ocean	
(C) bird:air (D) earth:worm	

Remember that you are to look for the pair that is the <u>best</u> match. It may not be a perfect match. Also be careful about choices that reverse the relationship. Item D reverses the relationship you are trying to match.

Practice: Each question below consists of a related pair of words or phrases, followed by four pairs of words or phrases labeled A through D. Select the pair that best expresses the relationship in the original pair.

1. SODIUM:CHEMISTRY::
    (A) nail:carpentry   (B) snakes:biology
    (C) textbook:history   (D) students:school

1. _____

2. CRIME:RETRIBUTION::
    (A) felony:incarceration   (B) insult:outrage
    (C) jail:misdemeanor   (D) law:jury

2. _____

3. MAVERICK:INDEPENDENT::
    (A) doctor:patient   (B) cattle:stray
    (C) incumbent:candidate   (D) vagabond:aimless

3. _____

Name _____

How well do you remember the words you studied in Lessons 34 through 36? Take the following test covering the words from the last three lessons.

Part 1 Choose the Correct Meaning

Each question below includes a word in capital letters, followed by four words or phrases. Choose the word or phrase that is <u>closest</u> in meaning to the word in capital letters. Write the letter for your answer on the line provided.

Sample

S. FINISH	(A) enjoy	(B) complete	**S.** ____**B**____
	(C) destroy	(D) send	

1. BRAZEN   (A) dull   (B) brash   **1.** _____
(C) hardened   (D) distant

2. ANACHRONISM   (A) type of spider   (B) Asian religion   **2.** _____
(C) something out of its proper time   (D) inaccuracy

3. SALLY   (A) rush forth   (B) soil   **3.** _____
(C) delicate   (D) rearrange

4. RESOLUTE   (A) decide   (B) determined   **4.** _____
(C) promised   (D) arranged

5. INTRICATE   (A) accuse   (B) simple   **5.** _____
(C) thorough   (D) complicated

6. PALPITATE   (A) valuable   (B) worthless   **6.** _____
(C) flutter   (D) satisfy

7. TEMPORAL   (A) worldly   (B) tempting   **7.** _____
(C) ancient   (D) spiritual

8. CHRONIC   (A) painful   (B) temporary   **8.** _____
(C) habitual   (D) timely

9. DEXTEROUS   (A) clumsy   (B) skillful   **9.** _____
(C) annoying   (D) dull

10. NURTURE   (A) nourish   (B) disregard   **10.** _____
(C) insult   (D) starve

Go on to next page. ➤

11. VEHEMENT   (A) evil   (B) passionate   11. _____
                            (C) poisonous   (D) slight

12. APPRECIATE   (A) answer   (B) apply   12. _____
                            (C) dislike   (D) value

13. REDOUBTABLE   (A) forgetful   (B) complete   13. _____
                            (C) reformed   (D) causing fear

14. STALWART   (A) strong   (B) clever   14. _____
                            (C) overweight   (D) weak or tame

15. TEMPORIZE   (A) tenderize   (B) evade and delay   15. _____
                            (C) reduce   (D) quicken

Part 2   Matching Words and Meanings

Match the definition in Column B with the word in Column A.
Write the letter of the correct definition on the line provided.

Column A	Column B	
16. appall	a. calm and peaceful	16. _____
17. incursion	b. invasion	17. _____
18. contemporary	c. physical strength	18. _____
19. myriad	d. shock	19. _____
20. synchronize	e. fear	20. _____
21. anxiety	f. to cause to occur at the same time	21. _____
22. extemporaneous	g. belonging to the same time period	22. _____
23. serene	h. opposite	23. _____
24. stamina	i. numerous	24. _____
25. converse	j. carried out with little preparation	25. _____

Dictionary

Pronunciation Guide

Symbol	Example	Symbol	Example
ă	pat	oi	boy
ā	pay	ou	out
âr	care	ŏŏ	took
ä	father	ōō	boot
ĕ	pet	ŭ	cut
ē	be	ûr	urge
ĭ	pit	th	thin
ī	pie	*th*	this
îr	pier	hw	which
ŏ	pot	zh	vision
ō	toe	ə	about, item
ô	paw		

Stress Marks: ′ (primary); ′ (secondary), as in **dictionary** (dĭk′shə-nĕr′ē)

A

ab·er·rant (ă-bĕr′ənt) *adj.* Deviating from what is usual, normal, or correct. -**ab·er′rance, ab·er′ran·cy,** *n.* -**ab·er′rant·ly,** *adv.*

ab·ject (ăb′jĕkt′, ăb-jĕkt′) *adj.* **1.** Miserable; wretched. **2.** Contemptible; despicable. -**ab′ject′ly,** *adv.* -**ab·ject′ness,** *n.*

ab·nor·mal (ăb-nôr′məl) *adj.* Not usual, average, or normal; unusual. -**ab·nor′mal·ly,** *adv.* -**ab′nor·mal′i·ty,** *n.*

a·bridge (ə-brĭj′) *v.* a·bridged, a·bridg·ing, a·bridg·es. **1.** To restrict; curtail. **2.** To shorten; condense. -**a·bridg′ment,** *n.*

ac·cord (ə-kôrd′) *n.* An agreement; harmony. -*v.* **1.** To make agree. **2.** To grant. **3.** To agree.

ac·cre·tion (ə-krē′shən) *n.* Increase in size by gradual outside addition or natural growth.

ac·crue (ə-krōō′) *v.* -crued, -cru·ing, -crues. **1.** To grow in amount over time. **2.** To result as from natural growth or addition.

ac·cul·tur·ate (ə-kŭl′chə-rāt) *v.* To adapt or adjust to the cultural traits or patterns of another group as a result of conditioning. -**ac·cul′tur·a′tion,** *n.*

a·cer·bi·ty (ə-sûr′bĭ-tē) *n.,* pl. -**ties.** Sharpness or bitterness of words, temper, or tone. -**a·cer′bic,** *adj.* -**a·cer′bi·cal·ly,** *adv.*

ac·ro·pho·bi·a (ăk′rə-fō′bē-ə) *n.* An abnormal fear of being in high places.

ad·ja·cent (ə-jā′sənt) *adj.* Lying near; adjoining. -**ad·ja′cent·ly,** *adv.*

ae·gis (ē′jĭs) also, **e·gis.** *n.* **1.** Sponsorship. **2.** Protection.

af·fect (ə-fĕkt′) *v.* **1.** To produce an effect in; influence. **2.** To move the emotions of. -*n.* (af′-ĕkt′) An emotion or feeling.

af·front (ə-frŭnt′) *v.* To insult deliberately, especially openly. -*n.* A deliberate and open insult.

ag·nos·tic (ăg-nŏs′tĭk) *n.* A person who believes that the existence of God is unknown or unknowable. **-ag·nos′ti·cal·ly**, *adv.*

al·le·go·ry (ăl′ĭ-gô′rē, -gōr′ē) *n., pl.* **-ries.** A story in which the characters represent moral principles or ideas.

al·lu·sion (ə-lōō′zhən) *n.* An indirect reference made to something.

al·ter·ca·tion (ôl′tər-kā′shən) *n.* An angry and heated quarrel.

am·nes·ty (ăm′nĭ-stē) *n., pl.* **-ties.** A general pardon given by a government for offenses committed against it.

a·nach·ro·nism (ə-năk′rə-nĭz′əm) *n.* Anything out of its proper or historical time. **-a·nach′ro·nis′tic,** *adj.* **-a·nach′ro·nis′ti·cal·ly,** *adv.*

an·guish (ăng′gwĭsh) *n.* Great mental suffering or physical pain. *-v.* To suffer intense sorrow or pain.

an·nals (ăn′əlz) *pl. n.* **1.** Historical records; history. **2.** A written record of chronological events.

an·ni·hi·la·tion (ə-nī′ə-lā′shən) *n.* The act or result of destroying completely. **-an·ni′hi·late,** *v.*

a·nom·a·ly (ə-nŏm′ə-lē) *n., pl.* **-lies.** Something different from the usual or normal; abnormality.

an·tag·o·nism (ăn-tăg′ə-nĭz′əm) *n.* Strong feeling against; hostility; opposition.

anx·i·e·ty (ăng-zī′ĭ-tē) *n., pl.* **-ties. 1.** Worry or feeling of uneasiness about what may happen. **2.** A cause of this feeling.

ap·a·thy (ăp′ə-thē) *n.* **1.** Lack of interest or concern; indifference. **2.** Lack of emotion.

ap·pall (ə-pôl′) *v.* To dismay or horrify; shock.

ap·pre·cia·ble (ə-prē′shē-bəl) *adj.* Enough to be measured or noticed; perceptible. **-ap·pre′cia·bly,** *adv.*

ap·pre·ci·ate (ə-prē′shē-āt′) *v.* **-at·ed, -at·ing, -ates. 1.** To recognize the quality, value, or significance of. **2.** To be aware of or sensitive to.

ar·tic·u·late (är-tĭk′yə-lĭt) *adj.* Expressing oneself effectively and clearly. *-v.* (är-tĭk′yə-lāt) To state clearly and effectively. **-ar·tic′u·late·ly,** *adv.* **-ar·tic′u·la′tion,** *n.*

as·cribe (ə-skrīb′) *v.* **-cribed, -crib·ing, -cribes. 1.** To assign to a particular cause, source, or origin. **2.** To regard as belonging to.

at·mos·phere (ăt′mə-sfîr′) *n.* The gaseous mass surrounding the Earth or any celestial body.

au·dit (ô′dĭt) *v.* To examine financial accounts and records to determine whether they are correct. *-n.* A formal examination of financial records.

au·ton·o·my (ô-tŏn′ə-mē) *n., pl.* **-mies.** The state or condition of being free from outside control; self-governance. **-au·ton′o·mous,** *adj.*

a·venge (ə-vĕnj′) *v.* **a·venged, a·veng·ing, a·veng·es. 1.** To get revenge for. **2.** To take vengeance on behalf of. **-a·veng′er,** *n.*

B

bed·lam (bĕd′ləm) *n.* A place or condition of uproar and confusion.

bel·li·cose (bĕl′ĭ-kōs) *adj.* Inclined or eager to fight or start wars; warlike. **-bel′li·cos′i·ty,** *n.*

bel·lig·er·ent (bə-lĭj′ər-ənt) *adj.* Eager to fight; hostile. *-n.* A person or country that is engaged in war. **bel·lig′er·ence,** *n.*

ben·e·dic·tion (bĕn′ĭ-dĭk′shən) *n.* **1.** A blessing. **2.** An invocation of a blessing, especially at the end of a religious service.

ben·e·fac·tor (bĕn′ə-făk′tər) *n.* One who gives help, especially financial aid; patron.

be·nev·o·lent (bə-nĕv′ə-lənt) *adj.* Doing or wanting to do good; kindly. **-be·nev′o·lent·ly,** *adv.*

be·nign (bĭ-nīn′) *adj.* **1.** Having a kindly disposition. **2.** Favorable; beneficial. **3.** Not dangerous to health; not malignant.

bi·zarre (bĭ-zär′) *adj.* Odd or strange in appearance or manner; grotesque. **-bi·zarre′ly,** *adv.* **-bi·zarre′ness,** *n.*

bla·sé (blä-zā′) *adj.* Uninterested or bored, as from too much of worldly pleasures.

boy·cott (boi′kŏt′) *v.* To refuse to use, buy, or sell. *-n.* An organized refusal to do business with a person or group.

bra·va·do (brə-vä′dō) *n., pl.* **-dos** or **-does.** A false show of bravery.

bra·zen (brā′zən) *adj.* **1.** Shameless; impudent. **2.** Made of brass. **-bra′zen·ness,** *n.*

bu·reauc·ra·cy (byoō-rŏk′rə-sē) *n.* The administration of government officials following an inflexible routine. **-bu′reau·crat′ic,** *adj.*

C

cap·i·tal (kăp′ĭ-tl) *n.* **1.** Wealth in any form used or capable of being used to produce more wealth. **2.** The total amount of money or property owned.

car·di·ac (kär′dē-ăk) *adj.* Near, of, or relating to the heart.

car·tel (kär-tĕl′) *n.* A group of companies or businesses formed to control production, prices, and marketing of its members' goods.

cat·a·stroph·ic (kăt′ə-strŏf′ĭk) *adj.* Of or relating to a great and sudden disaster. **-ca·tas′tro·phe,** *n.*

char·ac·ter (kăr′ək-tər) *n.* **1.** All of the good and bad qualities of a person that constitute his or her moral nature. **2.** Moral strength; integrity.

char·is·mat·ic (kăr′ĭz-măt′ĭk) *adj.* possessing personal magnetism or charm that attracts many followers. **-cha·ris′ma,** *n.*

char·i·ty (chăr′i-tē) *n., pl.* **-ties. 1.** The giving of help or relief to the poor. **2.** Kindness or tolerance in judging others.

char·la·tan (shär′lə-tən) *n.* A person who claims to have knowledge or skill that he or she does not have; imposter.

cher·ish (chĕr′əsh) *v.* **1.** To regard with affection; hold dear. **2.** To hold in the mind; cling to.

chron·ic (krŏn′ĭk) *adj.* **1.** Lasting a long time or recurring frequently. **2.** Habitual. **-chron′i·cal·ly,** *adv.*

chron·i·cle (krŏn′ĭ-kəl) *n.* A detailed record of events in the order in which they happened. *-v.* To record the history of in a chronicle.

chron·o·log·i·cal (krŏn-ə-lŏj′ĭ-kəl, krō′nə-) *adj.* Arranged in the order in which the events took place. **-chron′o·log′i·cal·ly,** *adv.*

claus·tro·pho·bi·a (klô′strə-fō′bē-ə) *n.* An abnormal fear of being in an enclosed, narrow, or small place.

clem·en·cy (klĕm′ən-sē) *n., pl.* -cies. Leniency in punishing or judging.

cli·ché (klē-shā′) *n.* An expression or idea that has lost its effect because it has been over-used; a trite expression.

cli·en·tele (klī′ən-tel′, klē′än-) *n.* Clients and customers as a group.

cod·i·fy (kŏd′ĭ-fī, kō′də-) *v.* -fied, -fying, -fies. To arrange systematically. **-cod′i·fi·ca′tion,** *n.* **-cod′i·fi·er,** *n.I*

cog·no·men (kŏg-nō′mən, kŏg′-no) *n., pl.* -no·mens or -nom·i·na. **1.** A surname. **2.** Any name, especially a nickname or an epithet.

col·lat·er·al (kə-lăt′ər-əl) *n.* Property given as security for the repayment of a loan. **-col·lat′er·al·ly,** *adv.*

col·lide (kə-līd′) *v.* **1.** To come together with forceful impact; crash. **2.** To conflict; clash.

com·mod·i·ty (kə-mŏd′ĭ-tē) *n., pl.* Anything that can be bought and sold; article of trade.

com·po·nent (kəm-pō′nənt) *n.* An essential part, element, or ingredient. *-adj.* Being one of the parts of a whole.

com·port (kəm-pôrt′, -pōrt′) *v.* To behave or conduct (oneself) in a specified manner. **-com·port′ment,** *n.*

com·pos·ite (kəm-pŏz′ĭt) *adj.* Made up of separate parts or elements; compound. *-n.* Something that is made up of separate parts.

con·cise (kən-sīs′) *adj.* Expressing in a few words what is meant; brief and to the point; terse. **-con·cise′ly,** *adv.* **-con·cise′ness,** *n.*

con·found (kən-found′, kŏn-) *v.* To confuse or perplex; bewilder. **-con·found′er,** *n.* **-con·found′ed·ly,** *adv.*

con·jec·ture (kən-jĕk′chər) *n.* **1.** Judgment based on insufficient or incomplete evidence. **2.** A guess.

con·no·ta·tion (kən′ə-tā′shən) *n.* A meaning or idea that is associated with a word in addition to its literal meaning.

con·script (kən-skrĭpt′) *v.* To enroll by law to serve in the armed forces; draft. *-n.* (kŏn′skrĭpt) Draftee.

con·spir·a·cy (kən-spîr′ə-sē) *n., pl.* -cies. A secret plan to perform together an evil or wrongful act; plot.

con·tem·po·rar·y (kən-tĕm′pə-rĕr′ē) *n., pl.* -ies. A person who lives in the same time as another or others. *-adj.* **1.** Living at the same time. **2.** Modern.

con·ten·tious (kən-tĕn′shəs) *adj.* Argumentative; quarrelsome. **-con·ten′tious·ly,** *adv.* **-con·ten′tious·ness, -con·ten′tion,** *n.*

con·tig·u·ous (kən-tĭg′yōō-əs) *adj.* **1.** In contact; touching. **2.** Near; close. **-con·tig′u·ous·ness,** *n.*

con·tin·gent (kən-tĭn′jənt) *adj.* **1.** Dependent on uncertain conditions or events. **2.** Possible. **-con·tin′gen·cy,** *n.*

con·tin·u·al (kən-tĭn′yōō-əl) *adj.* Repeated frequently. **con·tin′u·al·ly,** *adv.*

con·tin·u·ous (kən-tĭn′yōō-əs) *adj.* Going on without interruption; unbroken. **-con·tin′u·ous·ly,** *adv.* **-con·tin′u·ous·ness,** *n.*

con·verge (kən-vûrj′) *v.* -verged, -verg·ing, -ver·ges. To tend to come together at a place or point. **-con·ver′gence,** *n.* **-con·ver′gent,** *adj.*

con·verse (kŏn′vûrs′) *n.* Something opposite or reversed; the opposite.

co·pi·ous (kō′pē-əs) adj. Abundant; plentiful. -co′pi·ous·ly, adv. -co′pi·ous·ness, n.

cor·dial (kôr′jəl) adj. Warm and friendly; gracious. -cor·dial′i·ty, cor′dial·ness, n. -cor′dial·ly, adv.

cov·et (kŭv′ĭt) v. To desire ardently (especially something that belongs to another). -cov′et·a·ble, cov′et·eous, adj.

coun·ter·mand (koun′tər-mănd′, koun′tər-mănd′) v. To cancel or reverse (an order or comand).

creed (krēd) n. 1. A statement of belief, principles, or opinions. 2. A formal statement of religious belief.

creep (krēp) v. crept, creep·ing. 1. To move with the body close to the ground, as on hands and knees. 2. To move slowly.

cul·mi·nate (kŭl′mə-nāt) v. -nat·ed, -nat·ing, -nates. 1. To reach the highest point or climax. 2. To come to an end. -cul′mi·na′tion, n.

cul·pa·ble (kŭl′pə-bəl) adj. Deserving blame. -cul′pa·bil′i·ty, n. -cul′pa·bly, adv.

cul·prit (kŭl′prĭt) n. A person accused or found guilty of a crime or offense.

cur·sive (kûr′sĭv) adj. Written in flowing strokes in which the letters are joined together. -cur′sive·ly, adv. -cur′sive·ness, n.

cur·so·ry (kûr′sə-rē) adj. Rapid; not thorough; hasty. -cur′so·ri·ly, adv. -cur′so·ri·ness, n.

D

de·pict (dĭ-pĭkt′) v. 1. To represent by drawing or painting; portray. 2. To picture in words; describe. -de·pic′tion, n.

de·port·ment (dĭ-pôrt′mənt, -pōrt′-) n. The manner in which a person behaves or acts; conduct.

des·o·late (dĕs′ə-lĭt, dĕz′) adj. 1. Devastated. 2. Uninhabited; deserted. -des′o·la′tion, n. -des′o·late·ly, adv.

des·pot (dĕs′pət) n. A ruler with unlimited and absolute power and authority. -des·pot′ic, adj. -des·pot′i·cal·ly, adv.

de·tract (dĭ-trăkt′) v. To take away value, quality, or importance; divert. -de·trac′tion, n.

de·vi·ate (dē′vē-āt′) v. -at·ed, -at·ing, -ates. 1. To turn aside from a course, standard, or subject. 2. To depart from a norm.

dex·ter·ous (dĕk′stər-əs, -strəs) adj. Skillful in the use of the hands, body, or mind. -dex′ter·ous·ly, adv. -dex′ter·ous·ness, n.

di·ag·nose (dī′əg-nōs′, -nōz′) v. 1. To identify a disease through careful analysis. 2. To analyze the cause and nature of a problem. -di′ag·no′sis, n.

dis·cord (dĭs′kôrd) n. A lack of agreement or harmony; conflict.

dis·cur·sive (dĭ-skûr′sĭv) adj. Wandering aimlessly from one topic to another. -dis·cur′sive·ly, adv. dis·cur′sive·ness, n.

dis·in·ter·est·ed (dĭs-ĭn′tə-rĕs′tĭd) adj. Not influenced by a personal interest; impartial. -dis·in′ter·est·ed·ly, adv. -dis·in′ter·est·ed·ness, n.

dis·po·si·tion (dĭs′pə-zĭsh′ən) n. 1. One's usual way of acting, thinking, or feeling; temperament. 2. A tendency or inclination.

dis·sen·sion (dĭ-sĕn′shən) n. Difference of opinion; disagreement; strife.

di·verge (dĭ-vûrj′, dī-) v. **1.** To draw apart from a common point. **2.** To differ, as in opinion.

doc·ile (dŏs′əl, -īl′) adj. Easily taught, trained, or managed; submissive. **-doc′ile·ly,** adv. **-do·cil′i·ty,** n.

doc·tri·naire (dŏk′trə-nâr′) adj. Adhering inflexibly to a practice or theory. -n. One who stubbornly adheres to a practice or theory.

doc·trine (dŏk′trĭn) n. **1.** A position, principle, or belief taught or held by a particular group. **2.** Teachings.

do·min·ion (də-mĭn′yən) n. **1.** Supreme authority; rule or power to rule. **2.** A country or territory controlled by a particular ruler.

du·ra·tion (dŏŏ-rā′shən, dyŏŏ-) n. **1.** The length of time something continues or lasts. **2.** Continuance in time.

E

ec·cen·tric·i·ty (ĕk′sĕn-trĭs′ĭ-tē) n., pl. **-ties.** An act or trait that differs from the usual; peculiarity.

ec·o·nom·ic (ĕk′ə-nŏm′ĭk, ē′kə-) adj. Of or relating to financial matters or concerns.

ef·fect (ĭ-fĕkt′) n. Anything brought about by a cause or agent; result. -v. To bring about or cause.

ef·fu·sive (ĭ-fyŏŏ′sĭv) adj. Showing more feeling than necessary; gushing. **-ef·fu′sive·ly,** adv. **-ef·fu′sive·ness,** n.

el·o·quent (ĕl′ə-kwənt) adj. **1.** Characterized by forceful and persuasive expression. **2.** Movingly expressive. **-el′o·quence,** n.

e·merge (ĭ-mûrj′) v. **e·merged, e·merg·ing, e·merg·es. 1.** To become visible; to come into view. **2.** To rise from or as if from a fluid.

em·is·sar·y (ĕm′ĭ-sĕr′ē) n., pl. **-ies.** An agent sent on a specific mission.

e·mit (ĭ-mĭt′) v. **-e·mit·ted, -e·mit·ting, -mits.** To give off or send out; discharge. **-e·mis′sion,** n.

em·pa·thy (ĕm′pə-thē) n. A sharing and understanding of another's feelings, situation, or state of mind.

en·sue (ĕn-sŏŏ′) v. **-sued, -su·ing, -sues.** To follow as a result. **2.** To come afterward.

en·trée (ŏn′trā, ŏn-trā′) n. **1.** The right, freedom, or privilege to enter. **2.** The main course or dish of a meal.

en·tre·pre·neur (ŏn′trə-prə-nûr′, -nŏŏr′) n. A person who organizes, manages, and assumes the risk of a business or enterprise.

er·rant (ĕr′ənt) adj. **1.** Roving in search of adventure; wandering. **2.** Straying from correct behavior; erring.

er·rat·ic (ĭ-răt′ĭk) adj. **1.** Having no regular course; wandering. **2.** Irregular; unpredictable. **-er·rat′i·cal·ly,** adv.

e·ven·tu·al (ĭ-vĕn′chŏŏ-əl) adj. Happening as a result of events that go before; ultimate; final. **-e·ven′tu·al·ly,** adv.

e·vict (ĭ-vĭkt′) v. To throw out or remove (a tenant) from property by legal procedure. **-e·vic′tion,** n.

e·vince (ĭ-vĭns′) v. **e·vinced, e·vinc·ing, e·vinc·es.** To show clearly; to make evident. **-e·vinc′i·ble,** adj.

ex·hi·bi·tion (ek′sə-bĭsh′ən) *n.* **1.** The act of showing publically. **2.** A public display.

ex·on·er·ate (ĭg-zŏn′ə-rāt′) *v.* **-at·ed, -at·ing, -ates.** To clear from blame or guilt. **-ex·on′er·a′tion,** *n.* **-ex·on′er·a′tive′,** *adj.*

ex·pe·dite (ĕk′spĭ-dīt′) *v.* To speed up the progress of; facilitate. **-ex′pe·dit′er, ex′pe·di′tor,** *n.*

ex·po·nent (ĭk-spō′nənt, ĕk′spō′nənt) *n.* **1.** A person who explains or interprets something. **2.** A person who represents, speaks for, or advocates.

ex·pound (ĭk-spound′) *v.* **1.** To set forth in detail. **2.** To explain in detail. **-ex·pound′er,** *n.*

ex·tem·po·ra·ne·ous (ĭk-stĕm′pə-ra′nē-əs) *adj.* Done, spoken, or made with little or no preparation; **impromptu.** **-ex·tem′po·ra′ne·ous·ly,** *adv.*

ex·tort (ĭk-stôrt) *v.* To get (something) by force or threats. **-ex·tor′tion,** *n.*

ex·tract (ĭk-străkt′) *v.* **1.** To draw or pull out with effort. **2.** To obtain or separate by pressing, distilling, etc. **-ex·trac′tion,** *n.*

ex·trin·sic (ĭk-strĭn′sĭk, -zĭk) *adj.* **1.** Not essential to the nature of a thing. **2.** Coming from the outside; external. **-ex·trin′si·cal·ly,** *adv.*

F

fa·cil·i·tate (fə-sĭl′ĭ-tāt′) *v.* **-tat·ed, -tat·ing, -tates.** To make easy or easier; help. **-fa·cil′i·ta′tive,** *adj.* **-fa·cil′i·ta′tor,** *n.*

fath·om·less (făth′əm-lĭs) *adj.* **1.** Too deep to be measured. **2.** Difficult to understand. **-fath′om·less·ly,** *adv.* **-fath′om·less·ness,** *n.*

feist·y (fī′stē) *adj.* **1.** Ill-tempered; touchy; quarrelsome. **2.** Spirited, frisky. **-feist′i·ness,** *n.*

fel·on·y (fĕl′ə-nē) *n., pl.* **-ies** A major crime, such as rape or murder, that is more serious than a misdemeanor.

fe·roc·i·ty (fə-rŏs′ĭ-tē) *n.* **1.** Fierceness; extreme savagery. **2.** Extreme intensity.

fi·nite (fī′nīt′) *adj.* Having measurable limits. **-fi′nite·ly,** *adv.* **-fi′nite′ness,** *n.*

fos·ter (fô′stər, fŏ′stər) *v.* **1.** To help the growth and development of; promote. **2.** To bring up; rear.

frat·ri·cide (frăt′rĭ-sīd′) *n.* **1.** The act of killing one's brother or sister. **2.** A person who kills his or her brother or sister.

frus·tra·tion (frŭ-strā′shən) *n.* A feeling of disappointment resulting from being unable to accomplish something or from a defeat. **-frus′trate,** *v.*

G

gal·va·nize (găl′və-nīz) *v.* **-nized, -niz·ing, -niz·es.** To rouse suddenly to awareness or action; startle; excite. **-gal′va·ni·za′tion,** *n.*

gar·ru·lous (găr′ə-ləs, găr′yə-) *adj.* Excessively talkative, especially about unimportant topics. **-gar′ru·lous·ly,** *adv.* **-gar′ru·lous·ness,** *n.*

gauche (gōsh) *adj.* Lacking social grace; awkward; tactless. **-gauche′ly,** *adv.* **gauche′ness,** *n.*

gaunt (gônt) *adj.* **1.** Very thin and bony; haggard. **2.** Bare; grim; bleak. **-gaunt′ly,** *adv.* **-gaunt′ness,** *n.*

gen·er·ate (jĕn′ə-rāt) *v.* **-at·ed, -at·ing, -ates.** To bring into existence.

gen·o·cide (jĕn′ə-sīd′) *n.* The systematic killing of a national, political, racial, or cultural group.

glib (glĭb) *adj.* **glib·ber, glib·best.** Speaking or spoken with little thought or sincerity. **-glib′ly,** *adv.* **-glib′ness,** *n.*

gra·tu·i·tious (grə-tōō′ĭ-təs, -tyōō′-) *adj.* **1.** Given without charge; free. **2.** Without justification; uncalled for. **-gra·tu′i·tous·ly,** *adv.* **-gra·tu′i·tous·ness,** *n.*

H

hale (hāl) *adj.* Healthy; vigorous; robust. **-hale′ness,** *n.*

hal·lowed (hăl′ōd) *adj.* **1.** Holy; sanctified. **2.** Highly respected.

ha·rangue (hə-răng′) *n.* **1.** A long, pompous speech. **2.** A tirade. *-v.* **-rangued, -rangu·ing, -rangues.** To give a harangue.

her·cu·le·an (hûr′kyə-lē′ən, hûr-kyōō′lē-) *adj.* **1.** Requiring great strength or exertion. **2.** Of great strength, courage, or size.

his·tri·on·ics (hĭs′trē-ŏn′ĭks) *n.* Overly dramatic behavior or speech for effect.

hue (hyōō) *n.* **1.** Color. **2.** A particular tint or shade.

hy·dro·pho·bi·a (hī′drə-fō′bē-ə) *n.* **1.** An abnormal fear of water. **2.** Rabies.

I

id·i·om (ĭd′ē-əm) *n.* A phrase or expression whose meaning is different from the literal meaning of its individual words.

id·i·o·syn·crat·ic (ĭd′e-ō-sĭn-krăt′ĭk) *adj.* Having a peciliar or distinguishing mannerism or characteristic. **-id′i·o·syn′cra·sy,** *n.*

il·lus·tri·ous (ĭ-lŭs′trē-əs) *adj.* Distinguished or renowned; famous. **-il·lus′tri·ous·ly,** *adv.* **-il·lus′tri·ous·ness,** *n.*

im·meas·ur·a·ble (ĭ-mĕzh′ər-ə-bəl) *adj.* That which cannot be measured; boundless; vast. **-im·meas′ur·a·bil′i·ty,** *n.* **-im·meas′ur·a·bly,** *adv.*

im·mense (ĭ-mĕns′) *adj.* **1.** Very large; huge. **2.** Of immeasurable size or extent. **-im·mense′ly,** *adv.* **im·mense′ness,** *n.*

im·ped·i·ment (ĭm-pĕd′ə-mənt) *n.* An obstruction; hindrance; obstacle.

im·per·i·ous (ĭm-pîr′ē-əs) *adj.* Overbearing; domineering; arrogant. **-im·per′ri·ous·ly,** *adv.* **-im·pe′ri·ous·ness,** *n.*

im·ply (ĭm-plī′) *v.* **-plied, -ply·ing, -plies.** To express or suggest indirectly; hint.

im·pos·tor (ĭm-pŏs′tər) *n.* A person who deceives or cheats others by pretending to be someone else.

im·pres·sive (ĭm-prĕs′ĭv) *adj.* Producing attention, wonder, respect, or admiration. **-im·pres′sive·ly,** *adv.* **-im·pres′sive·ness,** *n.*

in·ci·sive (ĭn-sī′sĭv) *adj.* Mentally sharp; cutting into; keen; penetrating. **-in·ci′sive·ly,** *adv.* **-in·ci′sive·ness,** *n.*

in·cog·ni·to (ĭn′kŏg-nē′tō, ĭn-kŏg′nĭ-tō′) *adv.* or *adj.* With one's identity hidden or disguised.

in·con·gru·ous (ĭn-kŏng′grōō-əs) *adj.* Lacking harmony; incompatible; unsuitable. **-in·con′gru·ous·ly,** *adv.*

in·cor·ri·gi·ble (ĭn′kôr′ĭ-jə-bəl, -kŏr′-) *adj.* Unable to be corrected or reformed; uncontrollable. **-in·cor′ri·gi·bil′i·ty,** *n.* **-in·cor′ri·gi·bly,** *adv.*

in·cur·sion (ĭn-**kûr**′zhən, -shən) *n.* A hostile invasion or raid.

in·de·fat·i·ga·ble (ĭn-dē-**făt**-ə-gə-bəl) *adj.* Untiring; incapable of being fatigued.

in·dem·ni·fy (ĭn-**dĕm**′nə-fī) *v.* -**fied, -fy·ing, -fies.** To insure against future loss, damage, or expense. **-in·dem′ni·fi·ca′tion,** *n.*

in·dif·fer·ence (ĭn-**dĭf**′ər-əns, -**dĭf**′rəns) *n.* **1.** Lack of interest, concern, or feeling. **2.** Lack of importance. **-in·dif′fer·ent,** *adj.*

in·dig·e·nous (ĭn-**dĭj**′ə-nəs) *adj.* Originating in or growing naturally in a particular region or country; native. **-in·dig′e·nous·ly,** *adv.*

in·doc·tri·nate (ĭn-**dŏk**′trə-nāt′) *v.* -**nat·ed, -nat·ing, -nates.** To teach a particular theory, belief, or principle. **-in·doc′tri·na′tion,** *n.*

in·duce (ĭn-**dōōs**′, -**dyōōs**′) *v.* -**duced, -duc·ing, -duc·es. 1.** To bring about; cause. **2.** To lead to an action; persuade. **-in·duc′i·ble,** *adj.*

in·fer (ĭn-**fûr**′) *v.* -**ferred, -fer·ring, -fers.** To conclude from facts or observations.

in·gre·di·ent (ĭn-**grē**′dē-ənt) *n.* Any one of the elements of a mixture.

in·her·ent (ĭn-**hîr**′ənt, **hĕr**′-) *adj.* Exisiting in someone or something as a permanent or basic characteristic. **-in·her′ent·ly,** *adv.*

in·sa·tia·ble (ĭn-**sā**′shə-bəl, -shē-ə-) *adj.* Not able to be satisfied. **-in·sa′tia·bly,** *adv.*

in·tact (ĭn-**tăkt**′) *adj.* Not damaged; unimpaired; untouched; uninjured. **-in·tact′ness,** *n.*

in·ter·de·pend·ence (ĭn′tər-dĭ-**pĕn**′dəns) *n.* A state of mutual reliance on the aid of each other. **-in′ter·de·pend′ent,** *adj.*

in·ter·mit·tent (ĭn′tər-**mĭt**′ənt) *adj.* Stopping and starting again at intervals; periodic. **-in′ter·mit′tence,** *n.* **-in′ter·mit′tent·ly,** *adv.*

in·ter·vene (ĭn′tər-**vēn**′) *v.* -**vened, -ven·ing, -venes. 1.** To come between to alter, affect, or prevent an action. To come between two things. **-in′ter·ven′tion,** *n.*

in·trac·ta·ble (ĭn-**trăk**′tə-bəl) *adj.* Hard to manage; stubborn; unruly. **-in·trac′ta·bil′i·ty,** *n.* **-in·trac′ta·bly,** *adv.*

in·tri·cate (ĭn′trĭ-kĭt) *adj.* **1.** Having elaborate detail; complicated. **2.** Hard to understand. **-in′tri·cate·ly,** *adv.* **-in′tri·ca·cy,** *n.*

in·vin·ci·ble (in-**vĭn**′sə-bəl) *adj.* Incapable of being subdued, conquered, or overcome. **-in·vin′ci·bil′i·ty,** *n.* **-in·vin′ci·bly,** *adv.*

i·o·ta (i-**ō**′tə) *n.* A very small amount.

J–K

jar·gon (**jär**′gən) *n.* The specialized vocabulary used by those in a particular profession or way of life.

jux·ta·po·si·tion (jŭk′stə-pə-**zĭsh**′ən) *n.* The placement of things side by side or close together, especially for comparison or contrast.

kin·dred (**kĭn**′drĭd) *adj.* Related; like; similar.

L

la·con·ic (lə-**kŏn**′ĭk) *adj.* Using few words to express much; concise; terse. **-la·con′i·cal·ly,** *adv.*

le·gion (**lē**′jən) *n.* A large number; multitude.

le·git·i·mate (lə-**jĭt**′ə-mĭt) *adj.* **1.** Lawful. Logically correct. **2.** Genuine. **-le·git′i·mate·ly,** *adv.* **-le·git′i·mate·ness,** *n.*

liq·ui·date (**lĭk**′wĭ-dāt′) *v.* -**dat·ed, -dat·ing, -dates.** *1.* To pay off or settle (a debt). **2.** To convert (assets) to cash. **-liq′ui·da′tion,** *n.*

lon·gev·i·ty (lŏn-jĕv′ĭ-tē, lôn-) *n., pl.* **-ties.** Long life.

lu·cra·tive (lōō′krə-tĭv) *adj.* Producing money or wealth; profitable. **-lu′cra·tive·ly,** *adj.*

M

mal·a·dy (măl′ə-dē) *n., pl.* **-dies. 1.** A disease or illness. **2.** Any unwholesome condition.

mal·aise (mă-lāz′, -lĕz′) *n.* A vague feeling of physical discomfort or unease.

ma·lev·o·lence (mə-lĕv′ə-ləns) *n.* The desire for evil or for harm to others; spitefulness.

mal·ice (măl′ĭs) *n.* The wish to harm, injure, or cause pain to another. **-ma·li′cious,** *adj.*

ma·li·cious (mə-lĭsh′əs) *adj.* Showing or having the desire to harm, injure, or cause pain to another; spiteful.

ma·lign (mə-līn′) *v.* To tell evil or harmful lies about. *-adj.* Evil; harmful.

ma·lig·nant (mə-lĭg′nənt) *adj.* **1.** Likely to spread through the body and cause death. **2.** Very harmful or evil. **-ma·lig′nant·ly,** *adv.*

man·date (măn′dāt′) *n.* An authorization or support given by voters to their representatives in government. *-v.* to require, as by law.

man·da·to·ry (măn′də-tôr′ē) *adj.* Required or commanded by a law, rule, or order. **2.** Of or having a mandate.

ma·nip·u·late (mə-nĭp′yə-lāt′) *v.* **-lat·ed, -lat·ing. 1.** To work or operate skillfully with the hands. **2.** To manage or control to one's own advantage.

man·u·mit (măn′yə-mĭt′) *v.* **-mit·ted, -mit·ting, -mits.** To free from slavery; emancipate. **-man′u·mis′sion,** *n.* **-man′u·mit′ter,** *n.*

maud·lin (môd′lĭn) *adj.* Excessively or foolishly sentimental.

mav·er·ick (măv′ər-ĭk, măv′rĭk) *n.* **1.** An unbranded animal. **2.** A person who thinks and acts independently of others in his or her group.

men·tor (mĕn′tôr′, -tər) *n.* A wise and trusted advisor or teacher.

mes·mer·ize (mĕz′mə-rīz, mĕs′-) *v.* **-ized, -iz·ing, -iz·es. 1.** To hypnotize. **2.** To spellbind; fascinate. **-mes′mer·i·za′tion,** *n.* **-mes′mer·iz′er,** *n.*

met·a·phor (mĕt′ə-fôr′, -fər) *n.* A figure of speech in which one thing is compared to another to suggest a similarity.

mil·i·tant (mĭl′ĭ-tənt) *adj.* **1.** Aggressive or vigourously active in support of a cause. **2.** Fighting. *-n.* One who acts aggressively.

min·i·mal (mĭn′ə-məl) *adj.* Smallest or least possible. **-min′i·mal·ly,** *adv.*

mis·sive (mĭs′ĭv) *n.* A written message; letter.

myr·i·ad (mĭr′ē-əd) *adj.* Too many to count; countless. *n.* A great number.

N

na·ive (nä-ēv′) *adj.* **1.** Lacking in experience or informed judgement. **2.** Childlike; unsophisticated. **-na·ive′ly,** *adv.*

nas·cent (năs′ənt, nā′sənt) *adj.* Coming into being; beginning to develop. **-nas′cen·cy,** *n.*

nem·e·sis (nĕm′ĭ-sĭs) *n., pl.* **-ses** (sēz). Something that causes one's defeat or failure. **2.** One that punishes wrongdoing.

non·cha·lant (nŏn′shə-länt′, non′shə-länt′) *adj.* Showing a lack of interest or enthusiasm; coolly unconcerned.

non·de·script (nŏn′dĭ-skrĭpt′) *adj.* Having no interesting or distinctive qualities or characteristics.

nov·ice (nŏv′ĭs) *n.* A person new to an activity; beginner.

nur·ture (nûr′chər) *v.* **1.** To feed; nourish, **2.** To educate; foster. *-n.* Something that nourishes. **-nur′tur·er,** *n.*

O

o·men (ō′mən) *n.* A sign or happening that is supposed to foretell something good or bad.

o·mis·sion (ō-mĭsh′ən) *n.* Failure to include or mention. **-o·mit′,** *v.*

op·por·tune (ŏp′ər-tōōn′, -tyōōn′) *adj.* **1.** Suitable for a particular purpose. **2.** Happening at the right time; well-timed; timely. **-op′por·tune′ly,** *adv.*

or·tho·dox (ôr′thə-dŏks′) *adj.* Conforming to traditional and established beliefs, attitudes, or doctrines.

os·tra·cize (ŏs′trə-sīz′) -cized, -ciz·ing, -ciz·es. *v.* To banish or exclude from a group. **-os′tra·cism,** *n.*

out·land·ish (out-lăn′dĭsh) *adj.* Strange; off; peculiar. **-out·land′ish·ly,** *adv.* **-out·land′ish·ness,** *n.*

P

pal·pi·tate (păl′pĭ-tāt′) *v.* -tat·ed, -tat·ing, -tates. **1.** To beat rapidly. **2.** To quiver or tremble. **-pal′pi·tat′ing·ly,** *adv.*

pal·try (pôl′trē) *adj.* -tri·er, -tri·est. Lacking in value; worthless. **-pal′tri·ly,** *adv.* **-pal′tri·ness,** *n.*

par·a·dox (păr′ə-dŏks′) *n.* A statement that seems to be contradictory but may be true. **-par′a·dox′i·cal,** *adj.* **-par′a·dox′i·cal·ly,** *adv.*

par·ody (păr′ə-dē) *n., pl.* -dies. A humorous or satirical literary or musical imitation of a serious work.

pa·thet·ic (pə-thĕt′ĭk) *adj.* Arousing pity or sadness combined with either sympathy or contempt.

pa·thol·o·gy (pă-thŏl′ə-jē) *n., pl.* -gies. The branch of medicine that deals with the nature, cause, and development of disease.

pa·thos (pā′thŏs, -thôs) *n.* The quality that evokes a feeling of pity, sadness, or compassion.

pat·ois (păt′wä′) *n., pl.* **pat·ois** (pă-twäz′). A regional dialect of a language, especially one other than the standard or literary dialect.

pe·cu·ni·ar·y (pĭ-kyōō′nē-ĕr′ē) *adj.* Of, consisting of, or relating to money.

ped·es·tal (pĕd′ĭ-stəl) *n.* **1.** The bottom support of a pillar, column, statue, etc. A foundation, support, or base.

ped·i·gree (pĕd′ĭ-grē′) *n.* **1.** A line of ancestors; lineage. **2.** A list of ancestors; family tree.

per·ish (pĕr′ĭsh) *v.* **1.** To die or be destroyed, especially in a violent way. **2.** To pass from existence; disappear.

pe·ti·tion (pə-tĭsh′ən) *v.* To ask or request formally. *-n.* A formal written request.

pil·fer (pĭl′fər) *v.* To steal small amounts. -**pil′fer·age**, *n.* -**pil′fer·er**, *n.*

pit·tance (pĭt′əns) *n.* **1.** A small amount of money. **2.** A small amount.

plain·tive (plān′tĭv) *adj.* Expressing sorrow or melancholy; mournful; sad. -**plain′tive·ly**, *adv.* -**plain′tive·ness**, *n.*

pleth·o·ra (plĕth′ər-ə) *n.* An overabundance; too much; excess.

po·di·a·trist (pə-dī′ə-trĭst) *n.* A doctor specializing in the branch of medicine having to do with the foot.

po·di·um (pō′dē-əm) *n., pl.* -**di·a** or -**di·ums.** **1.** A stand for holding notes of a speaker; lectern. **2.** A raised platform as for an orchestra conductor.

po·lem·ic (pə-lĕm′ĭk) *n.* An argument or dispute, often attacking a specific opinion.

port·a·ble (pôr′tə-bəl, pōr′-) *adj.* Able to be carried or moved easily. **port′a·bil′i·ty**, *n.* -**port′a·bly**, *adv.*

port·age (pôr′tĭj, pōr′-, pôr-täzh′) *n.* The carrying of boats or supplies from one navigable body of water to another.

port·fo·li·o (pôrt-fō′lē-ō, pōrt-) *n., pl.* -**os. 1.** A portable case for carrying loose papers, etc. **2.** A representative collection of a person's work.

port·ly (pôrt′lē, pōrt′-) *adj.* -**li·er**, -**li·est.** Large and heavy; stout; obese.

post·script (pōst′skrĭpt′, pōs′skrĭpt′) *n.* -*abbr.* **P.S., p.s., PS.** A note added to the end of a letter after the signature.

pot·pour·ri (pō′pōō-rē′) *n., pl.* -**ris.** A mixture or collection of different things. **2.** A mixture of dried flowers and spices used for fragrance.

pre·cur·sor (prĭ-kûr′sər, prē′kûr′sər) *n.* A person or thing that goes before and indicates the approach of another.

pre·em·i·nent (prē-ĕm′ə-nənt) *adj.* Superior to or above others; outstanding. -**pre·em′i·nence**, *n.* -**pre·em′i·nent·ly**, *adv.*

prem·ise (prĕm′ĭs) *n.* A statement that serves as the basis for an argument or from which a conclusion is drawn.

prev·a·lent (prĕv′ə-lənt) *adj.* Widely, commonly, or generally happening, existing, accepted, or practiced. -**prev′a·lent·ly**, *adv.*

pro·crus·te·an (prō-krŭs′tē-ən) *adj.* Exhibiting ruthless disregard for individual differences.

pro·found (prə-found′, prō-) *adj.* **1.** Showing great understanding. **2.** Deeply felt. **3.** Significant; far-reaching. -**pro·found′ly**, *adv.*

pro·pound (prə-pound′) *v.* To put forward for consideration; set forth. -**pro·pound′er**, *n.*

pro·sa·ic (prō-zā′ĭk) *adj.* **1.** Commonplace; dull. **2.** Matter-of-fact. -**pro·sa′i·cal·ly**, *adv.* -**pro·sa′ic·ness**, *n.*

pro·scribe (prō-skrīb′) *v.* -**scribed**, -**scrib·ing**, -**scribes. 1.** To condemn. **2.** To forbid. **3.** To banish. -**pro·scrib′er**, *n.*

pro tem·po·re (prō tĕm′pə-rē) *adv.* For the time being; temporarily.

pro·tract (prō-trăkt′, prə-) *v.* To lengthen or draw out; prolong. -**pro·tract′ed·ness**, *n.* -**pro·trac′tive**, *adj.*

psy·cho·path (sī′kə-păth′) *n.* A person having a serious mental disorder characterized by amoral or antisocial behavior.

pug·na·cious (pŭg-nā′shəs) *adj.* Eager and ready to fight; quarrelsome. **-pug·na′cious·ly,** *adv.* **-pug·na′cious·ness, -pug·nac′i·ty,** *n.*

pur·port (pər-pôrt′, -pōrt′) *v.* **1.** To claim, often falsely. **2.** To mean; intend. *n.* Meaning.

Q

quell (kwĕl) *v.* **1.** To crush; suppress. **2.** To quiet; pacify.

quix·ot·ic (kwĭk-sŏt′ĭk) *adj.* Extravagently chivalrous or too romantically idealistic. **quix·ot′i·cal·ly,** *adv.*

R

ran·cor (răng′kər) *n.* Deep or bitter resentment or ill will; hatred. **-ran′cor·ous·ly,** *adv.* **ran′cor·ous·ness,** *n.*

rap·port (ră-pôr′, -pōr′, rə-) *n.* A close, harmonious relationship.

rav·age (răv′ĭj) *v.* **-aged, -ag·ing, -ag·es. 1.** To ruin; devastate, **2.** To be destructive. *n.* Destruction; damage. **-rav′ag·er,** *n.*

re·ac·tion·ar·y (rē-ăk′shə-nĕr′ē) *adj.* Of, characterized by, or favoring a return to a former condition, especially in politics.

re·course (rē′kôrs′, -kōrs′, rĭ-kôrs′, -kōrs′) *n.* **1.** A turning to a person or thing for aid or safety. **2.** A person or thing that is turned to for aid.

re·cur·rent (rĭ-kûr′ənt, -kŭr′-) *adj.* Happening or appearing again or periodically. **-re·cur′rent·ly,** *adv.*

re·doubt·a·ble (rĭ-dou′tə-bəl) *adj.* Formidable; awesome. **2.** Deserving of respect. **-re·doubt′a·bly,** *adv.*

re·fine (rĭ-fīn′) *v.* **-fined, fin·ing, -fines.** To make or become more polished or elegant. **2.** Purify. **-re·fin′er,** *n.*

rel·e·gate (rĕl′ĭ-gāt) *v.* **-gat·ed, -gat·ing, -gates.** To banish, especially to an inferior position or place. **rel′e·ga′tion,** *n.*

re·lent·less (rĭ-lĕnt′lĭs) *adj.* **1.** Steady and persistent. **2.** Harsh; pitiless. **-re·lent′less·ly,** *adv.* **-re·lent′less·ness,** *n.*

re·mu·ner·a·tive (rĭ-myoo′nər-ə-tĭv, -nə-rā′tĭv) *adj.* Profitable. **-re·mu′ner·a·tive·ly,** *adv.*

re·mis·sion (rĭ-mĭsh′ən) *n.* **1.** A temporary lessening of the symptoms of a disease. **2.** The act of sending (money) in payment.

ren·dez·vous (rän′dā-voo′, -də-) *n., pl.* **ren·dez·vous. 1.** An agreement to meet at a certain place and time. **2.** The meeting itself.

re·nown (rĭ-noun′) *n.* Widespread fame. **-re·nowned′,** *adj.*

re·pos·i·to·ry (rĭ-pŏz′ĭ-tôr′ē, -tōr′ē) *n., pl.* **-ries.** A place where things may be stored or deposited for safekeeping.

rep·ro·bate (rĕp′rə-bāt′) *n.* An immoral or wicked person. *adj.* Wicked, sinful.

res·o·lute (rĕz′ə-loot′) *adj.* Determined, firm. **-res′o·lute′ly,** *adv.* **res′o·lute′ness,** *n.*

ret·ri·bu·tion (rĕt′rə-byoo′shən) *n.* Punishment given or demanded in repayment for evil done.

re·venge (rĭ-vĕnj´) *n.* A desire to inflict, or the act of inflicting, harm, injury, or punishment in return for a wrong.

ro·bust (rō-bŭst´, rō´bŭst´) *adj.* Strong and healthy; vigorous. Requiring strength or stamina. **-ro·bust´ly,** *adv.* **-ro·bust´ness,** *n.*

ruse (ro͞os, ro͞oz) *n.* A trick or action intended to mislead.

ruth·less (ro͞oth´lĭs) *adj.* Without mercy, pity, or compassion. **-ruth´less·ly,** *adv.* **-ruth´less·ness,** *n.*

S

sal·ly (săl´ē) *v.* **-lied, -ly·ing, -lies. 1.** To rush out suddenly. **2.** To go out quickly.

sanc·tion (săngk´shən) *n.* Authorization; official approval. *v.* To give authorization or official approval to.

sar·to·ri·al (săr-tôr´ē-əl, -tōr´-) *adj.* Of tailors or their work. **2.** Of clothing or dress. **-sar·to´ri·al·ly,** *adv.*

scourge (skûrj) *n.* A cause of serious destruction of affliction.

scrip·ture (skrĭp[t]´chər) *n.* A sacred or religious writing or book.

se·di·tion (sĭ-dĭsh´ən) *n.* Language or action causing discontent, resistance, or rebellion against the government in power. **-se·di´tious,** *adj.* **-se·di´tion·ist,** *n.*

se·rene (sə-rēn´) *adj.* Undisturbed; peaceful; calm. **-se·rene´ly,** *adv.* **-se·ren´i·ty,** *n.*

se·ren·i·ty (sə-rĕn´ĭ-tē) *n.* The state or quality of being calm; tranquility; peacefulness.

shroud (shroud) *n.* A cloth used to wrap a body for burial. *-v.* To hide; cover; obscure.

sol·e·cism (sŏl´ĭ-sĭz´əm, sō´lĭ-) *n.* An error in grammar or standard language.

so·lem·ni·ty (sə-lĕm´nĭ-tē) *n.* **1.** Seriousness. **2.** A dignified or impressive ceremony. **-so´lemn,** *adj.*

so·lil·o·quy (sə-lĭl´ə-kwē) *n.,* *pl.* **-quies.** The act of talking to oneself. **2.** Lines in a play that a character says aloud to himself or herself.

sov·er·eign (sŏv´ər-ĭn, sŏv´rĭn) *adj.* Not controlled by others; independent. *-n.* The supreme ruler. **-sov´er·eign·ty,** *n.*

spawn (spôn) *v.* To bring forth; produce.

spe·cif·ic (spĭ-sĭf´ĭk) *adj.* Definite; explicit; precise. **-spe·cif´i·cal·ly,** *adv.* **-spec´i·fic´i·ty,** *n.*

spor·tive (spôr´tĭv, spōr´-) *adj.* **1.** Playful; frolicsome. **2.** Interested in sports. **-spor´tive·ly,** *adv.* **-spor´tive·ness,** *n.*

stal·wart (stôl´wərt) *adj.* **1.** Firm and steadfast; unwavering. **2.** Strong. *-n.* A person who is firm, steadfast, or strong. **-stal´wart·ly,** *adv.* **-stal´wart·ness,** *n.*

stam·i·na (stăm´ə-nə) *n.* Resistance to illness, fatigue, or hardship; endurance.

staunch (stônch, stänch) *adj.* **1.** Loyal and steadfast. **2.** Having a strong or solid construction. **-staunch´ly,** *adv.* **-staunch´ness,** *n.*

stra·te·gic (strə-tē´jĭk) *adj.* Related to a skillful plan intended to achieve a specific goal. **-strat´e·gy,** *n.* **-stra·te·gi·cal·ly,** *adv.*

struc·ture (strŭk´chər) *n.* **1.** The arrangement or interrelation of the parts of a whole. **2.** Something composed of interrelated parts.

sub·jec·tive (səb-jĕk′tĭv) *adj.* Of or coming from an individual's own mind. **2.** A view based on a person's own feelings, thoughts, or experiences.

sub·side (səb-sīd′) *v.* **-sid·ed, -sid·ing, -sides. 1.** To sink to a lower level. **2.** To become quiet or less active. **-sub·si′dence,** *n.*

suc·cinct (sək-sĭngkt′) *adj.* Concise and clearly stated. **-suc·cinct′ly,** *adv.* **-suc·cinct′ness,** *n.*

sur·pass (sər-păs′) *v.* **1.** To go beyond; excel. **2.** Exceed. **-sur·pass′a·ble,** *adj.* **-sur·pass′ing·ly,** *adv.*

sus·tain (sə-stān′) *v.* **1.** To keep in effect; maintain. **2.** Support. **-sus·tain′a·ble,** *adj.* **-sus·tain′er,** *n.*

sup·po·si·tion (sŭp′ə-zĭsh′ən) *n.* **1.** An assumption that something is true for the sake of argument. **2.** A belief on uncertain grounds.

syn·chro·nize (sĭng′krə-nīz, sĭn′-) *v.* **-nized, -niz·ing, -niz·es.** To cause to occur at the same time and together. **-syn′chro·ni·za′tion,** *n.*

syn·tax (sĭn′tăks′) *n.* The manner in which words are arranged to form sentences.

syn·the·sis (sĭn′thĭ-sĭs) *n., pl.* **-ses** (sēz). The combining of separate parts or elements to form a whole.

T

tact (tăkt) *n.* Skill in dealing with people or delicate situations without offending.

tan·gent (tăn′jənt) *adj.* In contact at a single point; touching.

tan·gi·ble (tăn′jə-bəl) *adj.* **1.** Capable of being touched. **2.** Capable of being treated as definite or fact; real; concrete.

tem·po·ral (tĕm′pər-əl, tĕm′prəl) *adj.* Lasting for a short time; temporary. Pertaining to life on earth; worldly.

tem·por·ize (tĕm′pə-rīz) *v.* **-rized, -riz·ing, -riz·es. 1.** To evade action in order to gain time. **2.** To discuss in order to gain time.

ten·et (tĕn′ĭt) *n.* A principle, doctrine, or belief held as truth by a person or group.

the·o·ret·i·cal (thē′ə-rĕt′ĭ-kəl) *adj.* **1.** Not based on fact or experience. **2.** Speculative. **-the′o·ret′i·cal·ly,** *adv.*

to·tal·i·tar·i·an (tō-tăl′ĭ-târ′ē-ən) *adj.* Of or relating to a government in which one political party or group exercises complete control.

trans·mit (trăns-mĭt′, tranz-) *v.* **-mit·ted, -mit·ting, -mits.** To send or convey from one person, place, or thing to another.

tra·verse (trə-vûrs′, trăv′ərs) *v.* **-versed, -vers·ing, -vers·es. 1.** To pass over, across, or through. **2.** To cross and re-cross.

trek (trĕk) *n.* A difficult journey. *v.* **-trekked, -trek·king** To travel slowly or with difficulty.

trite (trīt) *adj.* **trit·er, trit·est.** Lacking freshness because of overuse; stale; hackneyed. **-trite′ness,** *n.*

U

un·in·ter·est·ed (ŭn-ĭn′trĭ-stĭd, -tər-ĭ-stĭd, -tə-rĕs′tĭd) *adj.* Not interested; indifferent. **-un·in′ter·est·ed·ly,** *adv.* **-un·in′ter·est·ed·ness,** *n.*

un·re·mit·ting (ŭn-rĭ-mĭt′ĭng) *adj.* Never stopping; persistent. **-un′re·mit′ing·ly,** *adv.* **-un′re·mit′ting·ness,** *n.*

u·surp (yōo-sûrp´, -zûrp´) v. To take and hold by force and without legal right or authority. **-u·surp´er,** n.

u·su·ry (yōo´zhə-rē) n., pl. **-ries. 1.** The practice of lending money at an excessive interest rate. **2.** An excessive interest rate.

V

val·i·date· (văl´ĭ-dāt´) v. **-dat·ed, -dat·ing, -dates. 1.** To prove to be true or correct; confirm. **2.** To make legally valid. **-val´i·da´tion,** n.

van·quish (văng´kwĭsh, văn´-) v. **1.** To defeat or overcome in battle. **2.** To overcome in a contest or conflict. **3.** To gain mastery over.

ve·he·ment (vē´ə-mənt) adj. Characterized by intense or strong feeling or conviction; passionate. **-ve´he·mence,** n. **-ve´he·ment·ly,** adv.

ver·bos·i·ty (vər-bŏs´ĭ-tē) adj. The use of more words than necessary; wordiness. **-ver·bose´,** adj.

ver·sa·tile (vûr´sə-təl, -tĭl´) adj. Capable of doing many things well. Having many uses. **-ver´sa·tile·ly,** adv. **-ver´sa·til´i·ty,** n.

vi·cin·i·ty (vĭ-sĭn´ĭ-tē) n., pl. **-ties. 1.** The area around a place; neighborhood. **2.** Nearness; proximity.

W

wield (wēld) v. **1.** To handle and use (a tool or weapon) with skill. **2.** To exercise (power, influence, etc.) **-wield´er,** n.

X

xen·o·pho·bi·a (zĕn´ə-fō´bē-ə) n. Fear or hatred of strangers or anything strange or foreign. **-xen´o·pho´bic,** adj.

Standardized Test Practice

In lessons 1 to 36, you have concentrated on building vocabulary, a skill that is an important aid in reading comprehension. However, the competent reader must master a variety of other skills. These include the following:

- **Identifying main and subordinate ideas**—deciding what the most important idea in the selection is and what items support that idea

Examples:

Main idea	Marcel Marceau is the master of mime, the wordless theater.
Subordinate ideas	Marceau admired Charlie Chaplin, Buster Keaton, and the Marx Brothers, all of whom used mime in their performances.
	Marceau tells most of his stories through Bip the clown, a character he created.
	Marceau's aim is to make his audiences see, feel, and hear the invisible.

- **Deciding on an appropriate title**—choosing a title that is closely related to the main idea of a selection

- **Drawing inferences**—coming to a conclusion that is not directly stated but is based on information given

Example:

If a woman is clasping her purse tightly and looking around her, you can infer that she is afraid her purse will be stolen.

- **Locating details**—scanning a selection to find the answer to a specific question

The following pages will give you a chance to practice the skills you use when you read. The questions they contain are the kinds of questions you will be asked to answer on a standardized test.

The reading selections include passages from science and social studies texts as well as informative essays and short narratives.

Reread the selection "Lincoln Begins His Second Term" on page 15 in this book. Then circle the letter before the BEST choice to answer each question.

1. Which statement can be inferred from the selection?

   A. Abraham Lincoln was extremely popular with the people.

   B. Both Lincoln and Washington gave short swearing-in speeches.

   C. Lincoln took his second oath of office on a bright sunny day in spring.

   D. Lincoln thought that the South should be punished for causing the Civil War.

2. Which group of words best describes Lincoln in the selection?

   A. angry, weary, grateful

   B. sad, resentful, exhausted

   C. happy, triumphant, proud

   D. dignified, charitable, peace-loving

3. Which sentence from the selection shows that Lincoln did not want to go to war?

   A. "Lincoln deeply desired that the nation become one again."

   B. "Lincoln had been forced to accept war rather than let the nation perish."

   C. "More than anyone else, Abraham Lincoln is credited with holding the union of states together."

   D. "When the assembled crowd saw their president, the solemnity of the occasion gave way to applause."

4. What word best describes the attitude of the author toward Lincoln?

   A. fear

   B. sympathy

   C. admiration

   D. indifference

5. What does the word *defining*, as used in the first paragraph, mean?

   A. limited

   B. very fine

   C. determining

   D. praiseworthy

Reread the article "Earthquake" on page 29 in this book. Then circle the letter before the choice that BEST completes each statement.

1. When the edges of the plates that make up the earth's crust meet and grind together,
   - A. a volcano results.
   - B. a long crack results.
   - C. the result is subduction.
   - D. they create an earthquake.

2. According to the article, the earth's core is
   - A. solid.
   - B. a gas.
   - C. liquid.
   - D. a vacuum.

3. The following statement expresses the main idea of the article:
   - A. Volcanoes are upwellings of hot molten rocks.
   - B. San Francisco suffered a great earthquake in 1906.
   - C. An earthquake struck the island of Cyprus in A.D. 365.
   - D. In the past hundred years, scientists have been able to discover what causes earthquakes and where they might occur.

4. Geologists have been able to use computers to map areas where earthquakes may occur. When these maps are publicized, it is likely that
   - A. laboratories will be built on the sites.
   - B. the areas will become vacation resorts.
   - C. people will leave the areas for safer places.
   - D. companies will build large factories in the areas.

5. The word *converge,* in the third paragraph, means
   - A. pass.
   - B. meet.
   - C. strike.
   - D. converse.

Reread the selection "Lightning" on page 71. Then circle the letter before the choice that BEST completes each statement.

1. Lightning is caused by
   A. an eclipse of the sun.
   B. a buildup of electricity.
   C. low temperatures in an area.
   D. changing light patterns in the sky.

2. Of the following states, lightning is most likely to occur in
   A Alaska.
   B. New York.
   C. New Mexico.
   D. Mississippi.

3. Another title for this selection might be
   A Kinds of Lightning.
   B. Causes of Lightning.
   C. The Earth as a Battery.
   D. The Dangers of Lightning.

4. One should always seek shelter in an electrical storm because
   A. such a storm brings heavy rain.
   B. one might slip on wet pavement.
   C. lightning is attracted to open areas.
   D. it is easier to appreciate the spectacle of the storm from indoors.

5. The word *inherent,* in the fourth paragraph, means
   A. harmful.
   B. available.
   C. sticking together.
   D. forming the essential nature.

Reread the selection "Jeanealogy" on page 141. Then circle the letter before the word or phrase that BEST completes each statement.

1. The first jeans were made from

    A. green duck.

    B. blue denim.

    C. khaki cotton.

    D. brown canvas.

2. The word *bolt,* as used in the third paragraph, means

    A. streak of lightning.

    B. roll of wallpaper or cloth.

    C. rod used as a door fastener.

    D. one who runs suddenly away

3. Jeans enjoyed a surge in popularity in the 1980s because

    A. they were inexpensive and durable.

    B. people were searching for comfortable clothing.

    C. many people wanted to wear an unofficial uniform.

    D. they were worn by an American actor in a popular movie.

4. The main idea of the selection is the following:

    A. Jeans are worn by people in many parts of the world.

    B. Jeans have maintained their popularity for over a century.

    C. The first Americans to wear jeans were miners in California.

    D. Designers have found ways to make new jeans look old and worn.

5. If you are interested in *sartorial* pursuits, you are most likely planning to become

    A. a chef.

    B. a tailor.

    C. a sculptor.

    D. an engineer.

Read the following passage and pay close attention to the main points the author makes. Then follow the directions.

Marc Chagall

1   The artist Marc Chagall was born in Vitebsk, Byelorussia (now Belarus), Russian Empire, in 1887. When he was twenty-three, he moved to Paris, where he lived from 1910 to 1914. During those years, French cubism was on the rise, so it is not surprising that Chagall's unique painting style was influenced as much by French cubism as it was by Russian expressionism—a form of art that depicts the emotions and the responses that objects and events arouse in an artist.

2   Like Kandinsky, a famous Russian expressionist with whom Chagall was familiar, Chagall rendered scenes in an evocative, dreamlike manner that aimed more at making a viewer feel a certain way than at depicting reality. To this kind of framework Chagall added images from traditional Russian folktales, biblical icons, and scenes from his personal life.

3   Chagall's years in Paris exposed him to cubism, the main principle of which was that the underlying shapes of things—"the sphere, the cone, the cylinder"—are important elements that earlier painters had ignored. Chagall's emphasis on shapes and his inclusion of violins (cubists appreciated instruments for their interesting shapes) in several of his works demonstrate this influence.

Circle the letter before the choice that BEST completes each statement.

1. Paragraph 2 is mostly about
   A. how Chagall was different from the Russian expressionists.
   B. the kinds of images Chagall included in his paintings.
   C. the influence on Chagall of Russian art.
   D. the Russian expressionist Kandinsky.

2. Paragraph 3 is mostly about
   A. the principal ideas of French art in the 1800s.
   B. the influence on Chagall of French cubism's exploration of new shapes.
   C. the importance of the underlying shapes of things to the cubist movement.
   D. why Chagall liked to paint violins and other instruments because of their interesting shapes.

3. The main idea of this passage is that
   A. Chagall was a better painter than Kandinsky because he painted more loosely.
   B. painters in Paris about 1914 were interested in the underlying forms of things.
   C. Chagall used images from folktales and religious icons in many of his paintings.
   D. Chagall's art shows the influences of Russian expressionism and French cubism.

4. When a painter *renders* scenes, he
   A. represents or depicts them.
   B. observes them very carefully.
   C. changes certain of their details.
   D. decides that he will not paint them.

A Game of Cat and Mouse

1   One morning, as Cymbeline the cat lay sunbathing in her garden, a careless mouse scampered across her outstretched paw. The agile feline quickly scooped up the troublesome intruder. She drew the trembling captive close to her face.

2   "You've interrupted my nap," she meowed. "I'm afraid I shall have to eat you to make sure that you do not tread on me again."

3   "I beseech you, let me live!" implored the terrified mouse. "If you grant me this favor, I promise that someday I shall return it!"

4   "Return it?" snickered Cymbeline incredulously. "You shall allow me to live? I could crush you beneath my paws or between my jaws in an instant, if I chose to." Cymbeline eyed her prisoner, then added, "But I don't choose to. You are a brave little rodent and clever, too—clever enough to save yourself. Let us hope you are clever enough to not cross my path again."

5   She released her diminutive hostage.

6   "Thank you!" called the mouse as he scurried away. "But I hope our paths do cross again so that I can return the favor."

7   *Impertinent!* thought Cymbeline as she resumed her nap. *Perhaps I should have eaten him.* But she was soon too lost in her dreams to consider the matter further.

8   As for the mouse, he took care to remain inconspicuous when Cymbeline occupied the garden and had all but forgotten the incident himself, until one afternoon when he heard a weak but plaintiff cry coming from deep within the dense bramble hedge that skirted the perimeter of the lawn. Making his way through the underbrush, he found the source. It was Cymbeline! The hapless feline was bound from head to tail in a seemingly endless tangle of yarn.

9   Cymbeline whispered weakly through a small gap in the mesh, "I was playing with a ball of yarn in the study. I chased it through the open door and across garden. When I followed the ball under the hedge, I somehow became entangled in the yarn. The more I struggled, the more entwined I became."

10   "Fear not!" replied the stalwart mouse. With alacrity, he bit through the menacing strands until one by one they fell away, unfettering the grateful cat.

11   "Oh, mouse," said Cymbeline in a weary but appreciative voice, "you did return the favor. You were clever enough and kind enough to save me, just as you promised you would. Now, as for our paths—"

12   "I know," interrupted the mouse, "they must never cross again."

13   "Oh no," countered Cymbeline, "they must never part again!"

14   And she and the mouse remained fast friends for the rest of their days.

Circle the letter before the choice that BEST completes each statement.

1. This story is probably most accurately categorized as

   A. science fiction.

   B. a news story.

   C. a biography.

   D. a fable.

2. The cat did not eat the mouse because

   A. the cat was impressed by the mouse's courage.

   B. the mouse was too thin to make a good meal.

   C. the mouse tied her up in yarn.

   D. the mouse scurried away.

3. Of the events in the story listed below, the last event is that

   A. the cat releases the mouse.

   B. the mouse makes a promise to the cat.

   C. the mouse finds the cat tangled in yarn.

   D. the cat chases the yarn ball into the garden.

4. At the end of the story, the cat probably feels

   A. embarrassed.

   B. grateful.

   C. worried.

   D. angry.

5. If you were asked to find the moral of this story, you would

   A. skim it quickly.

   B. think about what the cat learned.

   C. make an outline of the events as they occurred.

   D. decide who is the more important character in the story.

6. In the ninth paragraph, the word *mesh* refers to

   A. the underbrush.

   B. a net snare.

   C. the fence.

   D. the yarn.

Read the selection below and then follow the directions.

Chinese Treasures

When thinking about ancient cultures, some Westerners forget the rich history of China. Westerners might associate Chinese art with modern, mass-produced products and handicrafts rather than with magnificent ancient buildings and sculptures. However, generalizing about China's history solely on the basis of China's present production for the current market is a great mistake.

The buildings and sculptures from China's past are incredibly beautiful. These enormous constructions took decades to build and still stand today. The terracotta army, for example, created during the Qin Dynasty (about 210 B.C.), consists of six thousand larger-than-life-sized men in full battle armor. The soldiers were made from clay and fired in large brick kilns. No two soldiers' faces are alike. The incredible artwork was buried underground for thousands of years until farmers discovered it in March 1974. Today the public can view the enormous "army."

The Great Wall of China is an architectural marvel that was also built during the Qin Dynasty. Originally meant to serve as a blockade between China and Mongolia during wartime, the wall remains one of the most beautiful and complex structures of all time.

Circle the letter before the choice that BEST completes each statement.

1. According to the author, some people might associate China with modern, mass-produced products because
   A. all Chinese sculpture is mass produced.
   B. mass-produced products are common in Chinese markets.
   C. modern, mass-produced art is very popular in Chinese culture.
   D. mass-produced products are more interesting than ancient sculpture.

2. Organize the following details of the author's argument, which support the thesis statement: "However, generalizing about China's history solely on the basis of China's present production for the current market is a great mistake."

(1) "The terracotta army . . . consists of six thousand larger-than-life-sized men in full battle armor."

(2) "The buildings and sculptures from China's past are incredibly beautiful."

(3) "These enormous constructions took decades to build and still stand today."

(4) "The incredible artwork was buried underground for thousands of years until farmers discovered it in March 1974."

A. 1, 2, 3, 4

B. 2, 3, 1, 4

C. 2, 4, 1, 3

D. 4, 1, 3, 2

3. The series of details in the preceding question suggests that it is a mistake to judge Chinese history on the basis of its current market because

A. beautiful works of sculpture and architecture are part of China's past.

B. there is no evidence of sculpture or architecture in modern China.

C. the terracotta army was a powerful army in China's past.

D. farmers discovered the terracotta army in March 1974.

4. In this selection, the following conclusion can MOST REASONABLY be drawn:

A. The author was one of the farmers who found the terracotta army.

B. The author thinks that the Great Wall of China is the most beautiful structure of all time.

C. The author can see no differences between the faces of the sculptures in the terracotta army.

D. The author prefers ancient Chinese art to the mass-produced products of the modern Chinese market.

Read the selection below and answer the questions that follow.

A Special Yankee

On May 20, 1945, a crowd of thirty-six thousand packed Yankee Stadium to watch a double-header that pitted New York's finest against the American League champions, the St. Louis Browns. The Yankees, who had finished third the previous season, had something to prove that afternoon. Even though World War II had stripped their lineup of star players, their traditional Yankee pride inspired the belief that 1945 would be "their year."

Game one of the double-header got underway with the Browns' rookie outfielder, Pete Gray, leading off against former twenty-game winner "Spud" Chandler. . . . By the end of the afternoon, Gray had reached base five times with four hits. He scored twice and knocked in two runs while fielding his positions flawlessly. The Browns swept the double-header 10–1 and 5–2.

Any player would have been proud of that performance, but for the St. Louis rookie it was a dream come true. As a boy growing up in the coal region of Pennsylvania, Gray had committed himself to fulfilling that dream. More impressively, he managed it all with only one arm, having lost his right arm above the elbow in a truck accident at the age of six. A natural right-hander prior to the mishap, Gray learned to hit, catch, and throw with his left hand. "The only thing I ever wanted to do as a kid was to play in Yankee Stadium," Gray, now in his eighties, recalls.

—William C. Kashatus, from "Pete Gray"

Circle the letter of the BEST answer to each of the following questions.

1. Which of these facts from the selection would be MOST RELEVANT to use in a research project about Pete Gray?

    A. "A crowd of thirty-six thousand packed Yankee Stadium to watch a double-header that pitted New York's finest against the defending American League champions, the St. Louis Browns."

    B. "Even though World War II had stripped their lineup of star players, their traditional Yankee pride inspired the belief that 1945 would be 'their year.'"

    C. "A natural right-hander prior to the mishap, Gray learned to hit, catch. and throw with his left hand."

    D. "The Yankees, who had finished third the previous season, had something to prove that afternoon."

2. What would be the MOST EFFICIENT procedure to follow in preparing a presentation about Pete Gray?

   A. Buy a ticket to a baseball game, take notes while watching it, and present your findings to the class.

   B. Ask your parents whether they know anything about Pete Gray, find out their opinions about him, write a summary of their opinions and whether you agree with them, and give your presentation.

   C. Make a list of every team that Pete Gray has ever played on, write a one-paragraph history of each team, make note of the relevant data about each player, and find photographs of each team to show to your audience.

   D. Make an outline of what you plan to present, review encyclopedia and topical references, organize the data to fit within the outline, write a brief summary of your findings, and practice the presentation in front of your friends.

3. In planning a research paper on Pete Gray, which of the following series of steps is in the MOST EFFICIENT chronological order?

   A. Create an outline about how Pete Gray was discovered by the St. Louis Browns; go to the library and do research; fill in the outline with what you find.

   B. Go to the library and search for information on Pete Gray; consult several sources, taking the most relevant and interesting information from each source; compile your information according to an outline based on your findings.

   C. Read several articles about baseball; use the information you find to create an outline for your paper; go to the library and find more information about baseball and baseball players; complete your outline.

   D. Go to the library and create an outline about Pete Gray; read several different sources of information about this player; fill in your findings on the outline; make sure that your findings are relevant and interesting.

4. A player who fields his position *flawlessly* does so

   A. with no mistakes.

   B. with much effort.

   C. in spite of great pain.

   D. with only a few errors.

Read the selections below and then follow the directions.

Intelligent Airbags

Although automobile airbags have effectively decreased injuries and deaths from car accidents, they have created some new safety problems. There have been many reported cases of injuries caused by airbags. Because the airbags have a greater impact on smaller bodies, most of these injuries have affected children and light-weight adults. Small bodies have less mass to counter the tremendous force of the inflating airbag. However, systems are being developed to decrease the number of airbag-related injuries.

One device used in such systems that helps prevent injuries is the FSR, or force-sensing resistor. This device gathers information about the size and weight of a car's passenger and sends that information to the airbag system to regulate the force of inflation.

FSRs are usually used along with an OC, or an occupant classification, a device that is placed within a car's seat. The OC device classifies occupants on the basis of their weight and their position on the seat. Using the data from the sensors in the OC device, the airbag system can tell how much a person weighs and how that passenger's weight is spread across the cushion of the seat. In the event of a car accident, the airbag responds to the information and inflates only enough to protect the individual passenger, thereby decreasing the possibility of injury.

Systems like this are already being installed in several cars in Europe, while only a small number of American cars currently carry the system. However, these "intelligent airbags" will soon be required in many American vehicles, thanks to new rules set by the National Highway Traffic Safety Administration.

Watch the Pedestrian!

It's a rainy night, and someone is trying to cross the street. Although the pedestrian uses the road's clearly marked crosswalk, the driver of an oncoming car still might have a hard time seeing the pedestrian through the darkness and inclement weather. This was the concern that led Mike Harrison of Santa Rosa, California, to invent a system to protect pedestrians in crosswalks.

Harrison invented an electronic system that alerts drivers to pedestrians in the roadway ahead. The system consists of flashing yellow lights embedded in the road alongside a crosswalk. As a pedestrian steps into the street, the lights automatically start blinking. The lights turn off after fifteen to twenty seconds.

The system is inexpensive, costing a fraction of the price of a new traffic light. It has been proven effective in alerting drivers to the need to yield. As a result, the system is already being used in a number of towns in northern California, as well as in towns in Florida, Washington, and Nevada. Many other states and some foreign countries have ordered the system too. Soon it will be protecting pedestrians everywhere. Sal Rosano, a former chief of police in Santa Rosa, California, hopes it will be. "I am convinced this saves lives," he says.

Circle the letter before the choice that BEST completes each statement.

1. The MAIN idea of "Intelligent Airbags" is the following:
   A. Automobile airbags have been proven to decrease injuries and deaths in car accidents.
   B. A number of children and lightweight adults have suffered airbag-related injuries.
   C. New airbag systems will decrease the possibility of airbag-related injuries.
   D. New airbag systems are being used in Europe and in the United States.

2. The following statement about the new airbag systems is MOST accurate:
   A. The new airbag systems have been placed in every car in the United States.
   B. The new airbag systems have already saved several lives.
   C. The new airbag systems classify vehicles' occupants.
   D. The new airbag systems have not yet been tested.

3. As described in "Watch the Pedestrian," Mike Harrison's system has caused drivers to
   A. drive only in good weather.
   B. yield to pedestrians.
   C. drive more quickly.
   D. yield to other cars.

4. The lights in Harrison's system light up when a pedestrian
   A. reaches the curb.
   B. has crossed the street.
   C. sees an approaching car.
   D. steps into the crosswalk.

5. The inventions discussed in both of these articles are PRIMARILY concerned with
    A. traffic safety.
    B. pedestrian laws.
    C. health problems.
    D. cost effectiveness.

6. If the weather were *inclement,* most people would
    A. work in their gardens.
    B. cancel plans for a picnic.
    C. wear lightweight clothing.
    D. take long hikes in the country.

Word List

Word	Lesson	Word	Lesson	Word	Lesson
aberrant	23	chronological	36	effusive	2
abject	24	claustrophobia	18	eloquent	1
abnormal	25	clemency	29	emerge	4
abridge	13	cliché	8	emissary	30
accord	9	clientele	8	emit	30
accretion	26	codify	11	empathy	18
accrue	14	cognomen	6	ensue	28
acculturate	10	collateral	14	entrée	8
acerbity	32	collide	16	entrepreneur	8
acrophobia	18	commodity	31	errant	23
adjacent	24	component	33	erratic	23
aegis	28	comport	27	eventual	13
affect	17	composite	33	evict	3
affront	32	concise	3	evince	3
agnostic	6	confound	22	exhibition	16
allegory	20	conjecture	24	exonerate	29
allusion	20	connotation	20	expedite	12
altercation	32	conscript	21	exponent	33
amnesty	28	conspiracy	25	expound	33
anachronism	36	contemporary	36	extemporaneous	36
anguish	1	contentious	32	extort	29
annals	22	contiguous	24	extract	21
annihilation	1	contingent	24	extrinsic	31
anomaly	23	continual	17	facilitate	19
antagonism	32	continuous	17	fathomless	26
anxiety	34	converge	7	feisty	22
apathy	18	converse	34	felony	29
appall	34	copious	26	ferocity	1
appreciable	26	cordial	9	finite	26
appreciate	34	countermand	12	foster	19
articulate	2	covet	31	fratricide	3
ascribe	21	creed	13	frustration	13
atmosphere	16	creep	7	galvanize	13
audit	14	culminate	7	garrulous	2
autonomy	11	culpable	29	gauche	8
avenge	17	culprit	29	gaunt	4
bedlam	5	cursive	9	generate	25
bellicose	3	cursory	9	genocide	3
belligerent	3	depict	16	glib	2
benediction	15	deportment	27	gratuitous	31
benefactor	15	desolate	7	hale	22
benevolent	15	despot	11	hallowed	31
benign	15	detract	21	harangue	1
bizarre	23	deviate	23	herculean	5
blasé	8	dexterous	35	histrionics	2
boycott	5	diagnose	6	hue	28
bravado	2	discord	9	hydrophobia	18
brazen	35	discursive	9	idiosyncratic	23
bureaucracy	11	disinterested	17	idiom	20
capital	14	disposition	33	illustrious	28
cardiac	9	dissension	32	immeasurable	13
cartel	14	diverge	7	immense	7
catastrophic	25	docile	6	impediment	12
character	13	doctrinaire	6	imperious	11
charismatic	13	doctrine	6	imply	17
charity	4	dominion	10	impostor	33
charlatan	29	duration	7	impressive	16
cherish	4	eccentricity	23	incisive	3
chronic	36	economic	34	incognito	6
chronicle	36	effect	17	incongruous	23

Word	Lesson	Word	Lesson	Word	Lesson
incorrigible	29	ostracize	32	resolute	35
incursion	35	outlandish	23	retribution	32
indefatigable	13	palpitate	35	revenge	17
indemnify	14	paltry	26	robust	10
indifference	1	paradox	6	ruse	1
indigenous	10	parody	20	ruthless	10
indoctrinate	6	pathetic	18	sally	35
induce	16	pathology	18	sanction	22
infer	17	pathos	18	sartorial	31
ingredient	16	patois	20	scourge	28
inherent	16	pecuniary	14	scripture	21
insatiable	26	pedestal	12	sedition	11
intact	24	pedigree	12	serene	22
interdependence	34	perish	4	serenity	34
intermittent	30	petition	1	shroud	4
intervene	25	pilfer	29	solecism	20
intractable	21	pittance	26	solemnity	4
intricate	34	plaintive	10	soliloquy	20
invincible	3	plethora	26	sovereign	11
iota	26	podiatrist	12	spawn	25
jargon	20	podium	12	specific	25
juxtaposition	33	polemic	2	sportive	27
kindred	25	portable	27	stalwart	35
laconic	2	portage	27	stamina	35
legion	19	portfolio	27	staunch	31
legitimate	31	portly	27	strategic	31
liquidate	14	postscript	21	structure	7
longevity	22	potpourri	8	subjective	24
lucrative	14	precursor	9	subside	4
malady	15	preeminent	22	succinct	1
malaise	15	premise	30	supposition	33
malevolence	15	prevalent	16	surpass	16
malice	4	pro tempore	36	sustain	25
malicious	15	procrustean	5	synchronize	36
malign	15	profound	19	syntax	19
malignant	15	propound	33	synthesis	10
mandate	12	prosaic	19	tact	24
mandatory	12	proscribe	21	tangent	24
manipulate	12	protract	21	tangible	24
manumit	30	psychopath	18	temporal	36
maudlin	5	pugnacious	32	temporize	36
maverick	5	purport	27	tenet	19
mentor	5	quell	10	theoretical	7
mesmerize	5	quixotic	5	totalitarian	11
metaphor	20	rancor	32	transmit	30
militant	22	rapport	27	traverse	10
minimal	25	ravage	28	trek	1
missive	30	reactionary	11	trite	2
myriad	34	recourse	9	uninterested	17
naive	8	recurrent	9	unremitting	30
nascent	19	redoubtable	35	usurp	11
nemesis	5	refine	28	usury	14
nonchalant	8	relegate	22	validate	10
nondescript	21	relentless	19	vanquish	3
novice	19	remission	30	vehement	35
nurture	34	remunerative	28	verbosity	2
omen	4	rendezvous	8	versatile	31
omission	30	renown	13	vicinity	7
opportune	27	repository	33	wield	28
orthodox	6	reprobate	29	xenophobia	18

A VISUAL HISTORY OF COSTUME *The Nineteenth Century*

VANDA FOSTER

B T BATSFORD LTD, LONDON

Contents

Preface

A Visual History of Costume is a series devised for those who need reliable, easy-to-use reference material on the history of dress.

The central part of each book is a series of illustrations, in black-and-white and colour, taken from the time of the dress itself. They include oil paintings, engravings, woodcuts and line drawings. By the use of such material, the reader is given a clear idea of what was worn and how, without the distortions and loss of detail which modern drawings can occasionally entail.

Each picture is captioned in a consistent way, under the headings, where appropriate, 'Head', 'Body' and 'Accessories'; the clothes are not just described, but their significance explained. The reader will want to know whether a certain style was fashionable or unfashionable at a certain time, usual or unusual – such information is clearly and consistently laid out. The illustrations are arranged in date order, and the colour illustrations are numbered in sequence with the black-and-white, so that the processes of change can be clearly followed.

The pictures will be all the better appreciated if the reader has at least some basic overall impression of the broad developments in dress in the period concerned, and the Introduction is intended to provide this.

Technical terms have been kept to a reasonable minimum. Many readers will use these books for reference, rather than read them straight through from beginning to end. To explain every term each time it is used would have been hopelessly repetitive, and so a Glossary has been provided. Since the basic items of dress recur throughout the book, a conventional, full Index would have been equally repetitive; therefore the Glossary has been designed also to act as an Index; after each entry the reader will find the numbers of those illustrations which show important examples of the item concerned.

List of Illustrations

Note The subject is followed by the artist, where known, then the medium, and then the collection. An Asterisk * indicates a colour illustration, to be found between pages 96 and 97.

42 **Queen Adelaide**
Sir William Beechey
Oil on canvas
National Portrait Gallery, London

43 **Benjamin Disraeli**
After D. Maclise
Drawing
Victoria and Albert Museum, London

44 **Mrs Thomas Hood**
Anon.
Oil on canvas
National Portrait Gallery, London

45 **Interior of the Gallery of Watercolour Artists (detail)**
G. Scharf
Watercolour
Victoria and Albert Museum, London

46 **A woman in evening dress**
Watt after A.E. Chalon
Engraving
Courtauld Institute of Art, London

47 **A young girl**
T.M. Joy
Watercolour
Victoria and Albert Museum, London

48 **Florence Nightingale and her sister**
W. White
Watercolour
National Portrait Gallery, London

49 **Queen Victoria**
A.E. Chalon
Watercolour
Scottish National Portrait Gallery, Edinburgh

50 **The Duchess of Kent**
A.E. Chalon
Watercolour
Scottish National Portrait Gallery, Edinburgh

51 **Mrs Harris Prendergast**
A. Geddes
Oil on canvas
National Gallery of Scotland, Edinburgh

52 **Youth and Age**
J.C. Horsley
Oil on canvas
Victoria and Albert Museum, London

53 **Princess Victoire**
Sir Edwin Landseer
Oil on canvas
Reproduced by gracious permission of
Her Majesty the Queen

54 **Mrs Edward Elliot in evening dress**
After A.E. Chalon
Engraving
Courtauld Institute of Art, London

55 **Lady Elizabeth Villiers**
After A.E. Chalon
Engraving
Courtauld Institute of Art, London

56 **Unknown woman**
W. Buckler
Watercolour
Victoria and Albert Museum, London

57 **Unknown gentleman**
W. Huggins
Oil on canvas
The Walker Art Gallery, Liverpool

58 **Two Dandies**
A. 'Crowquill'
Engraved caricature from *Punch* magazine, 1843

59 **The Royal Railroad Carriage (detail)**
Anon. engraved caricature
B.T. Batsford Ltd

60 **Sisters**
J. Sant
Oil on canvas
Sotheby's, Belgravia

61 **Lady Ruthven**
Hill and Adamson
Original photograph
National Portrait Gallery, London

62 **The Bromley family**
F.M. Brown
Oil on canvas
Manchester City Art Galleries

63 **Mrs Barker**
Hill and Adamson
Original photograph
National Portrait Gallery, London

64 **The Milne sisters**
Hill and Adamson
Original photograph
National Portrait Gallery, London

65 **Mrs Bell**
Hill and Adamson
Original photograph
National Portrait Gallery, London

66 **Baroness Burdett-Coutts**
W.C. Ross
Watercolour miniature
National Portrait Gallery, London

9

Introduction

It was in the nineteenth century that fashion, in terms of an interest in dress and its changing styles, became a predominantly female concern. From the early years of the century, the two sexes began to adopt diverging roles in society. In a rapidly changing social order, the masculine ideal became one of stolid integrity and economic reliability, expressed in safe, conservative styles of clothing, in discreet and sombre colours. The female, on the other hand, was seen as a mere dependent, a decorative accessory, who could display the family wealth and social status in the quality and fashionableness of her dress. Thus, while men's clothing became increasingly standardized over the century, women's demonstrated a wide variety of styles, which changed more rapidly than in any previous period.

This variety in dress was made possible by the greater buying power of the growing *nouveaux riches*, coupled with the greater diffusion of information on fashion which resulted from improved communications. It was further promoted by the major technical developments in clothing production which were a feature of the nineteenth century. As early as 1808, Heathcote's invention of a Bobbin Net machine introduced a cheaper alternative to hand-made lace. In the 1830s, the import of the Jacquard loom into Great Britain revolutionized the production of woven silks. In 1845 in the United States of America Elias Howe invented a sewing machine, a version of which was soon widely sold in Britain, marketed by the American firm of Singer. From the mid-1860s, traditional hand sewing was replaced almost entirely by machine work. There was a rapid increase in the use of paper patterns, which received a further boost when Butterick's opened an English branch in 1873, while further developments of the sewing machine led to the greater mechanization of clothing and footwear trades, and the growth of ready-to-wear. The year 1856 saw Perkins' discovery of the first aniline dyes, and in 1892 the first synthetic silk was created, forerunner of the modern range of man-made fibres.

Yet despite these technical advances, there were many constants in the history of nineteenth-century dress. Even in women's clothing, certain standards were never challenged. Dresses were always shaped and supported by whaleboned stays and petticoats. Sleeveless dresses were unthinkable during the day. Hats or bonnets were essential out of doors, and skirts, despite their variety of shapes, never rose much above the ankle. When, in the early 1850s, the American reformer Mrs Amelia Bloomer tried to introduce a form of trousers for women, she found that, for the majority, she was way ahead of her time.

In the nineteenth century changes in fashion were limited and progressive. Waistlines rose and skirts expanded over a number of years. New styles generally took shape quite steadily, reaching an extreme form from which they then reverted more rapidly, giving way to a new emphasis, and the beginning of another fashion. Each new silhouette was created by its own substructure, in the form of stays, petticoats, crinoline or bustle, and individual garments and accessories were all adapted to create the total look of the moment. Thus, when presented with a chronological survey, it is usually possible to chart these modifications, and to pinpoint an outfit on the line of progress from one fashion to another.

In women's dress, in the first two decades of the century, the general look was high-waisted and narrow, owing much to the general wave of neo-classicism. Hair was short and tousled 'à la Titus', or long and bunched in ringlets on the crown, in the style of ancient Greece. Soft white cotton muslins were almost universal for day and evening wear, imitating the clinging draperies seen in antique marble statues. The *avant-garde* who followed fashion to its extremes were reputed to have renounced all forms of underwear in the attempt to recreate the classical silhouette. The more conservative majority, however, still retained the basic linen chemise, with stays and a single petticoat, finding, indeed, that longer stays were necessary if the average figure was to conform to the sinuous ideal.

With low, drawstring necks, or cross-over bodices, these muslin dresses were usually made with an apron front; the upper third of the skirt was slit at the sides, the front lifting up to fasten with ties round the waist. In many cases the bodice front was attached, and also lifted up to fasten to the shoulders by means of pins or cotton-covered buttons. In the early years, bodice, skirt and short sleeves were full and gathered, giving a softly rounded silhouette, but after 1805 a higher waistline, long, narrow sleeves and a less gathered skirt created a more rigid vertical line.

Headwear was small and neat, but included a wide range of styles and trimmings. Outerwear either followed the line of the dress in fitted spencers and pelisses, or provided additional draperies in the form of Indian shawls, enveloping cloaks and mantles and loose tunics. Footwear was flat, or made with a minute wedge heel; half boots were usual for outdoor wear, and simple kid or silk slippers for indoors, sometimes with ribbon ties across the instep in imitation of Roman sandals.

Even at its purest, this neo-classical style often included motifs from other cultures, such as Egyptian palm designs, or Elizabethan ruffs, but from 1815, the year of the long-awaited peace with France, Romantic influences began to dominate. Waists rose still higher, and the width across the bust was further emphasized by puffed sleeves. Hems were also raised, and were stiffened by flounces or padded ribbons, while skirts were now gored, producing an unmistakable A-line. By 1817, dresses and pelisses were encrusted with vandyke frills and rouleaux, the general cone-shaped outline completed by a tall-crowned, wide-brimmed bonnet, topped with ostrich plumes. Softly draped white muslins were being replaced by stiffer, printed cottons and light-coloured silks, while for evening lustrous satins were veiled by over-dresses of paler net, producing shimmering pastel shades.

In 1820 the waistline began to drop, reaching its natural level by 1827. Longer, fitted bodices were now fastened at the back by means of hooks and eyes of flattened brass wire, the usual method until the introduction of front-fastening jacket bodices in the 1840s. Sleeves and hems widened, and bonnet brims flattened or dipped in front, echoing the same line. By the middle of the decade, bonnets with soft crowns and wide, flat brims were virtually indistinguishable from hats.

By the late 1820s, female fashions were angular and exuberant. Width was given to the face by sausage-shaped curls at each temple, on top of which rested huge cartwheel hats, their crowns sprouting trimmings of grass, flowers, feathers and stiff ribbon bows. From 1824 evening hairstyles echoed this general shape in the Apollo knot, a virtual parody of the classical knot of curls, consisting of upstanding loops of plaited hair, decorated with feathers or skewered with Glauvina pins. Even daytime caps were large, a positive halo of stiffened muslin and ribbons. Dresses were equally expansive, with huge gigot sleeves, distended by down-filled pads or cane hoops. Tiny waists were tightly laced into heavily boned stays, and wide, gored skirts, supported by stiff cotton petticoats, were gathered at the back over flounced cotton bustles. Outerwear was adapted to the new shape. Spencers would have looked top-heavy with such large sleeves, but fitted pelisses followed the new line, while shawls and mantles were all-enveloping, and wide capes and pelerines gave additional emphasis to the shoulders. Even footwear reflected the angular silhouette, with toes becoming square by the end of the decade.

From 1830, steadily inflating sleeves and skirts began to billow and sag like overblown roses, and the centre of gravity began its descent towards the hemline. Hats and bonnets grew smaller, their upturned brims framing the face in a narrow oval. Wide, straight necklines cut across the points of the shoulders so that the huge balloon-like sleeves were set in low on the arm, and found their maximum width around the level of the elbow. Waistlines were still dropping, and from 1828, the downward movement was emphasized by a V-shape of pleated folds on the bodice front. From the same year a new full skirt was created by pleating straight widths of fabric to the tiny waist. For these softly draped forms, plain lightweight silks, or fine, flower-printed wool or cotton muslins were the popular fabrics.

In 1836 the sleeve had reached its ultimate width, and began to collapse. Initially, the top was pleated or gathered to the upper arm, and then the lower sleeve narrowed too, leaving only a puff at the elbow. By 1840, this too had disappeared, and the billowing curves were finally replaced by a new silhouette, the dominant shape of the 1840s, base on the Gothic arch. Its narrow apex was a neat, smooth hairstyle, in which the front hair was sleeked down from a centre parting, and looped over the ears, or, particularly for evening, draped in long side ringlets, and wound into a knot on the crown. By the end of the decade, this knot had slipped down towards the back of the neck, and all emphasis was on the sides of the face. Bonnets followed the same line. From 1838 a tubular shape appeared, the crown continuous with the brim, and throughout the 1840s the brim curved downwards at the sides, demurely enclosing the face and hiding the profile.

As sleeves narrowed, so did the bodice, extending in a long, curved, pointed waistline, stiffened with whalebone and emphasized by trimmings of stiffly pleated folds. Beneath this the skirt grew ever wider, supported by increasing numbers of stiff cotton petticoats, and from 1841 straight widths of fabric were gauged to the waistline, producing a distinctive dome-shape. Hemlines dropped, and footwear lengthened and narrowed, retaining the square toes. The look was one of modesty and reticence. Silks were plain, or figured in gently contrasting tones, and the subtle effects of shot silk were particularly appropriate. Decoration consisted chiefly of stiffly piped seams and flat, pleated draperies on the bodice.

From the mid-1840s, however, there were hints that the silhouette was opening out. By 1844 sleeves were widening below the elbow. Two years later, jacket bodices with basques were appearing, and flounced skirts were becoming increasingly popular. These were to be the dominant features of the 1850s, a decade in which the silhouette became a wide-based triangle, and the hard outlines of the 1840s were softened and blurred.

By 1850 bonnet brims opened more widely round the face and sloped towards the crown. By 1853 they were decreasing in size and had receded to the back of the head, providing only a narrow frame to the face. Wide-brimmed hats were a fashionable alternative for the young and for informal wear. Pagoda sleeves were flared and open at the wrist, softened by full, white, cotton undersleeves. The waistline rose, and basqued bodices blurred its exact position. Skirts grew still wider, with flounces *à disposition* emphasizing the horizontal line.

Opaque printed muslins, warp-printed silks, draped bodices, flounces, pinked edges and fringe decoration all added to the softer silhouette.

By the mid-1850s it was usual to wear as many as five stiffened petticoats, including one of horsehair, in order to create the fashionable full skirt. In 1856, however, this intolerable burden was relieved by the introduction of a hooped petticoat, not unlike that of the eighteenth century. Called a crinoline, after the horsehair petticoats which it replaced (from the French *crin*, hair), it had an immediate impact on female fashions, and although widely criticized for its impracticalities, it was adopted at almost every level of society. In the decade up to 1868 the crinoline dominated fashion, producing a wide-based triangular silhouette. At its apex, the head was small and neat, the hair smoothed into a neat, round chignon, topped by small hats or tiny, spoon-shaped bonnets. Bodices had fitted sleeves and round waists, slightly above natural level, and skirts, though large, were plain, since flounces (although occasionally worn) appeared excessive. Similarly, plain fabrics were popular, with perhaps a moiré effect, or just a simple pattern of applied braid. Loose-fitting shawls, jackets and mantles were the favourite forms of outerwear.

During the 1860s the crinoline itself was modified in shape. From 1860 it began to flatten at the front, and skirts were gored to follow this line. By 1865 tunic dresses or double skirts gave added emphasis at the back, with the lower skirt extending as a train. In the latter years the framework shrank to a half-crinoline, with half hoops at the back. Finally, by 1868, many crinolines were discarded altogether, leaving a fairly narrow skirt with a train. An alternative was found in the bustle, initially a variant of the half-crinoline, but soon reduced to a large flounced pad of horsehair, tied round the waist. In some cases this was worn on top of a half-crinoline, but by the early 1870s it was worn alone, above flowing, trained petticoats.

The dominant look of the years 1869-74 was frothy and curvaceous. The rising bustle was echoed in a rising chignon, the hair dressed high on the head, with a heavy plait or ringlets at the back, and from 1868, the American fashion for loose back hair was also popular. To accommodate these styles, small hats and bonnets were usually worn with a forward tilt, although after 1873 many were tilted back and sat on top of the chignon. Square necklines were popular, above a high, round waistline, and skirts were flat and narrow at the front, curving in a soft undulating line at the back. From 1872 tapes were attached inside the back of the skirt, holding the upper part in a puff over the bustle. Overskirts, either separate, or attached to the bodice in the polonaise form, were draped to give an apron front and an additional puffed pannier at the back. The whole was encrusted with layers of pleated frills and lace flounces. Now that the sewing machine was making light work of a straight seam, it was as if greater complexities were necessary to prove costly workmanship.

The year 1874 saw the revival of a narrower silhouette. The long cuirass bodice was introduced, fitting snugly over the waist and hips, and necessitating the revival of long stays. Skirts hung flat at the front with gores at the sides, and, in this year, additional tapes were set inside to tie across the back breadths, drawing the front of the skirt more closely to the body. At the same time the bustle grew smaller, and was brought down the skirt, the back fullness extending as a long train. By 1876, according to *The Ladies' Treasury*, skirts were now 'so tight that our sitting and walking are seriously inconvenienced'. Indeed, it was found necessary to reduce the volume of underwear by replacing the separate chemise and drawers with fitted combinations. To emphasize height and slimness, bodice and sleeves were made in contrasting fabrics, coats and mantles were cut to fit closely over the dress, and footwear developed Louis heels of up to two inches.

This narrow style continued into the 1880s, with variations created by the draping of the skirt and overskirt, and by the range of bodices, many of which were cut *en Princesse*, with an attached polonaise overskirt almost as long as the underskirt.

After 1880, the train disappeared except for evening dress, leaving the skirt as a straight tube, smothered in flounces, pleats and ruchings. It was soon replaced by a new form of bustle which dominated the decade, reaching its maximum size by 1887, and finally disappearing in 1889. This bustle was a narrow, angular construction, often made of small steel hoops, and producing a much harder outline than that of the previous decade.

Thus the dominant look of the 1880s was tall and angular. The hair was scraped back from the sides of the face, dressed in a small neat chignon, and, from the middle of the decade, topped by hats and bonnets whose trimmings emphasized their height. Vertical bows, plumes and birds' wings were popular, and the typical style was the hard, tall-crowned, post-boy hat. Collars were tall and military, bodices long, pointed and heavily boned, sleeves narrow, and skirts straight at the front, the bustle forming a shelf-like profile at the back. Formal day and evening dresses had skirts with elaborate and ingenious draperies, but after 1884 the general trend was towards a simpler style. This decade saw the increasing popularity of woollen tailor-made dresses for general day wear, as well as for travelling and sport, and the introduction of the jersey, a simple bodice of knitted wool or silk, worn with a simple skirt.

Although the crinoline had provoked criticism and mockery, the extremes of the late 1870s and early 1880s produced far more drastic reactions. In artistic circles the bright colours, heavy boning and complex draperies of contemporary fashion were compared unfavourably with the plainer forms of mediaeval dress. By the late 1870s, the aesthetes had developed a distinctive style of their own characterized by loose-fitting dresses with puffed sleeves, natural waists and simple trained skirts, in the soft, dull-coloured, oriental silks being popularized by Liberty's. The dress reformers were another vociferous minority group who rejected high fashion, but in their case on the grounds of health and practicality. They too recommended simpler, flowing styles, and many favoured natural woollen fabrics. Even the followers of high fashion sought an alternative to tight-lacing, and found it in the tea-gown, a loose (although still elaborate) garment for the less formal hours between afternoon visiting and dinner.

By 1890 high fashion had adopted many of the recommendations of both aesthetes and dress reformers. Bustles, trains, and complicated skirt draperies had finally been banished in favour of gored A-line skirts. Wool was popular for day wear. In the following decade, matching tailor-made jackets and skirts were even more popular, worn with blouses in an early form of the suit. Separate blouses and skirts were worn on all but the most formal occasions, and in their plainer, more masculine forms were complemented by straw sailor hats and neck ties. The ultimate theft from the male wardrobe came in the form of the wide knickerbockers sometimes worn for cycling. With the liberated 'new woman' of the 1890s, Mrs Bloomer's ideals had been given a reality.

Appearances were deceptive, however. As the informal blouse became more fashionable, it was shaped to the figure by a heavily boned lining and high stiffened collar. Gored skirts gave freedom to the legs but fitted closely to the hips, and the waists of the 1890s were narrower than ever. Finally, from 1890, the sleeve head began to grow, producing by the middle of the decade a revival of the huge, impractical, gigot sleeve of the 1830s. As then, this was offset by the wide hat, narrow waist and gored skirt, with the addition, in this decade, of wide yokes and lapels, and short capes and mantles.

From 1897 came the due reaction to this angular silhouette, and the line began to soften again. The hair was swept up over cushion-like pads to frame the head. Bodices were padded and pouched at the front. Sleeves narrowed, leaving just a puff at the shoulder. Skirts were cut to fit still more closely over the hips, but flared out from below the knee, extending once more as a train at the back, and as lightweight silks and fine wools replaced the heavier fabrics of the early 1890s, the result was a more fluid silhouette. With the introduction of a straight-fronted corset in 1900 which gave the body a characteristic S-bend, the flowing *art nouveau* curves of the Edwardian age were already apparent.

In contrast to these swings of fashion, men's dress was extremely conservative. Post-revolutionary Europe had seen a reaction against the brightly coloured silks and lavish trimmings of the *ancien regime*, so that by 1800 dark cloths and plain styles were the order of the day. Following the tenets of Beau Brummel, the fashionable emphasis was on fit rather than on exciting variations in cut and design. The fancy waistcoat was the only garment in which a sense of colour and pattern could be given free rein. (This was particularly true of the 1840s, the decade in which Charles Dickens, on his American lecture tour, was criticized for wearing bright waistcoats 'somewhat in the flash order'.)

The main developments in men's dress were in the introduction of new garments, and, in the second half of the century, a widening of the available options, with a move towards greater informality. Otherwise, variations in style were subtle and often hard to distinguish, even in the exaggerations of caricatures and fashion plates.

At the beginning of the period, the main coats were the dress tail coat, with its straight front waist, and the less formal morning or riding tail coat, with sloping fronts. From 1816, the nineteenth-century version of the frock coat, with its distinctive straight front edges, made its first appearance, becoming, in the second half of the century, the usual garment for formal day wear, a safe, conservative choice for the respectable middle classes. A short, loose-fitting pilot coat or paletot began life as an overcoat in the 1830s, but soon evolved into a variety of short, informal jackets. Of these, the lounging jacket was soon given the addition of matching waistcoat and trousers, producing, in the 1860s, the early form of the lounge suit. The Norfolk jacket was fashionable country wear in the second half of the century. The 1880s saw the dinner jacket competing with the tail coat for evening wear, and in the 1890s the reefer and blazer jackets evolved from sporting garments as popular leisure wear.

From the late eighteenth century knee breeches were being replaced by tight-fitting, calf- or ankle-length pantaloons, and between 1807 and 1825, these were themselves gradually superseded by trousers. At first these two garments were virtually indistinguishable (hence the American usage of the word pants, the shortened form of pantaloons, as an alternative to trousers). By 1817, however, trousers had lengthened to reach the instep, and in their new form became increasingly popular. By 1850 fly fronts had replaced falls, and in the 1890s front creases and turn-ups became fashionable features. Pantaloons were retained until the middle of the century for evening dress. Similarly, breeches were worn for the rest of the period, but only as full court dress, riding dress, and as unfashionable wear, particularly in the country.

Fine white linen shirts were a status symbol throughout the period, and in the second half of the century, collars, cuffs and fronts were often heavily starched to keep them clean as well as smooth. Initially, collars were attached and swathed in fine linen cravats, but during the 1840s detachable collars appeared, and the cravat narrowed around the neck to be fastened as a loose scarf or large bow at the front. Turn-down collars and shaped neckties finally appeared in the 1860s.

The top hat was worn throughout the century, but again, from the 1850s, a range of less formal styles appeared, including the straw sailor hat, and the hard felt bowler. The soft felt hat with a dented crown, later known as a trilby, appeared in the 1870s, and by the 1890s there was also the harder Homburg, together with a range of caps, helmets and boaters.

Light shoes or pumps were worn with evening dress, but for day wear boots were general. With the advent of trousers, hessians and top boots were replaced by half boots. From 1837 an elastic gusset was a common alternative to front-lacing, while buttons were popular from the 1860s.

Apart from the steady evolution of informal clothes, and their gradual acceptance for more formal occasions, general stylistic changes can also be traced, many of which reflect those of female dress. In the first two decades, the neo-classical ideal was expressed in hair 'à la Titus', and in a narrow, high-waisted silhouette, produced by short-bodied coats and waistcoats, and almost skin-tight pantaloons and trousers. In the 1820s men's coats, like women's dresses, featured full, gathered shoulders and low narrow waists, whose baggier trousers matched widening skirts. In the 1840s men's coats fastened higher to the neck, and waistcoats share not only the same fabrics, colours and patterns as women's dresses, but also their pointed waistlines. Small feet were fashionable for both sexes, and shoes became narrow and square-toed. Waistcoats of the 1860s featured the same higher, rounded waist as dresses, although in other ways men's clothes at this period provided a complete contrast to women's. As the crinoline reached its widest circumference, top hats became tall, narrow 'chimney-pots', coats straightened, and peg-top trousers reversed the wide-based, triangular silhouette of the fashionable female. From then on, men's clothes remained fairly straight and easy-fitting, except for the pointed shoes and high shirt collars of the last two decades, features found also in women's dress.

These were the main developments in male and female fashions, but there were, of course, as many variations in actual dress as there were variations in social gradation, level of income and individual preference. The poorer classes could rarely afford to follow fashion, except perhaps in the general style of the hair, or the trimming of a bonnet. Their clothes were usually home-made and simple, or second-hand and out of date. Alternatively, some sections of working-class society developed their own distinctive garments, such as the countryman's smock, which were outside the influence of high fashion. Even among the middle classes there was often a time lag in the spread of styles from London to the provinces and the countryside, so that the small-town belle might be coveting an outfit already rejected by the *beau monde* of the city. Again, the thrifty might try to update an existing garment, producing an outfit fashionable only in certain features. The elderly frequently clung to the styles of their youth, and different age groups developed different tastes. Caps, for example, were retained by older women long after they were discarded by the young.

Further variations were prompted by the occasion and the time of day, a concept alien to our informal tastes. Morning was the time for household duties, requiring an outfit that was fashionable but fairly plain. More elaborate dress was worn for formal afternoon visiting, although more practical variations were acceptable in the country or for going out walking. The fashionable changed again for dinner, a meal which grew later and more formal as the century progressed, and a further distinction was made between an evening dress suitable for dinner or the theatre, and the still more *décolleté* ball

dress. These distinctions are specified in the illustrations and descriptions found in contemporary fashion magazines, but social variations become apparent only when comparing a number of different sources. Fortunately, there is an enormous range of visual material available for the study of dress in the nineteenth century.

The most obvious source of information is to be found in the garments themselves, for a large number survive in museums and private collections. When studying the fabric, colour and construction of individual items, there is no substitute for actual clothes (although the patterns found in tailoring guides, and after the mid-century in magazines, provide invaluable evidence on cut). For an understanding of the total look, however, shaped by the appropriate underwear, completed by a suitable hairstyle and accessories and worn with the correct posture, one must turn to other forms of documentation.

Of these, the one most widely used is the fashion plate. These charming, often hand-coloured, prints showing figures dressed in the latest styles were issued by contemporary magazines, together with a description of the outfits depicted. They provide for us, as for their oringinal purchasers, a view of the current silhouette, garment and accessories, complete with a description in contemporary terminology. Although depicting actual garments (indeed, some advertised the work of specific dressmakers) these drawings were highly stylized, for they aimed to show the fashionable ideal rather than the reality. (They can be misleading, too, in the depiction of colours, since the range is limited by the print-maker's palette.) There are many histories of dress which use fashion plates to trace the changes in the fashionable ideal. In this book, however, I have tried to redress the balance between ideal and reality by using a variety of visual sources.

The fashion plate had its origins in the early pseudo-scientific surveys of national or occupational dress. This idea was still popular in the nineteenth century, and produced contemporary counterparts in such publications as Pyne's *Costume of Great Britain* (1808), Walker's *Costume of Yorkshire* (1814), and White's *Sketches of Characters* (1818). These series of engravings provide a major source of information on working-class dress, and the variations between different occupations and regions. Some leeway must be granted in their dating, however, for they were often the work of several years, and, in some cases, plates were copied from earlier publications rather than direct from life.

For the middle and upper classes an obvious record is to be found in portraiture. This was still regarded in the nineteenth century as one of the lowest forms of art, and sculptors in particular, used to working on a more grandiose scale, tended to swathe their sitters in classical draperies, or, where appropriate, in civic robes, in order to set them above the mediocrity of everyday life. Nineteenth-century painters, however, although often critical of contemporary dress, were usually content to depict it in their portraits, reserving their grand style for other types of painting. In the hands of a master like

Ingres even a simple pencil sketch can convey a wealth of information on cut, construction and drape, while a full oil painting can express still more about colour, pattern and texture. From the most detailed it is possible to distinguish a satin from a plain-weave silk, or a blonde lace from a linen. Where the painter does attempt to idealize his sitter, however, the usual result is a simplification of hairstyles, draperies and fabric patterns, and a reduction in the range of jewellery and accessories.

In some ways a more accurate rendering of dress is to be found in what Christopher Wood has called 'modern-life' narrative paintings (Christopher Wood, *Victoria Panorama*, 1976). This tradition, dating back to Hogarth, and supported by the Pre-Raphaelite painters, was given a new impetus in the mid-nineteenth century by the work of W.P. Frith. Working from sketches, photographs and posed models, his minutely detailed paintings of contemporary scenes and events were so vast that they often took several years to complete. Nevertheless, his subjects are a valuable source of information on costume, being deliberately chosen to demonstrate a variety of contemporary characters in typical dress.

Even Frith's broad social range was confined to the socially acceptable, however. The widely held view that 'Picture Galleries should be the townman's paradise of refreshment' (Charles Kingsley), did not allow for any representation of the seamier side of life. Only in the 1870s and 1880s did a school of social realism enjoy a brief popularity. Then, painters like Holl, Herkomer and Fildes attempted to depict the real poverty and misery of contemporary life, but even they succumbed to sentiment and melodrama, and their dramatic use of light and shade tends to blurr details of dress.

By the 1890s painstaking detail and social realism were almost entirely superseded by the painterly, atmospheric designs of artists influenced by the Impressionists and inspired by the concept of 'art for art's sake'. Even a portrait painter like John Singer Sargent, while brilliantly conveying the character, pose and silhouette of his fashionable sitters, frequently presents their gowns in a shimmering haze of brushstrokes, expressing general effect rather than specific detail.

A complementary viewpoint is provided by the caricaturists, many of whom treated fashion or the fashionable. Through the wit of artists like Gillray, Cruikshank and du Maurier, we are shown not the fashion-plate ideal, but clothing as it was being worn, albeit in an exaggerated form. In his 'Monstrosities of 1818', for example, Cruikshank satirizes the current fashion for shorter skirts. Judging by contemporary fashion plates and portraits, the rise in hemlines was only a matter of an inch or two, and would be almost imperceptible to modern eyes. Only through Cruikshank's exaggeration are we able to recognize a change in style which was obvious to contemporaries.

In the first half of the period such caricatures were usually published and sold individually, but the removal of the paper tax in 1861 produced a flood of illustrated newspapers and journals, providing new outlets for writers, caricaturists and illustrators alike. For the costume historian these publications are a mine of information, not only for the fashion plates, articles, and correspondence on fashion which many of them contain, but also for the wealth of non-fashion illustrations. Here, for the first time, are depicted the subjects of articles, advertisements and popular fiction. Ordinary people, from a variety of social backgrounds, are shown in a variety of situations, and portrayed without the bias of the fashion plate. Outside the magazine illustration, this combination of social range and informality can be found only in the later developments of photography.

Photography is, of course, the other major visual source for the study of Victorian dress. It was in 1837 that Louis Daguerre first produced a clear, permanent photographic image, and within a few years his daguerrotype technique was widely used to create small, mirror-image portraits. Poses were stiff and wooden, for exposures lasted up to a minute, and high costs restricted the process to the middle and upper classes. (Exceptions are found in a few working-class subjects, chosen by photographers like Hill and Adamson for their picturesque qualities.) Although unsophisticated by later standards, these photographs from the 1840s can provide surprisingly clear details of contemporary costume.

The cheaper improved ambrotypes of the 1850s brought portraiture to a wider social range, but the real impetus came with the craze for *cartes de visite* in the 1860s. Portrait photographs of friends, relatives and celebrities, from the royal family downwards, were printed the size of visiting cards and issued by the thousand to avid collectors. Usually studio portraits, with a very limited range of poses and backdrops, they are invaluable for details of fashionable, usually formal, dress.

Although variations on the *cartes de visite* were produced for the rest of the period, by the early 1870s the Anglo-American Edward Muybridge was already experimenting with the photography of moving objects. His discoveries, aided by new technical advances, led to the development of the snapshot. By the late 1880s, the work of Eastman and Walker, and the use of continuous 'American' film, enabled amateurs to capture crowd scenes and outdoor portraits, often without the knowledge of the subject. The latter are unique sources for the study of informal, working-class and occupational dress, although by the very nature of their technique and subject matter they usually lack the fine detail of the studio portrait.

These then, are the main visual sources from which it is possible to study almost every aspect of nineteenth-century dress. There are limitations, however. Underwear, for example, is rarely depicted, except by caricaturists or illustrators of fiction, and in the stylized forms of fashion plates and advertisements. Shoes, gloves, bags and other accessories are rarely shown in any great detail. Except in the work of a few social-realist painters and snapshot photographers later in the century, the poorer classes are usually 'cleaned up' and made acceptably picturesque, so that evidence on their dress may be unreliable. Nevertheless, there is more visual information available on the nineteenth century than on any previous period.

This book aims to show how this evidence may be read and understood, with a view to recognizing and dating the costume portrayed. The illustrations have been chosen to reflect the main developments in fashion. I have included a few examples of non-fashionable dress, however, as a reminder of the constant variations available, and to demonstrate that even these can sometimes reflect fashionable features. The illustrations are drawn from a wide range of sources, bearing in mind that some are more informative, and reproduce more clearly than others. Where a painting has taken a number of years to complete, a suitable date span is quoted. Similarly engravings after popular paintings have been given the date of the original work, since this is more relevent to the costume. In the descriptions, I have tried to use generic terms for the garments (e.g. mantle), since contemporary names (e.g. pardessus) changed so rapidly that they would require constant re-definition. Similarly, fabrics have been described in general terms, since it is now almost impossible to distinguish all the contemporary variations.

If my sin is one of omission, it is because the nineteenth century is so rich a period, both in known varieties of dress and in the range of visual sources for its study.

PLATES & CAPTIONS

20

1 George, Duke of Argyll, 1801
H. Edridge

Note From the 1790s male fashions were noted for their informality and understatement. For all occasions short of full court dress fabrics and styles were simple, colours limited.

Head The hair is short and dishevelled 'a la Titus'.

Body The ruffled linen shirt has a high pointed collar encased in a starched white linen cravat. The formal dress tail coat is of dark woollen cloth; the waistcoat, probably of wool or cotton, has a standing collar. The close-fitting knee-breeches are buttoned and tied at the knee.

Accessories He wears white silk stockings, flat lace-up leather shoes, and short gloves of cotton or fine leather.

2 Princess Augusta, 1802
H. Edridge

Note Although the short hair, bandeau and soft white draperies are overtly classical in inspiration, the skirt is full, supported by a bustle pad at the back waist, and the general effect remains full and rounded, as was fashionable until 1805. Trains were worn with day dresses until 1806.

Head Her short, tousled hair, 'a la Titus' is encircled by a bandeau.

Body The dress is of white muslin, the V-neck indicating a wrap-over front to the bodice. It has a high waist tied with a sash, and a skirt with a short train.

Accessories She wears a black silk mantle, edged with lace; elbow-length gloves of silk or fine kid; pointed shoes with ribbon ties and very low heels; and a necklace with an anchor pendant.

3 Princess Sophia, 1802
H. Edridge

Note For day wear, low necks were often filled in by a handkerchief, chemisette or tucker, and thin fabrics augmented by a variety of shawls, mantles, cloaks, tunics, 'vests' and pelisses.

Head The short tousled hair 'a la Titus', is encircled by a bandeau extending under the chin.

Body The apron-fronted dress is of white muslin, the skirt ties passing right round the body and forming a bow under the bust, the neckline edged with the frill of a tucker or chemisette. It has short full sleeves, and a skirt with a short train and tucked hem, a fashionable feature of this year. She wears an over-tunic or mantle with a frilled edge (the sleeves may belong to this rather than to the dress).

Accessories The pointed shoes have ribbon ties and very low heels. She wears a necklace and cameo brooch, in the classical style.

4 Thomas, Earl of Haddington, 1802
H. Edridge

Note Fashionable morning and walking dress had now adopted elements of military and country wear, in the form of the riding coat, with its curved fronts, and long boots. Breeches were being replaced by pantaloons, which were tighter fitting and extended to the mid-calf or below. They were usually worn with hessian boots made of patent leather, as developed in the 1790s.

Head The hair is 'a la Titus'.

Body He wears a fine white linen shirt and cravat; double-breasted riding coat; a short waistcoat; and light-coloured breeches or pantaloons.

Accessories He has V-fronted, tasselled hessian boots and short gloves of cotton or leather. Seals hang at the waist.

6 Self-portrait, 1804
J.C. Ibbetson

Note The artist wears fashionable morning dress. Pantaloons, as shown here, were usually made of light-coloured cloth or cotton, and cut on the bias of the fabric, causing it to stretch and cling to give the closest possible fit. Some were made in fine leather, such as doeskin, which gave a close fit with fewer creases.

Head The top hat is of dark silk or beaver, with a buckled band.

Body He wears a ruffled shirt and black silk stock; a double-breasted morning coat with gilt buttons and high stand-fall collar; and pantaloons.

Accessories Short hessian boots.

5 Bella Ibbetson, 1803
J.C. Ibbetson

Note In this period the pelisse was half way between an over-tunic and a coat. Generally long-sleeved and high-waisted, at the beginning of the decade it usually reached just below the knees, but soon extended to the ankles.

Head The small hat of swathed fabric is trimmed with feathers.

Body Her dress is of white muslin, the high-waisted, wrap-over bodice forming a V-neck, edged with a frill. It is worn under a darker pelisse with a shawl collar and wrap-over front, fastening under the bust with a belt. The long tight sleeves have frilled cuffs to match the frilled front edges and hem. The puffed over sleeves caught up at the outer arm are also found on dresses at this date.

Accessories Short gloves and hoop earrings.

7 Miss Ross, 1804
Sir Thomas Lawrence

Head The hair is in classical coils and ringlets.

Body Her day dress is of light silk or cotton muslin with a high-waisted, V-necked bodice and short, puffed sleeves. The skirt of this dress appears to be caught to the bodice at the front and sides, suggesting the popular form of the apron front by which the upper third of the skirt front was slit down the sides, and the flap thus formed was gathered to a drawstring or tape and tied round the waist. The bodice front would fasten separately. Here, the V-neck suggests a wrap-over front, which might lie over or under the top of the skirt. An alternative was for the bodice front to be attached to the skirt flap, and pinned to the shoulders. In both cases buttons, pins or brooches were used as fastenings.

Accessories The pointed shoes are of silk or kid, with very low heels. She has a necklace, brooch and pendant.

8 The Bridges Family, 1804
J. Constable

Note Trousers were fashionable for children
before they were introduced for adults. Both
sexes wore dresses until about four years old.

Head Mrs Bridges has her cropped curls
wound in bandeaux, while the older girls have
long hair combed back in classical coils.

Body All the women wear day dresses of white
muslin with high waists and short, full sleeves,
although the adult version has a more modest
frilled wrap-over front. Father and elder son
both wear frilled shirts with high collars and
white cravats, and dark cloth coats with high
stand-fall collars. The younger boy has a simpler
shirt with frilled collar, a double-breasted tail
coat and high-waisted trousers. The baby
follows adult fashions, but also wears a frilled
muslin cap, threaded with ribbons.

9 The Prince of Wales (George IV), 1804
R. Dighton

Note A stylish riding outfit which would have been equally acceptable as fashionable morning or walking dress. Country clothes were high fashion, but only when beautifully tailored in fine quality fabrics. The 'Jean de Bry' riding coat was popular among the Dandies between 1799 and 1808.

Head The hair is 'a la Titus' beneath a top hat of silk or beaver.

Body He wears a shirt with high pointed collar; a wide starched cravat; a 'Jean de Bry' riding coat, distinctive for its high stand-fall collar, almost horizontal lapels, and full gathered shoulders; M-notch collar and gilt buttons; and tight pantaloons.

Accessories He has hessian boots with spurs and wears the Star of the Order of the Garter. The fine leather gloves have decorative points. He carries a rustic-style cane.

10 Robert Southey, 1804
H. Edridge

Note The poet wears informal dress and eschews fashionable extremes. Originally a functional garment worn by sailors, trousers were adopted as informal seaside wear around 1800, and were popularized by the fashionable at Brighton in 1807. At this time, they were usually made of stout buff cotton, and ended well above the ankle. Although looser than pantaloons, they often required a short slit at the hem. They were accepted as general day dress by 1825.

Head The hair is short but avoids the windswept style of high fashion.

Body The shirt collar and cravat are of moderate height. The double-breasted morning coat has a stand-fall collar and M-notch lapels, and he wears matching waistcoat with stand collar. The trousers have a slit at the outside leg.

Accessories Light stockings and lace-up shoes.

11 Vauxhall Gardens (detail), 1805
Anon. engraving

Note Vauxhall Pleasure Gardens were
frequented by all ranks of society.

Head The women wear their hair trimmed with
jewelled bandeaux, ornamental combs and
feathers.

Body Outfits include several formal afternoon
or evening dresses, similar in style to day
dresses, but with lower necklines and longer
trains. Frilled V-necks are popular, with short
puffed sleeves draped, or caught up and
buttoned on the outer arm. The men's outfits
range from the stylish full evening dress of the
man in the centre, with his crescent-shaped
opera hat, or 'chapeau bras', dark evening coat
and pantaloons and lace-up shoes, to the old
man on the left, who still wears the three-
cornered hat, curled wig, loose frock coat and
breeches with stockings and buckled shoes,
which were last fashionable in the mid-eighteenth
century.

12 Portrait of a young lady, 1806
H. Edridge

Note Supposedly out sketching, she poses in fashionable walking or
morning dress. From 1805 skirts and sleeves were less gathered, and with
the disappearance of trains for day wear after 1806, the silhouette became
straighter and narrower.

Head Her hair is tied in a classical knot of curls under a half
handkerchief.

Body The dress is probably of cotton lawn or muslin, the high-waisted
bodice with a frilled V-neck indicating a wrap-over front. The skirt has an
apron front, shown by the ties passed round the waist and fastened in a
bow at the front. The upper sleeves are short with narrow lower sleeves
extending over the hand (these may be detachable).

Accessories Straw bonnet with ribbon ties and trimmings; low-heeled
pointed shoes; matching necklace and bracelet, probably of coral.

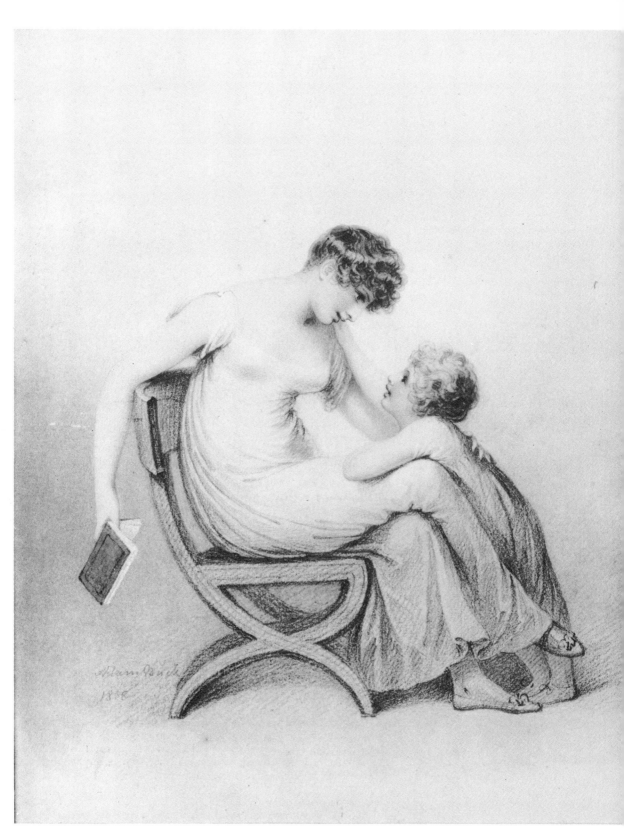

13 Mother and child, 1808
A. Buck

Note An idealized portrait in neo-classical style, but revealing all the basic elements of contemporary fashions.

Head Both adult and child have short, tousled hair.

Body The dresses are of white cotton muslin or lawn. The mother's sleeves are caught up on the outer arm in the style of classical drapery, a common feature in fashionable dresses of 1800-10. The wide, square neckline was common in both day and evening dresses from 1806, and for less formal day dress was worn over a chemisette, which reached to the neck.

Accessories Her shoes are low-cut with very low heels, pointed toes, and decorative ribbon ties. The child's are flat, with high uppers and narrow ribbon laces.

Progress of the Toilet — THE STAYS. Plate.

14 Progress of the Toilet: the Stays, 1810
J. Gillray

Note Despite the ideal of body-revealing draperies, the fashionable, willowy silhouette of 1810-20 was achieved by hip-length boned stays (Gillray exaggerates the length). To maintain the narrow line, drawers were sometimes preferred to layers of petticoats, but did not become general wear until the 1840s.

Head The fashionable lady being dressed has short hair under a ribbon-trimmed morning cap of fine muslin or lace. The maid wears a cornette.

Body The lady has a short-sleeved chemise with frilled neck, boned stays (into which she inserts a busk), and knee-length drawers. The maid's dress has a fashionably high waistline and long, tight sleeves, but the coloured cotton fabric and ankle-length skirt, and the addition of an apron, are governed by practicality. Her chemisette is normal daytime wear for all classes.

Accessories The lady's silk stockings with decorative clocks and elegant low-cut shoes contrast with the maid's practical lace-ups.

16 Two country women, 1813-18
W.J. White

Note The combination of the loose wrap-over bedgown and simple petticoat (right) was an outfit common to working-class country women from at least the mid-eighteenth century.

Head The old woman on the right wears a silk bonnet with stiffened peak and soft crown, peculiar to the working classes. Her more fashionable companion wears a straw 'cottage' bonnet, with a continuous crown and brim.

Body The old woman's kerchief or small shawl is worn over a long-sleeved, hip-length bedgown, apron and petticoat. Her companion wears a short spencer over a high-waisted dress, in the style fashionable from 1810 to 1815, before the introduction of decorative shoulders and hems.

Accessories The umbrella is a fashionable as well as practical accessory.

15 Portrait of Miss Bathurst, 1812
H. Edridge

Note The pelisse now follows the lines of the dress very closely. Mancherons and tucks introduce a new emphasis on shoulders and hem.

Head The curled hair is combed to the sides of the face with a centre parting, as introduced in 1810. The brimmed hat is trimmed with ribbons.

Body She wears a pelisse which has button fastenings and a belt, a turn-down collar, very long sleeves with mancherons, frogging on the bodice front and tucked hem.

Accessories The low-heeled sandal shoes have ankle ties and three bars across the vamp. She has a knotted neck scarf and long rectangular shawl.

17 Lady Mary Cavendish Bentinck, 1815
J.D. Ingres

Note At the end of the Napoleonic Wars, upper-class visitors to Rome were immortalized by Ingres in a series of souvenir portraits. Stiffened by the frills at the hem, skirts become more angular, while the gathers in the pelisse reveal a new emphasis on the back skirt. Outdoors, gloves and a hat or bonnet would be essential.

Head The hair is in full ringlets on each side of the face.

Body The day dress, with a ruff collar, waist sash and pleated frills at the hem, is worn under a silk pelisse with fur lining, mancherons and cuffs.

Accessories The flat, pointed sandal shoes have ribbon ties and patterned toes (possibly kid with cut-out decorations). She wears a heavy brooch, perhaps a cameo.

18 The Montagu sisters, 1815
J.D. Ingres

Note Well-to-do young girls (the elder is thirteen years old) were dressed in a similar style to adults, except that their sleeves were always short, shoes more substantial, and they often wore white cotton trousers or drawers instead of petticoats. (These became apparent only with the shorter skirts of the 1820s.) Drawstring necks were a popular alternative to wrap-over fronts for adults as well as children.

Head The girls wear low-crowned, wide-brimmed summer hats of fine straw with ribbon ties and trimming.

Body Their pelisses, probably of silk, are thrown open to reveal dresses of light cotton lawn or muslin, with low drawstring necks, high waists tied with a sash, and tucks at the hem.

19 Lord Grantham, 1816
J.D. Ingres

Note The gathered shoulders, very long tight sleeves and high waistline echo those of female dress. Here, the fall front to the pantaloons is obvious, as is the crossways pull of the fabric. Baggy hessians enjoyed a briefly popularity at this time.

Head He has short, tousled hair with side-whiskers.

Body He wears a shirt with high pointed collar swathed in a white starched cravat. The double-breasted dress coat, with a high stand-fall collar and M-notch lapels, slightly gathered shoulders, and flapped pockets at the waist, is worn over a waistcoat with a stand collar. He has pantaloons.

Accessories He wears hessian boots with tassels and carries a top hat and short gloves.

20 Sir David Wilkie, 1816
A. Geddes

Note The dressing-gown was a long, loose garment, worn indoors over the shirt, waistcoat and legwear, as an informal alternative to the coat. Although straight-fronted, with an easy shawl collar, this one has a gore in the side to give a flare to the skirt and emphasize the waist, so following a general trend in menswear for a closer fit.

Head He has short, tousled hair.

Body He is dressed in a frilled white shirt and cravat; a dressing-gown of silk or wool damask, patterned with leaves and flowers; and trousers with the legs buttoning at the outer ankle.

Accessories He has light stockings and slippers in the form of flat, heelless mules with a pointed vamp, in the Turkish style.

21 Mr and Mrs Woodhead and the Rev. Comber as a youth, 1816
J.D. Ingres

Head Mrs Woodhead's hair is coiled and held by a comb and bandeau.

Body She wears a spencer, probably of cotton, decorated with bands of ruching caught down with narrow cords, over a dress featuring the very high waist of 1815-20. Both men wear versions of the greatcoat, a form of overcoat fashionable about town and typically long and loose, with straight fronts and buttons to the waist. Woodhead's (left) has a shawl collar, and Comber's a high 'Prussian' collar. When decorated with braid and loop or frog fastenings, like Comber's, they were called 'Polish', 'Hungarian' or 'Russian' coats, and were sometimes fur-lined. Around this date they began to be cut with a close fit and were worn as informal coats with trousers, early versions of the straight-fronted frock coat.

Accessories Mrs Woodhead's neckline is filled in with a handkerchief fastened with a brooch. The dress buttons are almost certainly ornamental. She has a fashionable fringed shawl.

22 Princess Charlotte, 1817
Anon. printed textile

Note This commemorative handkerchief shows the Princess wearing fashionable ball dress. The dominance of white clinging muslins has given way to brightly coloured lightweight silks, which can be puffed and ruched at shoulders and hem, and stiffen a flared skirt. Stripes were particularly fashionable from 1816 to 1820. Indian shawls, with their distinctive pine-cone patterns, were fashionable from the beginning of the century. Copies and variations were produced in France, and in Britain at Norwich and Paisley.

Head The Princess's hair is in a coil, trimmed with a bandeau and flowers.

Body She wears a back-fastening dress, the bodice and puffed sleeves of light silk held by bands of darker silk. The skirt is flared, and the hem decorated with puffs and swags of fabric.

Accessories She has light silk stockings and flat sandal shoes. Her long shawl or 'scarf' is of silk or fine wool, the borders woven with formal flower patterns.

23 The Cloakroom, Clifton Assembly Rooms, 1817
R. Sharples

See colour plate between pp. 96 and 97.

Her Royal Highness,
PRINCESS CHARLOTTE of WALES,
And of SAXE COBURG Saalfield.
Born 7th Jan.t 1796. Died 6th Nov.r 1817.

& MONSTROSITIES of 1818

24 Dandies of 1817 Monstrosities of 1818, 1818
G. Cruikshank

Note The Dandies were leaders of male fashion, and excessively clothes-conscious. Both they and their female counterparts demonstrate high fashion at its most extreme. Cruikshank emphasizes the women's larger bonnets, shorter and more decorated hemlines, and the wearing of bustles in the form of semi-circular pads at the back waist.

Head The men's small top hats, or tiny flat hat (an exclusively Dandy style) are in complete contrast to the women's tall-crowned or wide-brimmed bonnets.

Body The men wear excessively high collars and cravats. Their morning coats, or the new straight-fronted frock coat, are cut with high waists, padded chests and gathered shoulders, echoing the high waists and puffed sleeves of the women's pelisses. The men wear either breeches or short wide trousers.

Accessories Footwear is pointed, with top boots and spurs for the men, and flat shoes or sandals for the women. The woman on the right wears a neck chain with watch or scent bottle, and carries a fringed parasol and an embroidered reticule.

25 Mrs James Andrew, 1818
J. Constable

Note Brightly coloured, lustrous silks were
softened by being overlaid with soft nets or
'aerophanes'. As the wearer moved, a shimmering
effect was produced in the skirt and sleeves,
highlighted by the silk trimmings on bodice,
sleeves and hem.

Head She wears her hair with a centre parting
and side curls, under a full-crowned cap of fine
lawn or muslin, tied under the chin, and
trimmed with flowers and ribbons.

Body She is dressed in a high-waisted dress of
silk gauze or net, with an under-dress of plain
silk or satin. Bust and shoulders are emphasized
by applied bands of silk. The long, full sleeves
are frilled at the wrist.

Accessories There is a silk sash at the waist
and, beneath the dress, a chemisette with a
frilled neck. Her other accessories are
neckchains, a brooch and rings.

26 The Duke of Argyll, 1819
R. Dighton

Note The Duke is dressed in fashionable
outdoor wear. Early frock coats are still very
similar to greatcoats, although perhaps more
fitted, since they are no longer top coats. This
one is in the latest style, with its roll collar,
straight fronts, buttons down to the waist, long
tight sleeves with cuffs, and a back vent with side
pleats. It features the longer waist which
appeared from about 1818. This gave a closer fit
which soon required a dart or seam at the waist,
although these were not general until 1823.

Head He has a top hat.

Body His shirt has a high pointed collar,
swathed in a cravat. The striped waistcoat has a
stand collar. He wears an early form of the frock
coat and trousers.

Accessories Boots and gloves.

27 Lady Catherine Manners, 1819-20
Sir William Beechey

Note She is dressed in fashionable full evening dress. Most fashionable skirts of this date had their hems decorated and stiffened with flounces, rouleaux, or other applied trimmings. The plain flowing lines of this one may be influenced by the painter's preference for flowing draperies.

Head Her centrally parted hair with side curls and back ringlets is worn under a silk turban trimmed with pearls and feathers.

Body The high-waisted silk dress has a low neck edged with a lace frill or tucker, short puffed sleeves caught up by bands of darker silk and a skirt with a train.

Accessories As well as a lace 'scarf' shawl she has pearl drop earrings, a neck chain with pendant or scent bottle, chain bracelets and a rectangular brooch.

28 Court dress, 1820
Engraving from *Ackermann's Repository of Arts*

Note The fashion plate ideal of court dress.
The elaborate costumes worn for official
occasions at the royal court were governed by
strict regulations, and were slow to reflect
changes in fashion. An ostrich feather headdress,
long gloves and a train were essential
requirements, and the components of robe and
separate stomacher, bodice and petticoat, were
based on eighteenth-century styles. It was only
with the accession of George IV in 1820 that the
eighteenth-century hoop was finally discarded.
Here the narrow skirt, short puffed sleeves and
relatively high waist are the main concessions to
current fashions.

Head The ostrich plume headdress has a pearl
bandeau and lace lappets.

Body Her short-sleeved, trained robe of silk is
trimmed with lace and pearls, and the silk
bodice, with stomacher-style front, is ornamented
with pearls. A separate satin petticoat trimmed
with silver and artificial roses is worn beneath a
shorter lace petticoat.

Accessories She has white kid gloves, white
satin shoes, pearl necklace and earrings and an
embroidered silk fan.

29 Tom and Jerry at the Royal Academy (detail), 1821
I.R. and G. Cruikshank

Note Fashionable day dress is shown in this scene.

Head Women's headwear includes (from the left) a feathered turban, a high-crowned hat and a range of wide-brimmed bonnets trimmed with ostrich plumes and a veil.

Body Women's pelisses are still very high-waisted, with mancherons and braid trimming. Hem lengths vary, but puffs and vandyking are a feature. On the left is a riding habit, trimmed with military-style braid. The men wear morning coats or (at the back) a frock coat, while the parson (right) wears clerical dress. Greatcoats feature cape collars (back view right). Breeches still compete with straight trousers of varying lengths, including (centre) voluminous 'Cossacks', pleated to the waist and gathered to the ankle, a style inspired by the Czar's visit to London in 1814.

Accessories Women carry reticules of fabric or leather.

30 Tom and Jerry in the Saloon at Covent Garden (detail), 1821
I.R. and G. Cruikshank

Note The men generally wear day dress, but many of the women are in full evening dress.

Head Evening headdresses for women include curled hair in a knot, with combs and feathers, or feathered turbans.

Body Evening dresses have low décolletage with puffed sleeves and padded hems. Day dress necklines are modestly filled in with a chemisette, while the woman in the riding habit (left) demonstrates the fashionable obsession informality and the popularity of riding dress for all occasions. The men generally wear morning coats and knee breeches or pantaloons. An exception (right) is the frock coat with military-style frogging, and trousers with instep straps to keep them taut (popular from 1817).

31 Walking dress, 1821
Engraving from *Ackermann's Repository of Arts*

Note This fashionable ideal has the slightly dropped waistline, puffed shoulders and padded decorations at the hem.

Head She has centrally-parted hair with side curls. The watered silk bonnet has a slightly turned-up brim lined with tufted gauze and tied with silk ribbons. According to the fashion-plate description, the crown is trimmed with silk leaves, plaited straw, and flowers.

Body A ruff with double frill is attached to the chemisette. The silk spencer, with its V-shaped satin panel, small falling collar, shoulder puffs and tight sleeves are all edged with frills and bands of satin. Beneath is a dress of cotton muslin, the hem trimmed with a rouleau, puffs of muslin, and a pleated flounce.

Accessories Black kid shoes.

32 Hannah More, 1822
H.W. Pickersgill

Note This elderly playwright and reformer wears a simple day dress which, with its very high waistline and smooth, ungathered shoulders, is in the fashionable style of 1815-20.

Head The centrally-parted hair is slightly curled at the sides. The high-crowned, frilled muslin cap ties under the chin, and is trimmed with silk ribbons.

Body She wears a silk dress with high waist, the V-neck filled in by a chemisette with a ruff collar. The sleeves have muslin frills at the wrist.

Accessories A scarf shawl of silk or fine wool, with fashionably patterned borders and ends is draped over her shoulders. She holds a scent bottle.

33 The Countryside in May (detail), 1822-4
Anon. engraving

Note City fashions were copied in the country, but were usually less extreme and were modified according to the wearer's occupation.

Head The woman on the right wears a fashionable 'Marie Stuart' bonnet, while the barmaid has a simple high-crowned day cap.

Body and Accessories The more fashionable woman wears a pelisse with concealed front fastening, frilled collar, puffed shoulders and frilled hem. The barmaid's dress has fashionably puffed shoulders, but the neckline is covered with an old-fashioned handkerchief, crossed at the front. This is tucked into the bib of her barmaid's apron, which is pinned to her bodice. The country man wears the long, flap-pocketed greatcoat. Its loose fit is unfashionable, as are his large neckcloth, which he wears instead of a cravat, and his top boots. The girl has the hat, low neckline and short sleeves common to children's fashions.

34 Lord Byron, 1823
Count D'Orsay

Note Newly recovered from an illness, his fashionable day clothes hang rather loose upon him. In this decade the clothes of both sexes featured fuller shoulders and a narrower waistline.

Head His hair is short and tousled.

Body His shirt is finely gathered to a high, pointed collar and he wears a black silk stock and a morning coat with a roll collar cut high at the back and M-notch lapels. The cut-away fronts are now squared off, and the tails broad and square. The shoulders are gathered and the sleeves long and tight. The waistcoat is cut in the latest fashion with a slightly pointed waist. The trousers have instep straps.

Accessories He is probably wearing light-coloured gaiters over square-toed boots. There is a decorative, perhaps jewelled, pin fastening the shirt front. He carries a cane with plain short handle, less showy than those with strings and tassels.

35 Woman in day dress, 1824-7 'Mansion'

Note Between 1822 and 1827 the waistline drops to its natural level, sleeves widen, and with 'Marie Stuart' caps and ruffs, the look is self-conciously Elizabethan.

Head Fashionably parted hair with side curls and a knot on the crown is worn under a 'Marie Stuart' morning cap of fine muslin, the double frill edged with lace, and silk ribbon ties under the chin.

Body A matching neck ruff is attached to a chemisette and she has a bow of striped silk gauze ribbon. Her dress is of fine lawn or muslin, the fan-shaped gathers emphasizing shoulders and waist. The straight edge of the cotton lining is visible level with the shoulder. The sleeves are gathered at the shoulder over short puffed undersleeves. The flared skirt is gathered to the bodice at the sides and back (probably over a small bustle pad).

Accessories Watered silk belt with metal buckle.

36 Beauties of Brighton, 1825
A. 'Crowquill'

Note Under the Prince Regent Brighton became a centre of fashion frequented by Dandies.

Head The Dandies wear top hats, the women fashionable wide-brimmed hats. The man in the centre has the newly fashionable long side-whiskers which merge with his lady-friend's curls.

Body The men's high-pointed shirt collars and cravats are worn with tight morning coats (left), open to reveal waistcoats with shawl collars and pointed waists. Tight pantaloons and patterned stockings (left) are still an alternative to trousers with instep straps (centre). Tight-waisted coats (centre) echo women's pelisses, now cut with huge gigot sleeves and ever wider gored skirts with decorated hems.

37 The Rev. Ryland, 1827
D. Maclise

Note This is fashionable day dress for men. In the 1820s men's coats reflect women's fashions with their gigot sleeves, dropped waistline and tight fit. Some Dandies wore chest padding and stays to achieve the fashionable hour-glass silhouette.

Head His short hair is still worn brushed forward rather than back, as was usual in this decade.

Body He wears a high, pointed shirt collar with cravat; a high-cut waistcoat; a morning coat with roll collar cut very high at the back, M-notch lapels, long, narrow sleeves, gathered at the shoulder and extending over the hand; and light trousers.

Accessories Watch or seals attached to the waist.

39 Woman in dinner dress, 1830
F. Cruikshank

Note Although painted in 1830, the sitter's dress is in the style fashionable in the late 1820s. Berets were popular evening wear throughout the 1820s and early 1830s, and were usually worn at an angle after 1827. Cut steel and chased gold were used for buckles as for other jewellery.

Head Centrally-parted hair with sausage-shaped side curls and a knot on the crown is worn under a silk or velvet beret, trimmed with ribbons and feathers.

Body The silk dress features a vandyked neck and cuffs and a horizontal neckline emphasizing full gigot sleeves. The skirt has a deep flounced hem headed by a twisted rouleau.

Accessories She wears a silk belt with ornate metal buckle, silk shoes with square toes, a short necklace and rings. Her glove, probably of kid, is fashionably short, but plain (many had frilled or scalloped wrists).

38 'Nothing extenuate nor aught set down in malice', 1827
Anon. engraving

Note From 1825 hats, sleeves and skirts grew steadily wider. Down-filled sleeve puffs padded the shoulders, heavy corded and flounced cotton petticoats stiffened the skirt, tight, boned stays narrowed the waist, and a bustle made of cotton flounces gave fullness to the back of the skirt. This caricature exaggerates the shape for 1827, but by 1830 this was almost a reality.

Head The wide-brimmed hat has a wide ribbon tie left hanging loose. The trimmings are bows, leaves and sprigs of feathers or grass. She has centrally-parted hair with sausage-shaped side curls and a knot on the crown.

Body The dress consists of a draped bodice, narrow waist (now at natural level), large gigot sleeves and a wide skirt, gathered at sides and back, with a flounced hem.

Accessories Her accessories include a ribbon bow and sash, long drop earrings, short kid gloves with vandyked wrists, square-toed sandal shoes and an embroidered handkerchief.

40 An Irresistible Arming for Conquest, 1828-30
Anon. engraving

Note A fashionable woman in her underwear, being dressed for the evening. Stays and bustles were essential to achieve the hour-glass shape fashionable from 1825 to 1835.

Head The hair, in a high chignon (a variant on the Apollo knot) with curls and ringlets, is decorated with an ornamental comb and ostrich plumes. The maid has a be-ribboned cotton day cap.

Body The lady wears tightly laced boned stays over a sleeveless chemise, and a bustle of cotton flounces tying round the waist. The maid's dress, although plain, features a fashionably fitted waist, full skirt and gigot sleeves.

Accessories The mistress has the white silk stockings, square-toed black satin sandal shoes, drop earrings and short necklace fashionable with formal dress.

41 Mrs Ellen Sharples, 1829-31
R. Sharples

Note The artist's mother in fashionable day dress. Still wider gigot sleeves are emphasized by wide caps, pelerines and capes. Within a year or two, bodice pleats will converge well above the waist, adding another almost horizontal line.

Head The hair in side curls and a knot is hidden by a cap of pleated, stiffened blonde lace.

Body Her neckline is filled by a handkerchief and she wears a double pelerine of blonde lace. The silk dress has a bodice decorated with flat pleats converging at the waist and padded gigot sleeves. The cloak, apparently of figured or brocaded silk, has a plain lining and an attached cape.

Accessories Brooch and armlet, probably set with a cameo, mosaic, or semi-precious stone.

42 Queen Adelaide, 1831
Sir William Beechey

Note The Queen poses in evening dress.
Blonde lace, with its distinctive sheen of silk, was
fashionable for veils, trimmings etc. throughout
the 1820s and 1830s.

Head The Queen's hair is dressed in a chignon
formed from stiffened loops of hair (a variant on
the Apollo knot), with sausage-shaped side curls.
She has a pearl bandeau and veil.

Body The muslin tucker is edged with a lace
ruff and the dress, apparently of velvet, has a
wide neck trimmed with a vandyked frill
extending over the shoulders. The large gigot
oversleeves are of blonde lace. The waist is
emphasized with a belt. Her skirt is set flat to the
waist at the front (clearly not the full pleated
dome-shape of the current fashion plates).

Accessories She wears drop earrings, matching
pendant brooch, and a gold watch and chain. A
bouquet and a handkerchief were both popular
evening accessories.

44 MrsThomas Hood, 1832-4
Anon.

Note She is wearing evening or dinner dress, with the addition of a pelerine. Sleeves were at their fullest between 1830 and 1833, with pelerines emphasizing the width.

Head The hair is centrally-parted with a knot on the crown and side curls. Her hat probably consists of wired puffs of brocaded or embroidered silk, edged with a fringe (a similar type in a fashion plate of 1827 was called a 'Vienna toque').

Body The double pelerine is probably of embroidered white muslin. It appears to extend at the front, and may be a fichu-pelerine, with its two ends tucked into the belt. The dress has decorative lapels resting on large gigot sleeves, a wide belt and a skirt pleated to the waist.

Accessories These include drop earrings, brooch and neck chain, probably with a watch, eyeglass, or scent bottle tucked into the belt.

43 Benjamin Disraeli, 1833
After D. Maclise

Note Young Disraeli's style of morning dress reflects his Dandified tastes. In this decade, lavish tastes found expression in colourful patterned waistcoats and a variety of jewellery, including studs, pins, rings etc.

Head The hair is fashionably mid-length with a side parting.

Body The shirt has frilled front and cuffs and the wide cravat is tied in the 'waterfall' style, with a decorative pin (he favoured white satin cravats). His shawl-collared waistcoat is very tight. Fitted, and possibly padded, the morning coat has a roll collar and lapels cut high at the back, M-notch lapels, and very long sleeves, worn open to reveal cravat and waistcoat. His trousers have instep straps.

Accessories His footwear consists of square-toed pumps with ribbon bows and he has a watch and chain tucked into the waistcoat watch pocket.

45 Interior of the Gallery of Watercolour Artists (detail), 1834
G. Scharf

Note The middle-class visitors to the gallery are in outdoor dress.

Head The women wear bonnets with deep oval brims hiding the sides of the face, and bavolets. Fashionable trimmings are ribbon bows and feathers, and broad ribbon ties under the chin (lace veils to shade the face, or hang down one side from the brim, were also popular).

Body Broad white muslin pelerines are worn or (right) a fichu-pelerine. Pelisses have large gigot sleeves. The men demonstrate the popularity of frock coats and trousers.

Accessories The seated woman has an umbrella (as opposed to the smaller parasol), and the one on the right wears a neck chain, probably suspending a watch, scent bottle, or eyeglass. She carries an embroidered reticule.

47 A young girl, 1834
T.M. Joy

Note Day dress for young girls was a simplified form of adult evening dress, with the addition of long drawers. Around the middle of the decade, neater hairstyles, with the hair drawn back at the sides in a loop or plait, were replacing elaborate knots and side curls.

Head The girl's hair is plaited at the sides and arranged in a knot on the crown.

Body The dress has a low décolletage, beret sleeves, and waist sash. The skirt is gathered with a deep hem. She wears frilled drawers of white linen or cotton.

Accessories Silk or cotton stockings and square-toed sandal shoes, probably of black satin. She has neck chains and a pendant.

46 A woman in evening dress, 1834
Watt after A.E. Chalon

Note A fairly plain evening outfit, perhaps simplified by the artist. Popular accessories would have included flowers in the hair, long pendant earrings, short necklace, elbow-length white kid gloves with frilled tops, and a small fan or bouquet of flowers.

Head Centrally parted hair with side curls is arranged in stiffened loops on the crown, a version of the Apollo knot.

Body The silk evening dress has a low décolletage trimmed at the back and sides with a standing collar, probably of stiffened blonde lace. The bodice is draped *à la Sevigné*, in horizontal folds divided by a boned band. Beret sleeves are trimmed with bows. The waistline is round, and she wears a belt. (From 1832 some evening bodices were slightly pointed at the front and back waist.) The full skirt is pleated to the bodice.

48 Florence Nightingale and her sister, 1836-7
W. White

Note These are middle-class girls in informal morning dress. From 1836 shoulder lines dropped-sleeves began to deflate, and hemlines fell from the ankle to the instep. Mittens were fashionable for day and evening in the 1830s and 1840s.

Head Both women have centrally-parted hair smoothed into a plaited knot on the crown.

Body They are wearing white muslin pelerines and day dresses with simple draped bodice and belted waist. The smooth, dropped shoulder line leads to versions of the full gigot sleeves: (right) the 'Imbecile', full to the cuff, and (left) the 'Donna Maria', full to the elbow, and then tight to the wrist. Their skirts are full and gathered.

Accessories The sister on the left has square-toed shoes, short mittens of black net or lace and a linen or cotton apron.

49 Queen Victoria, 1837-8
A.E. Chalon

Note The young Queen is seen here in ordinary day dress. Embroidered aprons were fashionable 'at home' wear, proclaiming domesticity, although too ornate to be practical.

Head Her hair is looped over the ears into a knot at the back.

Body She wears a deep-caped lace pelerine and a dress of watered silk with dropped shoulders, with a type of 'Victoria' sleeve, full in the middle below a pleated mancheron. There is a buckled waist belt above the full pleated skirt.

Accessories Her shoes are flat and square-toed. Other accessories are neck chains, a brooch, bracelets and an embroidered black satin apron. On the ground is a silk bonnet trimmed with a bird of paradise, the brim lined with ruched tulle or lace.

50 The Duchess of Kent, 1837-8
A.E. Chalon

Note Queen Victoria's mother in fashionable outdoor dress.

Head The hair is plaited over the ears, with a knot at the back, and a velvet band across the brow. She wears an oval-brimmed bonnet with mentonnières and lining of ruched net or lace and flowers, the crown trimmed with ribbons and a bird of paradise.

Body The double collar is of net or lace. She wears a watered silk pelisse dress, with cross-over draped bodice; sleeves with multiple bouffants, a belt with ornate metal buckle; and a skirt trimmed with lace frills *en tablier*.

Accessories She has short gloves and square-toed shoes. Hanging from her neck chain is a watch or scent bottle tucked into the belt. Her bracelets include a fashionable matching pair of bands.

51 Mrs Harris Prendergast, 1838
A. Geddes

Note This is fashionable evening dress at a time
when fashion favoured a revival of mid-
seventeenth-century styles including ringlets,
lace berthas, and bows on shoulders and gloves.
The draperies emphasize width, while the
curved bertha creates the popular drooping
shoulder line.

Head Her hair is drawn into a plaited knot, with
a plaited band and ringlets.

Body The satin dress has a heart-shaped
décolletage, horizontal drapes across shoulder
and bust, and obvious vertical boning. The short
sleeves are trimmed with ribbon bows, falling
loosely at the elbow. The curved bertha of
blonde lace falls low over the outer arms, giving
the effect of a ruffled oversleeve. She wears a
full, pleated skirt.

Accessories On her right arm she wears an
evening glove, probably of kid, edged with
ribbon bows (she holds the other). Other
accessories are a neck chain, a pearl bracelet
with cameo clasp, and rings.

52 Youth and Age, 1839
J.C. Horsley

Head and Body The old country labourer wears the soft, wide-brimmed
'bullycock' hat and linen smock – characteristic country wear of the late
eighteenth and most of the nineteenth centuries. These smocks, in white,
brown or blue, were often elaborately embroidered in the same colour, on
chest, shoulders and wrists. He wears cord or leather breeches. The little
girl's bonnet, pelisse and drawstring reticule imitate adult fashions, but her
ankle-strap shoes with ribbon bows are typical child's wear.

Accessories Gaiters and sturdy leather boots were worn by country
labourers long after trousers had become fashionable.

53 Princess Victoire, 1839
Sir Edwin Landseer

Note The Princess is wearing formal summer day or evening dress. As the knot of the hair drops to the back of the head, the shoulder line slopes, and the sleeve fullness drops to the elbow and below, the whole silhouette deflates, introducing the elongated, angular shape of the 1840s.

Head Her long hair is drawn from a centre parting into a plaited knot at the back, and into side ringlets which Landseer wittily compares with the spaniel's ears.

Body The dress of sprigged muslin has a low décolletage edged with a deep lace bertha. Victoria sleeves are trimmed with bows. The gathered skirt has a flounced hem.

Accessories She carries a lace-edged handkerchief. On the balustrade is a parasol of silk or lace, with a tasselled cord.

54 Mrs Edward Elliot in evening dress, 1839-40
After A.E. Chalon

Note This is very similar to the evening dress worn by Mrs Harris Prendergast in 1838 (fig. 51), but the pointed waist is now essential. Concurrent with a revival of seventeenth-century motifs is the popularity for evening wear of silks brocaded with flowers in eighteenth-century style. Many eighteenth-century dresses were altered for re-use between 1835 and 1845.

Head Her hair is arranged in a knot at the back and in ringlets, although the very loose flowing ringlets may be artistic licence.

Body The evening dress is of figured or brocaded silk, the wide décolletage trimmed with a lace bertha and ribbon bows. It has a pointed waistline, with obvious boning. Loose draped and ruffled sleeves are caught up with a bow. The dress has a full, pleated skirt.

Accessories Her mittens are probably of embroidered net. She wears a bracelet with fashionable heart-shaped locket and holds a lace-edged handkerchief.

55 Lady Elizabeth Villiers, 1841-3
After A.E. Chalon

Note She is wearing fashionable day dress. Although the fullness is still centred on the back, skirts are becoming wider. From 1841 they contain more material which is gauged to the waist, a technique whereby the fabric is finely gathered and attached by alternate pleats. This produces a characteristic dome-shaped skirt. Here, the width is emphasized by the horizontal bands of trimming.

Head Her long hair is arranged in a knot and ringlets.

Body The dress of watered silk is trimmed with bands of velvet and black lace flounces, giving the effect of a bertha on the bodice. The long, tight sleeves have a band of trimmings as the only remnant of the bouffants of 1837-40. The skirt is full and gathered.

Accessories She carries the ubiquitous lace-edged handkerchief.

56 Unknown woman, 1842
W. Buckler

Note Another example of fashionable day dress of the early 1840s.

Head The hair is draped over the ears into a knot at the back (a neater alternative to ringlets, popular for daytime).

Body A lace pelerine is trimmed with rosettes. The dress of silk, figured or brocaded with a trailing stem pattern has a pointed waist, with obvious boning, long, tight sleeves and a full, gathered skirt.

Accessories A long scarf shawl was a popular summer wrap and this one features the traditional cone pattern of embroidered Kashmir shawls. This may be an Indian import, or one of the many woven imitations made in France, or in Britain, in centres like Paisley (whose name became synonymous with the pattern). The flat, square-toed shoes are probably of black satin. A lace-edged handkerchief and bouquet were both fashionable accessories. Her bonnet is in the almost tubular shape typical of 1838-50, trimmed with silk ribbons and ostrich plumes.

57 Unknown gentleman, 1842
W. Huggins

Note Fashionable day dress is shown here. Gathered sleeves and chest padding are reduced, waists lengthen, and waistcoats are cut with a pointed front, all features which echo changes in women's fashions, and which produce a more streamlined silhouette. His trousers feature a fall front, although the fly fastening, first used around 1823, became general in the 1840s.

Head He has smoothed hair with a side parting (many wore it longer and curled under at the back).

Body He wears a high shirt collar with a large silk cravat or 'scarf', covering the shirt. The double-breasted frock coat has a velvet collar, narrow sleeves and cuffs. The waistcoat, of embroidered or brocaded silk, has a wide roll collar and lapels, and pointed waist. The narrow trousers probably have instep straps.

Accessories Chained cravat pin, watch chain and ring.

63

58 Two Dandies, 1843
A. 'Crowquill'

Note As the male silhouette becomes more streamlined, flamboyance is expressed in brightly patterned neckwear, waistcoats and trousers. Paletots had many versions. These may be (left) the short pea- or monkey-jacket, and (right) the pilot coat, noted for its large buttons and slanted pockets.

Head They have long hair and flat-brimmed top hats.

Body They wear high shirt collars with (left) a brightly patterned silk cravat tied in a bow, and (right) a scarf cravat. Their paletots have fashionable turn-down collars, and horizontal slit or flapped pockets. The narrow trousers have gaiter bottoms. By contrast, the shopkeeper is unfashionable with his short hair, frilled shirt front and baggy trousers.

Accessories Footwear consists of narrow, square-toed shoes. They wear short gloves and carry thin canes, probably of ebony or bamboo, with gold knobs and tassels.

59 The Royal Railroad Carriage (detail), 1843
Anon. engraving

Note Prince Albert and Queen Victoria with their children and attendants in fashionable day dress.

Head The women wear tubular bonnets with dipped sides, decorated with ostrich feathers and bonnet veil.

Body All the women wear lace-trimmed pelerines and dresses with pointed waists (the Queen's being the longest and most fashionable). The attendants have slightly less fashionable Victoria sleeves. The Queen wears a mantle with armhole slits. Prince Albert wears a scarf cravat, probably a frock coat, and trousers apparently with gaiter bottoms. His fashionably sloping shoulders, pointed waist and small feet echo female styles. The infant Prince of Wales (right) in his plumed hat, is still young enough to wear a dress like his sister's. The baby wears a cap and formal long lace carrying robe.

61 Lady Ruthven, 1843-8
Photograph by Hill and Adamson

Note Summer outdoor clothes are shown here. The skirt of the 1840s is long enough to hide the feet and form a slight train.

Head The tubular bonnet has dipping sides, a brim which appears to be openwork straw plaits, a crown covered with fabric and simple ribbon trimmings. Her short bavolet juts out at the back as she looks downwards.

Body She has a white muslin collar. The folded square shawl is of black net (both hand-made and machined net were worn). The frilled edging is probably embroidered net rather than bobbin lace. The day dress is of striped silk or one of the popular mixed fabrics of silk and wool, or wool and cotton. The fitted, boned bodice puckers where it fastens down the back. Long tight sleeves fit below a line of dark piping at the shoulder.

60 Sisters,1842-6
J. Sant

Head Both girls have centrally-parted hair with ringlets. The elder has a knot and single ringlets.

Body The elder wears a satin day dress with a lace collar, long, tight sleeves and frilled cotton undersleeves. The sloping shoulders, long pointed waist, dome-shaped skirt and plain, clean-cut outlines are typical of the 1840s. Pleats, folds (and perhaps piped seams) are the only trimmings. Converging to the waist, and set *en tablier* on the skirt, they serve to emphasize the main structure. The younger girl's muslin dress, trimmed with ribbon and lace, has the low neckline, short sleeves and calf-length skirt of childhood, although the deep bertha and long pointed waist imitate adult styles. She has frilled cotton drawers (which were beginning to be worn by adults).

Accessories They both wear flat, square-toed shoes with ribbon ties.

62 The Bromley family, 1844
F.M. Brown

Head and Body The three women on the right follow the fashions, with centrally-parted hair draped over the ears into a knot, deep lace berthas, formal day dresses with low necks and very long, pointed waists. Two have narrow sleeves with lace cuffs, the third the new bell-shaped sleeve worn over separate white cotton undersleeves or *engageantes*. The woman on the left still retains the sausage-shaped side curls, long earrings, and wide frilled lace cap of the mid-1830s. (The fashionable cap, when worn, would have been flat and close-fitting, with lappets hanging over the ears.) Her round-necked dress with sleeves puffed below the elbow is equally unfashionable.

Accessories The bouquets, in holders of metal or cut paper, are popular accessories with formal dress.

64 The Milne sisters, 1843-8
Photograph by Hill and Adamson

Note For dresses of fashionable cut, the skirts are surprisingly narrow, showing little evidence of the usual layers of stiffened petticoats. Bare arms, without undersleeves, would be unacceptable for an older woman. Flounced skirts become more popular after 1843.

Head Both have hair looped over the ears into a knot.

Body The sister on the left wears a day dress, probably of cotton, printed with fashionable stripes. The bodice is draped to emphasize the long, pointed waist, finished with a sash and rosette. The skirt is flounced.

Accessories Sideways on the table is her bonnet, the brim lined with pleated fabric. Her sister wears a dark mantle or shawl, and carries a straw bonnet trimmed inside with flowers.

63 Mrs Barker, 1844
Photograph by Hill and Adamson

Head Her hair is looped over the ears into a knot.

Body The collar of white muslin has whitework embroidery. Her day dress, probably of cotton or a light wool mixture is printed with fashionable stripes and has a long pointed waist; the material is cut on the cross, with a centre front seam, so that the stripes echo the line of the waist. Separate panels are draped in folds at the front. Long tight sleeves are also cut on the cross to give a close fit, with decorative folds. Narrow undersleeves probably match the collar. The skirt is gauged to the bodice, allowing maximum material in the ever-widening skirt.

Accessories She wears a plaid shawl and has a long neck chain, probably suspending a gold watch.

66 Baroness Burdett-Coutts, 1847-50
W.C. Ross

Note The evening dresses of this decade were restrained in style, characterized by the contrast of plain silk and rich lace. This is probably expensive hand-made bobbin lace, but the cheaper machined laces were stylish and popular. The fashion plate ideal would have a wider skirt, and flowers in the hair.

Head Her hair is looped back in a plaited knot.

Body The silk dress has a décolletage edged with a tucker and a flounced lace bertha, sleeves with lace ruffles and a flounced skirt.

Accessories She wears a lace shawl, neck ribbon with pendant and bracelets, including two of black velvet ribbon with a decorative clasp or locket.

65 Mrs Bell, 1843-8
Photograph by Hill and Adamson

Note The self-conscious mediaevalism of the 1840s was reflected in dress as in other art forms.

Head She has centrally-parted hair with plaited knot, comb and ringlets.

Body Her day dress is of silk, figured or damasked with stylized scrolling leaves, recalling mediaeval designs and has trimmings of tucks, velvet ribbon and black lace. The neck is edged with a frill of muslin or lace. The bodice has a cape-like front panel, emphasizing the sloping shoulders, low-set sleeves, and long, pointed waist. A trimming of ornamental, thread-covered toggles and beads runs down the centre front (a precursor of the front-buttoning jacket bodice of the 1850s). The long, tight sleeves have braid trimming at the cuffs.

Accessories Her neck chain has a watch and key or seal. She wears a brooch of delicate intertwined flowers and stems, with pendant flower, in the Romantic style.

67 The County Hunt Ball (detail), 1850
Anon. engraving

Note The provincial middle and upper middle classes here wear full evening dress.

Head The women usually wear their hair looped into a plaited knot, trimmed with flowers or feathers (although ringlets are still worn).

Body The short-sleeved silk ball dresses have the décolletage edged with a lace bertha decorated with ribbons and flowers, long pointed waists and full skirts, often trimmed with lace flounces, or plain but open at the front to reveal a flounced underskirt. The men wear black or white ties. Evening tail coats were cut long in the waist until 1855. The single-breasted, shawl-collared waistcoats are usually black or white. Narrow trousers are now generally without straps.

Accessories Men's evening pumps were often buckled.

68 Answering the Emigrant's Letter, 1850
J. Collinson

Note A country labourer and his family.

Head The wife wears her hair smoothed into a knot, under a simple
gathered cotton day cap of the type worn by the fashionable classes only in
the morning.

Body Her short-sleeved dress of linen, cotton or wool, reveals
unfashionably bare arms, and lacks the boned bodice and stiffened
petticoats essential to the fashionable silhouette. Her linen apron is purely
functional. The husband wears a neck scarf. His linen shirt has the square-
cut body, shoulder band, and full sleeves common to all classes for most of
the century (the chief variable was the quality of the material). His short
waistcoat and breeches are old-fashioned. The seated boy wears a plain
country smock.

Accessories Both males have coarse stockings and sturdy leather boots.

69 Bloomerism, an American Custom, 1851
J. Leech

Note Around 1850, Mrs Bloomer, an American reformer, demanded that women be allowed to wear trousers instead of the burdensome long skirts and layers of heavy petticoats. She promoted a 'Bloomer' costume, consisting of wide-brimmed hat, loose, knee-length tunic and ankle-length baggy trousers, not unlike children's outfits of the period. Although worn by a number of Americans, it appears to have been too advanced for Britain. However, Englishwomen had worn neck ties with day dresses throughout the 1840s, a basqued jacket bodice had become acceptable by 1851, and wide-brimmed hats were being introduced for informal wear.

Head and Body The conservative Englishwoman (right) wears an oval-brimmed bonnet, wide-sleeved mantle, and long, dome-shaped skirt. The Americans (left) wear Leech's version of 'Bloomer' costume, consisting of a wide hat, neck tie, basqued jacket bodice, flounced skirt and baggy trousers.

70 The Awakening Conscience, 1853
W.H. Hunt

Note A fallen woman and her lover, in a rare depiction of women's informal undress.

Head The man has fashionably short hair and full side whiskers (a centre parting was the mode with elegant young men).

Body He wears a dashing scarf neckcloth, velvet coat, and contrasting trousers with decorative banding. The woman wears a striped cotton dressing jacket trimmed with lace and a silk ribbon bow, the sleeves of fashionable pagoda shape. Probably to add colour and drapery, the artist has swathed her hips in a fashionable shawl, whose borders are woven or embroidered with Indian cone patterns. Her waist-length cotton petticoat is trimmed with tucks and *broderie anglaise.*

Accessories Her square-toed shoes probably have the newly fashionable one-inch heels. His ankle boots have side buttons, or, more probably, elastic sides and decorative buttons. Elastic-sided boots were patented in 1837.

71 The Last of England, 1852-5
F.M. Brown

Note Middle-class emigrants to Australia, dressed for the long sea voyage.

Head The man wears an informal, wide-brimmed, beaver or wool felt hat, called a 'wideawake' ('because of having no nap', *Punch*, 1849), secured to his coat button by a cord. His wife's hair is fashionably draped over her ears into a knot at the back, with a plaited braid across the top of the head. This was a popular feature, typical of the fuller, rounder hairstyles of this decade. Her bonnet has the flared, elliptical brim of the early 1850s, revealing a trimming of puffed ribbon. A bonnet veil blows out over the umbrella.

Body The man wears a double-breasted heavy wool greatcoat, with checked lining; his wife a simple, non-fashionable, fringed shawl of finely checked wool, pinned together under the chin, over a plain day dress.

Accessories She has short leather gloves.

73 Ramsgate Sands (detail), 1854
After W.P. Frith

Note Apart from actual swimming costumes, no special clothing was worn at the seaside. The suntan was the mark of the country labourer, and so was consciously avoided by the fashionable.

Head The woman on the right wears a straw bonnet with flared brim, lined with ruched fabric, typical of the early 1850s. Her companion's ringlets are now more usually worn by young women, or restricted to evening dress. She has a silk bonnet, and both she and the child wear an ugly to protect them from the sun.

Body An alternative to the shawl (right) is the frilled silk mantle (left). The woman on the left has lifted the skirt of her day dress, revealing her white cotton petticoats trimmed with coarse lace or openwork embroidery.

72 Queen Victoria and Prince Albert, 1854
Photograph by R. Fenton

Note The royal couple in fashionable day dress. Transparent muslins, warp-printing, frills, flounces and trimmings all combine to create the characteristic blurred silhouette of women's dress in the 1850s.

Head The Queen's hair is draped over her ears into a knot at the back of the head. Her elaborate cap of frilled muslin, lace and ribbons, with hanging streamers, is worn on the back of the head, like fashionable bonnets.

Body Her dress of spotted muslin, warp-printed with bouquets, and trimmed with lace and threaded ribbons, has the fashionable pointed waist, pagoda sleeves and flounced skirt. The Prince wears a bow-tied cravat, and shirt with decorative studs. Patterned waistcoats were popular even, as here, with a dark, formal frock coat.

74 The Derby Day (detail), 1856-8
W.P. Frith

Note (centre left) A fashionable middle-class young couple dressed for a summer day at the races. Women's hats went out of fashion after the mid-1830s, but by the late 1840s a large round straw hat with turned-down brim was appearing for seaside and country wear. By 1857 more stylish versions, such as the mousquetaire, were accepted as fashionable, but only for the young.

Head The man wears a top hat with the straight sides and almost flat brim typical of this decade. The young woman has a mousquetaire hat.

Body The man's shawl-collared waistcoat is now cut without the pointed waist of the 1840s, and with the shorter length introduced by 1855. His dark coat is worn with contrasting trousers and a lighter greatcoat. (For details of the woman's dress, see next illustration.)

78

75 The Derby Day (detail), 1856-8
W.P. Frith

Note As fashion demanded ever wider skirts, the usual three or four cotton petticoats were supplemented by further layers, often including one of stiff woven horsehair. Skirt flounces emphasized the horizontal line, especially when they were patterned *à disposition*.

Head The woman wears her hair in a knot and ringlets, under a striped straw hat trimmed with ruched silk ribbons and feathers and tied under the chin with wide silk ties.

Body She wears a frilled cotton collar, and a dress of cotton muslin woven with a check, the flounces printed with flowers *à disposition*. The softly pleated bodice has a pointed waist trimmed with a sash. Pagoda sleeves have separate gathered undersleeves of *broderie anglaise*. Her shawl is of lace or embroidered net.

Accessories Short gloves; heavy chain bracelet with locket; leather purse with metal frame.

76 The Derby Day (detail), 1856-8
W.P. Frith

Head The fashionable women wear their hair turned under at the ears, into a low-set knot. Their silk bonnets have the wider brim and sloping crown, which grew progressively smaller and slid further down the head, throughout the 1850s. The one on the right has trimmings of artificial flowers with bobbin lace on the edge and inside the brim, and round the bavolet.

Body The woman on the right has a *broderie anglaise* collar and silk day dress with pointed waist, flounced sleeves, and fringe trimming.

Accessories One woman carries a fringed parasol. Fringe trimming on dresses and accessories was popular from the mid-1840s.

open coat and waistcoat reveal a three-button shirt front, patterned cravat and braces. His fashionably checked wool trousers, with their decorative bands, have the fly fastening which had become general in the 1840s. The riding coat (left) is distinguished by its curved front edges, flapped pockets and back pleats; its wearer and the thimblerigger both wear breeches.

Accessories The riding dress is completed by the new *Napoleon* boots with their high front peak, spurs, gloves, and metal-topped cane. The youth wears boots or shoes with the wide square toes typical of this decade.

78 The Empty Purse, 1857
J. Collinson

See colour plate between pp. 96 and 97.

79 Work (detail), 1852-65
F.M. Brown

See colour plate between pp. 96 and 97.

80 Eastward Ho, 1857
After H.N. O'Neil

Note Soldiers departing for the Indian Mutiny. The dress of the officer's wife at the top of the steps is contrasted with that of the poorer working-class woman at the bottom.

Head The fashionable woman has a small bonnet set well back on the head, the poorer the wider-brimmed bonnet of the early 1850s, sparsely trimmed.

Body The fashionable woman has a mantle and flounced dress, the poorer has only the plaid wool shawl of practical working-class wear, over a dress of wool or cotton with stripes rather than flounces. The three sailors on the quay wear traditional garments, including (far left) the knitted cap (also worn by fishermen and brewers); (centre) a sou'wester hat and knitted 'jersey' or 'guernsey' jacket (worn only by seamen until the 1880s); and (right) the coarse linen shirt with braces and loose-fitting trousers or 'slops'.

Accessories The poorer woman's cloth-topped boots were common to all classes.

77 The Derby Day (detail), 1856-8
W.P. Frith

Note A group of tricksters and their victims among the crowd display the variety of contemporary styles, including (back view) fashionable riding dress; (centre – the 'thimblerigger') old-fashioned country dress; and (right – the victim of pickpockets) the dress of a fashionable youth.

Head The youth's top hat is fashionably straight-sided. Curly brims and concave sides are old-fashioned, or retained only for riding.

Body The youth wears a greatcoat with wide sleeves which echo women's pagoda sleeves. His

82 The confidante, 1857
W. Gale

Note Jackets were fashionable informal wear in the 1850s and the style was reflected in day dresses with front-fastening jacket bodices. It was unusual to go bare-headed outdoors.

Head The confidante (left) wears her hair in ringlets beneath a fashionable feather-trimmed mousquetaire hat with a veil. Her companion has the more usual daytime hairstyle, with the hair turned under and drawn into a low chignon, with a plait across the top of the head.

Body The confidante's informal walking dress consists of a fitted jacket with pagoda sleeves, basques and decorative buttons, over a day dress open at the front, revealing a chemisette with fashionably plain, narrow collar. The undersleeves are plain and cuffed. Her companion has a simple plaid wool shawl, but her fashionably flounced skirt and lace-edged undersleeves suggest a more formal day dress.

81 Isambard Kingdom Brunel, 1857
Photograph by Howlett

Note Although jacket and trousers are of the same tone, this is not a matching suit. The heavy wool fabrics of the mid-century sag and crease, producing a totally different look from the fashion-plate ideal.

Head His top hat is fashionably straight.

Body He wears a pointed standing collar with bow tie. His morning coat, the popular coat of the decade, is distinctive in its slightly cutaway front skirts, combined with waist seam, stitched edges, and flapped pockets. An extra buttonhole in the left lapel (for a flower) was introduced in the 1840s. He has a fashionably short waistcoat with lapels and trousers with fly front, high-set slant pockets and buttons at the outer side seams.

Accessories The wide, square-toed boots have the high toe spring typical of this decade, and stacked heels. He has a watch and chain.

83 Woman in day dress, 1857-60
Anon. photograph

Note In the late 1850s, the chignon was low and wide on the back of the neck, and caps, like bonnets, were worn far back on the head. Pagoda sleeves were at their widest from 1857 to 1860, necessitating fuller undersleeves, which reached to the elbow. A balloon-like form, finished with a cuff, is typical of the late 1850s and early 1860s. Front-fastening bodices usually had basques.

Head The hair is drawn back into a low flat chignon, under a cap apparently of crocheted wool or cotton.

Body She wears a *broderie anglaise* collar and a dress of lightweight silk, with front-fastening bodice and wide pagoda sleeves; the *broderie anglaise* undersleeves are separate. The dress has a pointed waist and finely pleated skirt.

Accessories Brooch, and neck chain for a watch or scent bottle.

84 Pegwell Bay (detail), 1858-9
W. Dyce

Note During the 1850s, as rail travel made visits to seaside and countryside increasingly popular, women began to adapt their dress for outdoor pursuits. These three are gathering fossils on the beach, on a chilly October day.

Head The women wear informal hats and (left) a bonnet.

Body The two on the left wear burnous mantles, the one on the right a shawl. The skirts of their day dress are tucked up into the waistband, revealing petticoats (left) probably of striped flannel, and (centre) stiff enough to suggest horsehair, or the presence of the new cage crinoline beneath. A more formal method of hitching up walking skirts was developed in the 1860s (see illustration 96.)

85 Picnic, 1859-62
Anon. engraving

Note Throughout the 1850s, fashion decreed ever wider skirts, so that increasing layers of petticoats became an intolerable burden. The solution was a hooped petticoat called a cage crinoline. Introduced from 1856, it made layers of petticoats unnecessary, although drawers were now essential. For men, full side whiskers and moustaches were popularized by the Crimean War.

Head The women wear their hair in a low chignon, braided or held in a net. They have informal hats of felt or velvet. The men wear informal hats (left) of straw, and (right) probably of felt, in the popular muffin shape.

Body The day dresses have narrow collars and tie cravats, pagoda sleeves and undersleeves, and pointed waists. Flounced skirts are worn over crinolines and drawers. The men wear informal 'lounging suits', i.e. loose jackets and matching trousers.

Accessories The women wear low-heeled ankle boots.

86 Day dress, 1862
Anon. photograph

Note Velvet was a popular trimming on plain
silk, and was often echoed in hair nets of
chenille. Creases betray the tight fit of the boned
bodice. The pointed waist is now shorter, and
was often replaced by the princess line, cut
without a waist seam. High fashion preferred a
plain skirt over a crinoline.

Head The woman's hair is in a low chignon,
worn inside a net.

Body She wears a narrow white collar with tie
and a silk day dress with velvet-trimmed bishop
sleeves and cotton undersleeves. The skirt is
trimmed with pinked flounces and worn over a
crinoline.

Accessories These include earrings, a neck
chain with attached watch or scent bottle tucked
into the belt, and keys or seals hanging below.

87 Queen Victoria presenting a Bible at Windsor, 1860-2
T. Jones Barker

Note This is a ceremonial occasion on which the Queen wears court
dress, here, a form of fashionable ball dress, with the addition of feather
headdress and train.

Head Her hair is in a low chignon under a jewelled diadem and ostrich
plumes.

Body Her silk dress has a wide décolletage edged with a lace tucker, and
is trimmed with bands of silk, threaded ribbon, and lace, which merge into
the short sleeves, themselves finished with a puff of lace or net. The dress
has a pointed waist, and a skirt with flounces of bobbin lace (probably
Honiton, since the Queen supported the dying British hand-made lace
industry). The train is silk.

Accessories Across the bodice is the sash of the Order of the Garter. She
wears drop earrings, pearl necklace and matching bracelets with inset
cameo.

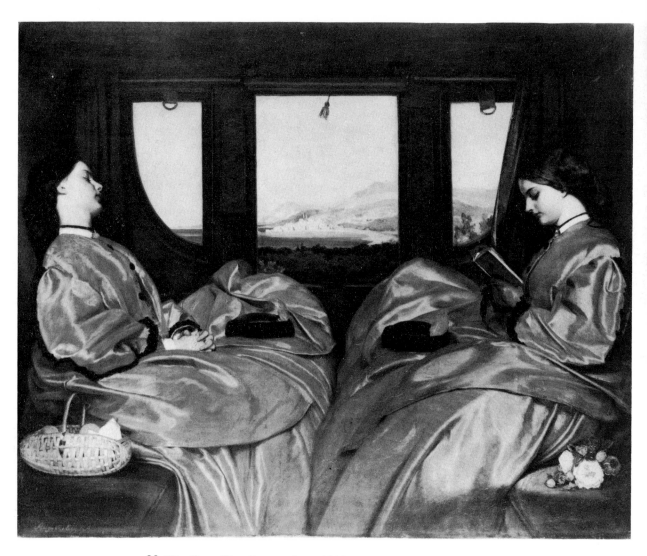

88 The Travelling Companions, 1862
A. Egg

Note Fashionable middle-class sisters, travelling through Europe, their balloon-like crinolines filling the railway carriage. When sitting, the hoops telescoped at the back, and rose slightly at the sides.

Head They wear their hair in a very large, low chignon (often supplemented by false hair).

Body They wear narrow collars. Their day dresses are worn under matching three-quarter length coats which, are loose or slightly waisted, buttoning at the front and with full, braid-trimmed sleeves (probably a paletot in contemporary terminology). They wear plain skirts over crinolines.

Accessories Ribbons with pendants are worn at the neck. On their knees are round hats of felt or velvet with turned-up brims, trimmed with a feather – a popular style for young women, often called a 'pork pie'.

89 Women in outdoor dress, 1862
H. Hilt

Note The characteristic triangular silhouette of mid-century fashion.

Head The ladies wear small sloping bonnets with high pointed brim and cut-away sides, producing the distinctive 'spoon' shape of the early 1860s (the trimmings of lace and artificial flowers inside the brim being all that is visible from the front). The flower-seller's patched suit and loose scarf proclaim his poverty. His peaked cap is of a type common to all five- to ten-year-old boys in the first half of the century.

Body The women's three-quarter length hooded cloaks of silk, fine wool or cashmere are worn over day dresses, the front one with a flounced hem. They have white undersleeves.

Accessories Short gloves and umbrellas.

90 Edward Lear, 1861-3
Photograph by McLean, Melhuish and Haes

Note Not a follower of high fashion, his clothes are still cut in the style of 1855-60. Fashion plates of the early 1860s show coats with peg-

top, rather than pagoda-shaped sleeves; peg-top trousers; and shorter waistcoats, with straight-bottomed edges, although, like his, they button high without lapels. His matching waistcoat and trousers follow the general trend towards the complete matching suit which became popular in this decade.

Head Full beard, moustache and side whiskers were increasingly common from the late 1850s.

Body He wears a bow tie, almost certainly with a standing collar; a tweed overcoat, apparently a loose paletot; and a darker cloth frock coat, distinctive by its straight front edges. The matching waistcoat and trousers are in popular fancy checked worsted.

Accessories Wide, square-toed shoes and watch chain.

91 Woman's Mission: Companion of Manhood, 1863
G.E. Hicks

Note Both wear informal morning dress. Braid edgings on men's coats became a general feature from the 1850s.

Head The husband has fashionably short, side-parted hair, with long drooping 'Dundreary' side whiskers (as popularized by a character in the play *Our American Cousin* in 1861). The wife wears her hair loose at the back, although a chignon, and perhaps a morning cap, were more usual, even before breakfast.

Body The husband wears the informal three-piece lounge suit, the jacket with the narrow cuffs and high-set button typical of the 1860s. His wife's day dress is fashionably plain, with bishop sleeves (popular since 1855). She appears to wear a crinoline.

Accessories The husband's Turkish-style slippers are informal indoor wear.

92 Charles Dickens and his daughters, 1862-3
Early photograph of anon. painting

Note In the early 1860s front-fastening bodices, often with separate skirts, featured a new, higher waistline, emphasized by wide belts.

Head The girls have crimped hair in the increasingly popular high chignon, with a plait on top.

Body The day dresses have short standing collars, button fronts and bishop sleeves. The dress on the left has fashionable epaulette trimming and the wide, double-pointed Swiss belt. Both dresses have crinoline skirts. Dickens himself wears an informal turn-down shirt collar, narrow tie, and three-piece lounge suit, with inside breast pocket.

Accessories The sister on the right wears the lace-trimmed silk apron of fashionable at-home wear, and cradles a round, flower-trimmed straw hat. Both wear drop-earrings and flowers.

**93 The Landing of H.R.H. Princess
Alexandra at Gravesend (detail), 1863**
H.N. O'Neil

Note The future Princess of Wales being
welcomed by her prospective bridegroom. Her
dress is fashionable, though simple, for the
Danish royal family had little money. The large,
dome-shaped crinoline looked best under a plain
skirt, and watered silk, or *moiré antique*, was a
popular choice.

Head and Body Her spoon-shaped bonnet has
a decorated brim, long bavolet, and wide ties.
The jacket or paletot of velvet, edged with fur, is
worn over a day dress of watered silk, with
crinoline skirt. The attendant 'maidens' wear the
loose or ringletted hair of girlhood, with
fashionable flower-trimmed straw hats, evening-
style cloaks, and crinoline dresses of white
muslin, decorated with wedding favours in the
form of ribbon rosettes.

of Chantilly, were especially prized. The crinoline of the early 1860s is flat at the front, and skirts are gored at the sides, with the back fullness extending as a short train.

Head The small, low-crowned hat of felt or straw has a ribbon rosette, an ostrich plume and a spotted net veil.

Body A black lace shawl (probably Chantilly lace) is worn over a silk day dress with fashionable epaulettes and round waist. She wears a white cotton petticoat, probably over a small crinoline.

Accessories Narrow, square-toed shoes or ankle-boots.

95 The dancing platform at Cremorn Gardens (detail)
P. Levin

See colour plate between pp. 96 and 97.

96 Queen Victoria and Princess Louise, 1865
Anon. photograph

Note Princess Louise (left) wears informal walking dress. With full crinoline skirts, jackets were either very short and bolero-shaped, in the 'Zouave' style, or hip-length, and cut very wide. Many had a ribbon trimming down the centre back. Walking skirts of the 1860s often had a series of internal cords passing from waist to hem, which, when manipulated at the waist, gathered up the skirt well clear of the mud, revealing brightly-coloured petticoats and stockings.

Head The Princess's hair is in a chignon under a round hat, probably of velvet and fur or feathers. The Queen now wears a widow's cap beneath her hooded mantle or jacket.

Body The Princess wears a jacket, probably of light wool or cashmere and a day dress, the skirt looped up to reveal a frilled petticoat over a crinoline.

94 Croquet player, 1864
G.E. Hicks

Note The contrast of black lace and white, or light-coloured, silk is characteristic of the late 1850s and early 1860s. Embroidered machine-made net was much used, but silk bobbin lace, particularly the flowing forms and clear ground

93

97 A widow, 1866
Anon. photograph

Note The mourning dress is fashionably cut, with its high round waist, fitted sleeves with epaulettes, and the trained skirt, which is now pleated and gored to fit the flat-fronted crinoline. A strict etiquette was followed in the choice of fabrics and colours and the duration they were worn. The white net widow's cap, with its two long streamers, and the deep crape band, were peculiar to first mourning, which lasted twelve months.

Head The hair is worn in a chignon under a widow's cap.

Body Her black silk dress is trimmed with deep bands of crape (a silk crimped to give a textured surface).

Accessories She wears black mourning jewellery, probably jet, together with commemorative lockets, and a watch and chain tucked into the belt.

98 Woman in evening dress, 1866
Photograph by Silvy

Note Pointed waists still vie with the princess line, or with a higher, rounded waist. The crinoline now has all the fullness at the back. This is emphasized by the overskirt, a form introduced in 1865, and soon to develop into a draped polonaise, worn over a bustle.

Head The hair is in a high-set chignon with ringlets.

Body The velvet dress has a slightly pointed décolletage edged with a pleated frill of net, threaded with ribbon, the bodice and puffed sleeves decorated with net, lace, and bands of velvet. She wears a lace-edged overskirt and a trained underskirt of ruched and puffed net over a crinoline.

Accessories These include drop earrings; a necklace of triple pendants in the heavy classical style, popular in this decade; a heavy chain bracelet; kid gloves; and a feather fan.

99 Interior at 'The Chestnuts', Wimbledon, 1867
J.L. Dyckmans

See colour plate between pp. 96 and 97.

100 On the Beach: a Family on Margate Sands (detail), 1867
C.W. Nichols

Note The bowler and lounge jacket, although informal, could be extremely stylish.

Head The young man has short hair, moustache and 'mutton-chop' whiskers. He wears an early form of bowler hat, a hard felt hat with distinctive bowl-shaped crown and curly brim, introduced for informal wear.

Body He has a narrow turn-down collar and neck tie. His dark cloth or velvet lounge jacket has a flower hole. He wears a fashionably short, plain, shawl-collared waistcoat and narrow trousers.

Accessories Striped stockings (also fashionable for women in this decade); short gloves; and a watch chain.

101 On the Beach (detail), 1867
C.W. Nichols

Note An innovation of this decade was the wearing of contrasting skirt and chemisette for country, 'at home' or seaside wear. The skirt often had a matching cape or jacket, forerunner of the tailor-made suit.

Head Over her high chignon, the young woman wears a straw hat with net and feather trimming and a net veil.

Body Her muslin chemisette is trimmed with lace and threaded ribbon. Beneath it are visible the low neckline and short sleeves (also ribbon-threaded) of her chemise, and across the bust, the top of her stays. She wears a Swiss belt and a silk skirt with braided hem (a protection against wear). The cotton petticoat with *broderie anglaise* hem, is probably worn over a crinoline.

Accessories These include lace-up boots; black lace shawl; short gloves with decorative points; and a silk and lace parasol.

102 An August Picnic, 1869
Anon. engraving

Head The older man wears formal day dress, including a top hat, but
more casual styles are favoured by the younger men. The one in the
foreground has a straw sailor hat, later called a boater. The man in the
centre has a protective veil, fashionable for men as well as women. The
young women wear a variety of small hats, now tilted forward to
accommodate the still rising and ever larger chignon. The girl in the right
foreground shows the fashion for loose back hair, introduced from
America in 1868.

Body and Accessories The older man's formal standing collar and frock
coat contrast with the casual lounge jackets of the younger men. The one
in the foreground may well be velvet, and is worn with fashionable braided
trousers and elastic-sided boots. The girl in the foreground has the looped
polonaise overskirt and bustle fashionable from 1868.

**23 The Cloakroom,
Clifton Assembly Rooms, 1817**
R. Sharples

Note Fashionable ball dress is worn here.

Head The women wear their hair in bandeaux
and flowers, or under silk turbans trimmed with
feathers.

Body They wear dresses of light-coloured
embroidered net or lace, over brightly coloured
silk or satin underdresses, featuring the puffed
sleeves and very high waists of 1815-20. The
flared skirts have deep flounced or vandyked
hems, often trimmed with artificial flowers. The
men wear white cravats and waistcoats, dark
dress coats and breeches or pantaloons.

Accessories The women's accessories include
low-heeled satin shoes, long kid gloves, shawls
and fans. The new arrival (seated right), is still
removing her fur-edged overshoes. The men
wear lace-up pumps, except for the two on the
left, whose military uniforms demand hessian
boots.

78 The Empty Purse
1857
J. Collinson

Note This is a fashionable middle-class woman at a bazaar.

Head Her bonnet is fashionably sloped and foreshortened to frame the head and reveal the trimmings of ruched net and flowers inside the brim. It has wide ribbon ties and a spotted silk bonnet veil.

Body She wears a silk dress with an unusual V-front, over a chemisette. The dress has a pointed waist; flounced pagoda-shaped undersleeves of muslin, threaded with ribbon; and a skirt with fashionable pinked flounces, striped *a disposition*.

Accessories She wears short kid gloves and holds a beaded stocking purse and one of its rings. On the stand is a woman's hat, trimmed with ribbons and feathers. Also visible are a pair of men's braces (above), and (left) a worked pattern for men's slippers, both hand-embroidered in wool.

79 Work (detail), 1852-65
F.M. Brown

Note This painting shows the range of London society, including a rare depiction of navvies.

Head The foreman (right) has a tasselled cap of a type commonly worn by small boys. The man on the left has a simple stocking cap, traditional headwear for working men, particularly sailors and brewers.

Body and Accessories The foreman's coarse linen shirt is cut like its fashionable counterparts, with low-set, full gathered sleeves. He follows fashion with a bow tie, fancy waistcoat and watch and chain under his linen apron. His men wear typical working clothes, including loose shirts or a plain smock (centre); old-fashioned breeches or cord trousers (left), hitched up at the knee with 'yarks'; thick woollen stockings; and lace-up 'blucher' boots. The two middle-class women (left) are dressed in the fashions of the late 1850s.

95 The Dancing Platform at Cremorne Gardens (detail) 1864
P. Levin

Note Expensively dressed ladies of the town in the popular pleasure gardens. Crinolines are still very large, but with more fullness at the back. This is emphasized by the use of basques and shaped overskirts, which by 1868 will have developed into bustles and pannier skirts.

Head To offset wide crinoline skirts, headwear is small and neat, whether it be a narrow-brimmed hat (left), the popular 'spoon' bonnet (centre), or an unusual toque (right).

Body The woman in the centre wears a lace mantle with an attached cape over her silk day dress, the contrasts of dark plain silk and pale lace being particularly fashionable in this decade. The woman on the left has a silk dress overlaid with multi-puffed sleeves and a draped overskirt of paler tulle or net. The third dress features a bodice with sash-like basques at the back, and a separate overskirt with cutaway sides.

99 Interior at 'The Chestnuts', Wimbledon, 1867
J.L. Dyckmans

Note Middle-class women in formal day dress.

Head The younger woman has fashionably crimped hair in a high chignon, tied with ribbon. The older married woman, as befits her age and status, wears a dress cap (although these confections of lace, net and ribbons were usually smaller and less enveloping by this decade).

Body The younger woman wears a dress of watered silk, with front-buttoning bodice, belted waist, shoulder trimming and the shaped sleeves which finally replaced bishop sleeves. Her skirt is gored and pleated to give a flat front and a train, now supported by a half-crinoline or by petticoats only. The child wears a dress of stiffened muslin over a miniature round crinoline, and the front-lacing boots with small heels which were also being introduced for adult wear.

Accessories A fashionably heavy brooch and fringed drop earrings are worn by the younger woman.

106 The Fair Toxophilites 1872
W.P. Frith

Note The artist's daughters in fashionable day dress. Mauve was one of the aniline dyes first developed in 1856. It remained fashionable until the mid-1870s.

Head Their hair is in heavy plaited chignons. Hats of felt and/or velvet are trimmed with ribbons and lace veiling (left) or feathers.

Body They wear lace-edged collars and jabots. The dress on the left has pagoda sleeves and basques at the back. The bustle is emphasized by the layered sash, basques and the overskirt, which is draped to give an apron front and a pannier at the back. The dress on the right has a bodice with attached overskirt and contrasting flounced skirt.

107 Too Early (detail), 1873
J. Tissot

Note London society girls in full ball dress.
Evening dresses of the early 1870s were frothy
confections. Pastel silks became misty seen
through overskirts and frills of white muslin, net
or gauze. Bustles, panniers and trains gave an
undulating line, softened by pleated frills, lace
flounces, ruched ribbons, and flower sprays.

Head They have fringed or centrally-parted
hair in high plaited chignons, decorated with
flowers, ribbons or feathers.

Body Their low-necked, short-sleeved dresses
have high, round waists, draped overskirts and
trained skirts, the fullness set in pleats at the
back and supported by a bustle.

Accessories Velvet ribbons decorate necks and
wrists. Kid evening gloves are still short, and
fans large.

136 St Martin-in-the-Fields (detail) 1888
W. Logsdail

Note Middle-class woman and child in fashionable winter outdoor dress. The tall-crowned, flower-pot shaped 'post-boy' hat was one of the most popular of the decade, matching the overall silhouette with its narrow angular forms. The 1880s and 1890s saw the importation of thousands of exotic birds which appeared on fashionable fans and headwear as plumes, wings, or even whole birds. Dark reds were typical of the late 1870s and 1880s.

Head The woman wears her hair in a knot under a tall 'post-boy' hat, probably of felt or beaver, trimmed with silk ribbon and feathers.

Body She wears a sheath-like cloth coat edged with fur over a dress with a bustle.

Accessories She has high-heeled shoes or boots with pointed toes, gloves and an umbrella.

103 Day dress, 1870
Anon. photograph

Note Light colours trimmed with dark braid or piping, together with fringes and narrow pleated flounces, are characteristic of 1868-75. Square necklines and yokes were fashionable from 1868. The waistband and overskirt may be attached to the bodice (i.e. a polonaise) or may be worn as a separate garment. It was usual to match the bow at the front with a larger version at the back, to emphasize the bustle.

Head The hair is worn in a high chignon with loose ringlets at the back.

Body The jacket bodice has pagoda sleeves and undersleeves. The overskirt is cut in handkerchief points. The short, walking-length skirt is apparently worn over a narrow crinoline or half-crinoline, and a bustle.

Accessories She wears a brooch and a heavy necklace.

104 The Marchioness of Huntley, 1870
Sir John Everett Millais

Note The Marchioness avoids fashion extremes to achieve romantic simplicity. Her square neckline and high round waistline are typical of 1868-74, although her epaulettes are no longer high fashion by 1870. The skirt, with its flat front, gored sides and long train, shows the transitional stage between crinoline and bustle. Here it is worn without either, but the trimmings suggest the more fashionable alternative of an apron-fronted overskirt, which high fashion would have worn draped and puffed over a bustle and half crinoline.

Head Her hair is in a high but plain chignon trimmed with ribbons.

Body Her summer day dress of muslin is trimmed with threaded silk ribbons and lace.

Accessories She wears drop earrings, a neck ribbon with a pearl drop pendant, and a bracelet. Her gloves are probably of very soft leather.

105 The Marquess of Townshend, 1870
Anon. caricature

Note The straight 'chimney pot' top hat of the mid century was reduced in height after 1865, while the years 1869-76 saw a fashion for very short coats, their hems, like this one, well above the knee. The artist exaggerates the waisted effects, however, and has missed out the waist seam.

Head Moustache and side whiskers were both fashionable in this decade. Beards were general for older men. He wears a top hat.

Body He has a turn-down collar with narrow tie; a pale waistcoat; a double-breasted 'top frock' overcoat with silk-faced lapels and breast pocket. His trousers have gaiter bottoms, a popular alternative to the narrow cut.

Accessories Fashionable square-toed shoes and tasselled cane.

106 The Fair Toxophilites, 1872
W.P. Frith

See colour plate between pp. 96 and 97.

107 Too Early (detail), 1873
J. Tissot

See colour plate between pp. 96 and 97.

108 Mrs Bischoffsheim, 1873
Sir John Everett Millais

Note She wears formal afternoon or dinner dress. A flowered bodice with sleeve ruffles and panniers, worn with a flounced underskirt, was a fashionable revival of the polonaise robe and petticoat of the 1770s. The bow-trimmed front panel recalls the stomacher. This is a dressier version of the chintz 'Dolly Varden' bodices of 1871-2.

Head The hair is in a full chignon, trimmed with ribbons or lace.

Body The square-necked jacket bodice of brocaded silk is trimmed with lace, the front cuffs and turn-back panels in plain silk, matching the flounced skirt. The overskirt is draped in panniers, the whole dress worn over a bustle.

Accessories She has pearl earrings and pendant on a velvet ribbon, long kid gloves and a fan.

109 The Ball on Shipboard (detail), 1874
J. Tissot

Note For this daytime event at Henley Regatta both formal and informal
day dress are acceptable.

Head The men wear informal straw sailor hats, or curly-brimmed
bowlers. The women have full braided chignons with forward-tilted straw
sailor hats, or more formal bonnets at the new backward-tilted angle.

Body The tight jacket bodices with basques are worn with draped, apron-
fronted overskirts, puffed at the back over a bustle. The figure coming up
the stairs wears the newly introduced cuirass bodice, which fits tightly over
the hips, and the ruffled, elbow-length sleeves of formal dress.

Accessories Some of the men have two-tone brogue shoes, popular for
informal wear.

100

110 Travelling scene, 1874

Anon. engraving

Note A middle-class couple dressed for travelling.

Head The fashionable wife wears her hair in a full chignon, with an exaggeratedly small, forward-tilted hat. Her husband has full side whiskers and the curved and curly-brimmed top hat of the first half of the 1870s.

Body He wears a greatcoat or paletot over his cut-away morning coat and waistcoat. She wears fashionable day dress, the square-necked jacket bodice with slightly pagoda-shaped sleeves and ruffles, the skirts draped to give an apron front and puffed back. Her matching underskirt has a flounced hem and train, supported by a bustle.

111 The Ulster, 1874
G.F. Watts

Head Hair drawn back into a high chignon. Forward-tilted hat, probably of hard felt, trimmed with feathers. The hat is very plain and masculine in style, suitable for informal walking or travelling.

Body She wears an Ulster coat, an overcoat worn by both sexes and also called a 'waterproof', 'dust-cloak', or 'travelling wrap'. The female version was distinctive for its fitted waist, shaped by darts, or pulled in by a half belt, and for its length (some were cut with a train). Many, like this one, had a detachable hood. The male version usually featured a hood and a belt.

112 The Dinner Hour, Wigan, 1874
E. Crowe

Note The dress of women working in the textile mills of the industrial North makes few concessions to the fashionable ideal.

Head Long hair is secured in a net for practicality and safety.

Body The basic dress consists of a short-sleeved linen overall with draw-string neck and open back, worn over chemise, stays and coarse linen or woollen petticoats. No bustles are worn (although in the 1860s many factory girls had worn crinolines).

Accessories Most wear wooden-soled leather clogs with metal clasps. Some have stockings of coarse wool or cotton. Others go without – 'slip-shod'. Simple plaid wool shawls are cheap and practical, and can be drawn over the head to form a hood. A few wear drop-earrings and necklaces, perhaps of glass or wood.

113 Poor Relations (detail), 1875
G.G. Kilburne

Note The years 1874-5 saw the introduction of
the cuirass bodice, which extended in sheath-like
form over the hips, making the bustle impossible.
The fullness in the back of the skirt slipped
downwards, in waterfall draperies, producing, in
a few years, a narrow, tie-back skirt with a train.
Here, the middle-class daughter of the house
demonstrates the transitional stage.

Head The hair is worn in a simple plaited
chignon.

Body The day dress consists of a bodice with
cuirass front but a high-waisted polonaise form
at the sides, which appears to be looped up
towards the back, still giving the effect of a
bustle. She has a lace or muslin neck frill and
long sleeves with frilled mousquetaire cuffs. The
flounced skirt may be tied back, but is still fairly
full.

Accessories She wears low-heeled shoes with
pointed toes.

114 Poor Relations (detail), 1875
G.G. Kilburne

Note The impoverished middle-class girl is
dressed neatly, with all the essential accessories,
but is too poor to follow fashion, except in the
style and angle of her hat.

Head Her hair is in a chignon, under a round
hat set on the back of the head.

Body Her day dress is of silk or wool (its
plainness suggests that it is home-made, or a
hand-me-down, perhaps worn by her mother in
the 1860s). The well-to-do child wears a silk
dress with basque bodice and sash, simulating a
bustle; a linen overall and stockings with fancy
clocks.

Accessories The young woman has an
inexpensive checked wool shawl, short gloves of
unfashionably thick leather, and a plain umbrella.
The child wears low-heeled shoes with the
pointed toes and decorative rosettes that are also
fashionable adult wear.

115 Day dress, 1875-7
Anon. photograph

Note This mixing of cuirass, princess and polonaise forms is typical of 1875-85, when dress construction was highly complex. The chief aim was to offset the narrow vertical line with graceful draperies.

Head The hair is worn in a neat braided chignon.

Body She wears a dress of contrasting materials, probably silk and velvet. The bodice front appears to be continuous with the skirt in the princess style, with the velvet side pieces extending as a long polonaise overskirt. The panel on the skirt front is draped in the fashionable apron shape, emphasizing the cuirass effect of the bodice. The back of the skirt is slightly puffed and gathered, the remnant of the bustle, but with the fullness extending as a train.

116 Woman in day dress, 1876
J. Tissot

Note By 1876 the overall silhouette was sheath-like, the bustle giving way to a waterfall of drapery extending as a train. Trimmings of flounces, pleats and ruching became more elaborate as the decade progressed.

Head The curly-brimmed hat is decorated with feathers (probably ostrich).

Body The dress of striped muslin, trimmed with silk bows, has a short polonaise bodice, the frilled edge forming the fashionable high standing collar and frilled cuffs. There is a separate overskirt with frilled edge dipping down at the back and a flounced underskirt.

Accessories A large, plain parasol was a fashionable alternative to those with lace edgings or trimmings of ribbon bows or ruchings.

117 The Gallery of HMS *Calcutta* (detail), 1876
J. Tissot

Note In the most fashionable dresses, bodices are carefully seamed to fit like sheaths, while draping and elaborate frills produce a waterfall effect in the skirt.

Head Hair is worn in long braided chignons under a curly-brimmed silk bonnet (left) and a hat (right), decorated with ribbons on the outside and flowers or pleated net under the brim.

Body The day dresses of silk (left) and striped muslin (right), have high frilled collars of lace or net. The long polonaise bodices are in princess style, tied and draped at the back under ribbon bows and frills. The matching tie-back skirts are decorated with rows of frills (those on the left are pinked), the fullness gathered at the back in a short train.

Accessories Fans are becoming larger, reaching up to sixteen inches in length in the 1880s.

118 Day dress, 1876-8
Anon. photograph

Note Contrasting materials were frequently used to emphasize the narrow, vertical line of the body and to give a cuirass effect, even in jacket bodices. Similarly, the fashion for asymmetrical skirt draperies is imitated in bands of trimming. Concealed pockets were no longer feasible in such narrow skirts, and the years 1876-8 saw a brief fashion for large, decorative pockets, set low on the skirt.

Head The parted hair is drawn into a neat, low chignon.

Body Her dress is of contrasting materials, probably silk and velvet. She wears a simple jacket bodice, narrow white collar and cuffs, a tie-back skirt with flapped pocket, and a train decorated with bows.

Accessories She has a heavy brooch and pendant. Her watch chain is tucked into the bodice front.

119 The Arrest, 1877
After W.P. Frith

Note The bailiffs serve a writ on the upper-class gambler. He and his family wear informal morning dress.

Head The husband has fashionably parted hair and moustache. His wife wears an oval-shaped 'Charlotte Corday' morning cap of muslin, lace and ribbon.

Body The husband's standing collar and necktie are those of formal day dress, but at present worn beneath a patterned dressing-gown, probably of thick wool, with contrasting shawl collar and cuffs, cord tie and edgings. His wife has a princess-style dressing gown or informal morning robe, with high collar and lace-edged front opening. The girl wears her silk day dress under a linen or cotton overall. The boy has a velvet knickbocker suit.

120 Evening dress, 1877-80
Anon. photograph

Note Although a simple chignon was now usual for daytime, full ringlets were often retained for evening. The squarish neckline, stomacher-like front, sleeve ruffles and delicate jewellery, particularly the pendant brooch, are all features consciously revived from the eighteenth century, a period much copied throughout the 1870s and early 1880s.

Head The hair is in a chignon with long back ringlets, decorated probably with lace or feathers.

Body Her dress is of contrasting materials, probably silk and velvet, edged with lace. The cuirass bodice has contrasting panels forming a stomacher front, and lacing together down the centre. The heart-shaped neckline is edged with a frill of lace or pleated net. There is a seperate, tie-back skirt with vandyked hem, and a separate or attached overskirt, extending as a train.

121 Two women in day dress, 1878
Photograph by Elliot and Fry

Note Skirts were now so sheath-like that long stays were essential, and combinations were introduced to dispense with the bulk of separate chemise and drawers. Petticoats were few and narrow, with extra flounces at the back to support the fall of drapery which replaced the bustle from 1876-80.

Head They wear their hair in chignons under (left) a hard felt Tyrolean hat, trimmed with ribbons and a bird's wing, and (right) a soft-crowned toque, trimmed with feathers.

Body Both wear a narrow white collar and a dress in the form of a princess-style polonaise, with narrow cuffed sleeves, a centre-front opening decorated with bows, and a tie-back skirt with back draperies and train. The pleated flounces at the hem may belong to a separate underskirt, but more probably are attached directly to the lining of the main skirt.

122 Couple in formal day dress, 1878
Photograph by Elliot and Fry

Note For both sexes the fashionable head is small and neat, the body tall and slender.

Head The woman wears her hair in the increasingly popular frizzed fringe and a plaited chignon.

Body Her polonaise dress, in the princess style, with a tie-back skirt, gives a narrow line, emphasized by narrow sleeves and the ruched panel in contrasting material down the centre front. Both the dress and the plain silk underskirt are draped at the back to give a train. His narrow winged collar and bow tie are almost hidden by his high buttoning frock coat, its straight cut echoed by narrow sleeves and trousers. (The outside breast pocket went out of fashion in 1877.)

Accessories Her high frilled collar is finished with a black lace jabot. She carries a fashionably large feather-trimmed fan with a tasselled cord. She may have a chatelaine bag on the cord around her waist.

123 A railway smoking saloon, 1879
Anon. engraving

Note Cigarette smoking became popular for men during the Crimean War. 'Fast' young ladies also indulged, but respectable women generally objected to the smell of smoke on clothing, encouraging their menfolk to adopt special caps and jackets for the purpose. The caps were always pill-box shaped, made of silk, wool or velvet, and often embroidered by their loved ones in vaguely Turkish patterns. The typical jacket was easy-fitting, with a quilted silk collar, and decorated with braid or frogging. Both were popular till the end of the century.

Head and Body The men wear informal day dress consisting of narrow standing or (right) turn-down collar, and lounge suits with very high buttoning jackets and waistcoats. The man on the right wears a smoking cap with button and hanging tassel.

124 Scarborough Spa at Night, 1879
F.S. Muschamp

Head The women wear small hats or toques, trimmed with flowers and feathers, or high-crowned hat with birds' wings. The men favour the tall, straight-sided, small-brimmed top hats of the late 1870s, or bowler hats, both high- and low-crowned.

Body The princess polonaise is the most popular dress, decorated with bows and pleated frills. The woman on the right loops up her train for walking. On a warm summer night, lace shawls are the most popular outerwear, tied fichu-style (right). The men wear high-buttoning frock coats or overcoats. The little boy has the long hair more usually associated with aesthetic dress, and a sailor hat and suit with knickerbockers.

125 Aesthetic dress, 1879
G. du Maurier

Note In artistic circles in the late 1870s the extremes of high fashion were rejected in favour of 'aesthetic dress'. For women this meant romantically loose hair, loose dresses worn without stays or stiffened petticoats, and large puffed sleeves in the Renaissance style. For children, it was mixed with a revival of early nineteenth-century fashions, as depicted in the drawings of Kate Greenaway.

Head The fashionable girls on the right wear adult-style hats but the aesthetic children favour old-fashioned, wide-brimmed bonnets.

Body The fashionable mother wears a polonaise dress, and her daughters' princess-style coats follow the same line. The aesthetic girls have shoulder capes and high-waisted printed cotton dresses as popular between 1810 and 1830. The older girl's puffed sleeves are typical of aesthetic dress.

Accessories Peacock feathers and sunflowers were favourite aesthetic motifs.

127 Couple in aesthetic dress, 1880
G. du Maurier

Note Among aesthetes, exotically embroidered or brocaded silks in the 'Renaissance' style were an alternative to the soft oriental silks in the muted 'greenery-yallery' colours, which they obtained at Liberty's.

Head The man's long hair and clean-shaven face brand him as an aesthete, as does the woman's loose, frizzed hair, in the style popularized by the Pre-Raphaelite painters.

Body The man's turn-down collar, soft tie, and lounge jacket (probably of velvet with a quilted silk collar), are fashionable informal dress, although velvet jackets were particularly associated with aestheticism. The woman's dress, probably of brocaded silk, has the low neck, puffed 'Renaissance' sleeves, lack of waist seam and loose, flowing skirt typical of aesthetic gowns.

126 Day dress, 1879-81
Anon. photograph

Note After 1878 hems rose and trains became less fashionable, leaving skirts as straight tubes, smothered with horizontal bands of ruches, puffs and narrow-pleated frills. In the early 1880s, the upper skirt was often curved to form panniers over the hips.

Head Her toque is swathed in ostrich feathers.

Body The cuirass bodice is probably of the popular Genoa velvet (a satin ground, patterned with a velvet pile). She wears a narrow, standing collar, and fancy buttons; jabot and frilled cuffs, probably of lace or muslin; and a contrasting skirt, the upper front arranged in horizontal pleats and a pleated frill, the back arranged in vertical pleats and slightly puffed.

Accessories She carries a Japanese paper parasol. The flow of Japanese imports produced by the 1868 revolution reached new levels in the 1880s.

115

OSCAR WILDE.
NEW YORK.

128 Oscar Wilde, 1882
Photograph by Sarony

Note Photographed in New York, when Wilde
was on his famous lecture tour of the United
States. Aesthetes and dress reformers favoured
the mediaeval forms of men's dress, consisting of
a loose tunic and knee-breeches. Wilde himself
admired cavalier dress, and from 1880 wore his
version (velvet jackets and breeches) to evening
parties. The breeches and stockings shown here
were bought from a theatrical costumier
especially for the tour.

Head Wilde has aesthetic-style long hair and a
clean-shaven face.

Body and Accessories He wears an informal
turn-down collar and unfashionably large silk
tie; a double-breasted cloth lounge or smoking
jacket with quilted silk collar and cuffs, and
decorative frogging; knee-breeches with silk
stockings; and flat or low-heeled shoes with wide
ribbon ties.

129 Outdoor dress, 1883-6
Anon. photograph

Note The soft leather of the gloves outlines the cuffs of the shorter sleeve introduced in 1883. The panniers of the early 1880s have now filled out and softened as the skirt widens to incorporate the new bustle. Woollen walking outfits like this one are plainer in style than more formal day dresses, and set the trend for the more tailored lines of the second half of the decade.

Head The hat of fur or beaver is trimmed with ostrich feathers.

Body The cravat of figured net is tucked into the bodice front to give a plastron effect. She wears a day dress, probably of wool, with a cuirass bodice; a separate overskirt, draped in panniers over the hips and back; and a straight skirt with the back arranged in vertical pleats over a bustle.

Accessories She carries a fur muff and wears gloves, probably kid.

130 Marion Hood, 1884
Photograph by Elliot and Fry

Note This is fashionable formal day dress, the draperies of which were at their most exuberant in the mid-1880s, just before they disappeared almost entirely.

Head She wears her hair with a fringe (fashionable sine 1882), and a loose version of the low-set chignon.

Body The velvet bodice has a standing collar, fashionably short sleeves and a pointed front waist, with a lace neck frill, sleeve ruffles and plastron. The silk skirt, with train, is made up from panels of draped and ruched silk, intermingled with swags and frills of lace, attached to a plain lining, which is tied with tapes inside the back, and worn over a bustle.

Accessories She wears a necklace, possibly of amber, and kid or suede gloves. Her fancy-mesh, machine-knit stockings probably match the dress. Her shoes are of fancy leather, with pointed toes, decorative rosettes, and probably one-and-a-half to two-inch heels.

117

132 Lady Dilke, 1887
H. von Herkomer

Note An artist's version of fashionable ball dress. (Compare this with the contemporary photograph in the previous plate.) The second half of the decade saw a slow return to a narrow vertical line, and the gradual decrease of the bustle. From 1887 straight pleats replaced apron draperies in skirts. Here, the gathered shoulder 'kick-up' of 1889 is already predicted in the ribbon bows on the sleeves.

Head The hair is swept up to a knot on the crown.

Body She wears a dress of silk figured with flowers in eighteenth-century style, with asymmetrical draperies of silk and heavy lace. The heavily-boned bodice has a low V-neck front and back. The skirt hangs straight at the front, the sides tied back over a bustle and extending as a train.

Accessories She is holding long evening gloves.

131 Ball dress, 1886
Anon. photograph

Note A V-shaped or heart-shaped décolletage was the most fashionable for ball dresses by the mid-1880s, and coupled with the sheath-like bodice and vestigial sleeves, gave a vertical emphasis and a starkness echoed in the cap-like hairstyle. Gloves reaching to, or even above, the elbow fastened with up to twenty buttons.

Head The hair is dressed in a tightly curled fringe, and a small knot on the crown, a style often decorated with flowers or feathers.

Body The heavily-boned bodice has a low V-neck front and back, emphasized with pleated net. Her skirt has a draped apron front and puffed and gathered back, worn over a bustle, and probably extending as a train.

Accessories The gloves would be of silk, kid or suede. She has cameo brooches and fashionably heavy bangles (now worn over the gloves).

118

133 The First Cloud, 1887
Sir William Quiller Orchardson

Note This upper-class couple are in full evening dress. The bustle of the 1880s was much narrower and more angular than that of the 1870s, and when worn with a train, gave a greater sense of movement.

Head The woman wears her hair swept into a knot, with flower or feather trimming.

Body Her silk gown has the extreme décolletage and vestigial sleeves typical of the late 1880s. Her draped tie-back skirt is worn over a bustle. The man has the fashionable standing collar, white bow tie, starched shirt front and cutaway dress coat (although by the mid-1880s lapels were generally superseded by the roll collar for evening).

134 Will it Rain? 1887
J. Charles

Note An old country woman in unfashionable outdoor dress. Without the appropriate substructure of crinoline or bustle, there is little to date a simple, working-class dress. Shawls went out of fashion with the demise of the crinoline, but remained popular among the poorer classes. This one probably dates from before 1840, when they became larger and more densely patterned.

Head The parted hair is drawn into a knot. The black bonnet has the slightly raised brim, trimmings on top of the crown, and wide ribbon ties most fashionable in the early 1880s.

Body She wears a shawl with fringed and patterned border, pinned at the front. Her dress, probably of inexpensive printed cotton, has an unfashionably simple gathered skirt, worn without a bustle.

Accessories Large, practical apron, umbrella and shopping basket.

135 Sir Arthur Sullivan, 1888
Sir John Everett Millais

Note Sir Arthur wears fashionable formal day dress. Coats were buttoned very high in this decade. Collars, shirt fronts, and cuffs were heavily starched in the latter half of the century.

Head He has short hair, probably sleeked with macassar oil (a side-parting was equally fashionable). Moustaches were usual, with or without short side whiskers.

Body He wears a winged collar and unusually wide tie; a double-breasted frock coat with cuffs; stiffened shirt cuffs; and contrasting trousers.

Accessories A monocle hangs from a cord round his neck, a popular accessory since the 1850s, and particularly associated with fops and 'swells'.

136 St Martin-in-the-Fields (detail), 1888
W. Logsdail

See colour plate between pp. 96 and 97.

137 Frances Hodgson Burnett, 1888
Anon. photograph

Note The Anglo-American authoress of *Little Lord Fauntleroy*, wears an evening dress in Grecian style. Classical robes were admired by the aesthetes for their artistic flowing lines, and by dress reformers for their healthy lack of constriction. In her imitation of classical draperies she rejects the separate bodice and skirt, although the draperies follow fashionable lines in the cross-over bodice, and skirt with apron front, bustle and train. She appears to be wearing stays and fashionable lace-trimmed petticoats.

Head Her frizzled hair, has a low 'aesthetic' fringe.

Body The dress of light silk is applied to a firm lining. The short sleeves have lacings, which are a classical motif. The hem is trimmed with applied braid in a pattern reminiscent of the Grecian key design.

Accessories She wears a simple pearl necklace and carries a fashionably large feather fan, decorated with a whole bird or bird wing.

138 A Royal Academy Private View (detail), 1888-9
H.J. Brooks

Head The standing women wear their hair swept back into a high-set knot, beneath (left) a tall pointed hat, and (right) a bonnet trimmed with feathers and ribbons. The seated woman (left), shows the fashionable tilt of the bonnet, with its cut-out back revealing the hair.

Body and Accessories Over their day dresses, with fitted bodices and bustle skirts, the women wear (left) a fur boa, and (right) a fur mantle, cut in the style of the late 1880s, with its wide sleeves and long pointed fronts, descending from a short flared back, which rests on the bustle. This woman also carries a be-ribboned fur muff, a popular winter accessory for most of the century. The men wear the ubiquitous silk top hats and frock coats.

139 Dulcie Delight and the Curate, 1889
Anon. engraving

Note A middle-class country girl in a tailor-made costume (originally informal outdoor dress and now fashionable morning wear). In very fashionable dresses, this year saw the bustle reduced to a mere pad.

Head She wears her hair in a knot under a be-ribboned straw hat, in shape half way between a 'post-boy' and a wide-brimmed 'Gainsborough'. The curate's flat hat is typical clerical wear.

Body Her dress is probably of light wool or flannel, trimmed with plain cloth or velvet (stripes were very popular in the late 1880s). The high standing collar is typical of 1880-1900. The dress has a mock waistcoat front with lapels, a variant of the plastron. Three-quarter-length sleeves were fashionable from 1883, and here they have the slightly gathered shoulders of 1889, the beginnings of a new gigot sleeve. Her simple draped skirt, a feature of the tailor-made is worn over a bustle.

140 City day dress, 1890
Anon. engraving

Note A middle-class couple in simple, conservative, outdoor dress.

Head The woman has a fashionable frizzed fringe and high-set knot of hair, under a toque trimmed with ribbons and a bird's wing. The man wears a semi-formal felt hat.

Body The woman's fitted jacket is a less dressy alternative to the popular mantle, and is probably made of cloth trimmed with darker fabric or fur. Her day dress has a simple draped skirt worn over a bustle. The man wears a Chesterfield overcoat (distinctive by its straight lines and outside pockets).

Accessories Her reticule or dress bag is probably home-made, for during the 1880s soft drawstring bags were being superseded by commercially-made leather handbags with metal frames and fastenings, more stylish versions of the man's travelling bag.

141 The Countess of Aberdeen, 1891
Anon. photograph

Note The Countess wears formal day dress. The bustle has now disappeared, leaving a flared skirt with back pleats. Jackets were popular with skirts and dresses, in either matching or contrasting fabrics.

Head Her hair is swept high into a knot, under a velvet bonnet trimmed with flowers, tying with a velvet bow.

Body The high-collared bodice is of dark fabric, probably silk, with an unusual inset pleated panel in a lighter colour, and a high waist sash. The fitted jacket of silk or cloth has the gathered shoulders typical of the early 1890s. The skirt is shaped and gored to hang straight at the front, with pleats at the back. Trimming of applied braid in scrolling patterns was popular from the 1880s.

Accessories She wears short day gloves and a chatelaine hangs from her waist.

142 The Royal Academy Conversazione (detail), 1891
G. Manton

Note The guests wear fashionable evening dress. From 1889-92, the main emphasis in female dress was vertical, particularly at the shoulder.

Head The women's hair is arranged with a fringe or centre parting and a high knot, to create a small neat head, undecorated except perhaps for an ornamental comb.

Body Sleeves are cut with a kick-up at the shoulder (fashionable from 1889). Even the shoulder straps of the full evening dress (left) have vertically arranged frills. Waists may be round or pointed. Bustles are no longer worn, although trains are still retained for evening. The shadow on the bodice of the woman on the right reveals the line of her stays.

Accessories Fashionable accessories are elbow-length gloves of kid or suede, and very large fans.

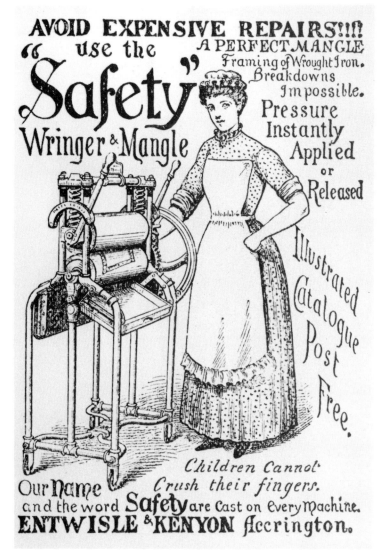

143 Magazine advertisement, 1892
Anon. engraving

Note The kitchen maid wears the basic uniform of female domestic servants – frilled cap, cheap printed cotton dress and apron. Although her outfit is plain and simple in construction, it reflects high fashion in the following features.

Head Her hair is worn in a knot on the crown. Her small cap is worn, like fashionable hats, flat on top of the head.

Body Her dress has a high collar, front-fastening bodice, narrow sleeves (although without the fashionable gathered shoulder), round waist at natural level and a skirt supported only by petticoats, with the fullness at the back. A more expensive skirt would be gored and pleated rather than gathered.

Accessories Her shoes have slight heels and pointed toes.

144 Woman in walking dress, 1893
Anon. photograph

Note The blouse became increasingly fashionable in the 1890s, but, whether frilly or plain, its apparent informality was belied by its heavily boned lining. It was worn with a simple skirt or, outdoors, a tailor-made costume. For walking, cycling and sports, masculine styles were adopted.

Head Her frizzed hair is in a knot. The coarse straw sailor hat, trimmed with silk ribbon, is worn fashionably flat on the head.

Body The blouse has a high standing collar and masculine tie. Her tailor-made costume is of checked wool. The jacket has the wide gigot sleeves of 1893-7, emphasized by wide lapels. She wears a waistcoat with the still fashionable pointed waist and a plain gored skirt with waist darts.

Accessories Short day gloves and fashionably heavy charm bracelets.

145 Middle-class couple, holidaying in the country, 1894
Anon. engraving

Note Their dress is smart but informal.

Head The woman wears her hair frizzed and probably padded, in a heavy knot or coil. Her wide-brimmed hat is trimmed with either ribbon bows or bird's wings. Her husband wears the soft, peaked cap which was originally sportswear, but popular in the 1890s for general leisure activities.

Body The woman wears a contrasting jacket and skirt, probably with a blouse. Fashionable features are the high standing collar, gigot sleeves and applied trimmings of braid or ribbon. The cut of the skirt is typical of 1890-7, when gores and darts gave a snug fit on the hips, while deep pleats, cut on the cross, gave a flowing line at the back. The man's lounge suit displays the large checks often used for informal suits in this decade.

146 Mother and daughter, 1895
Anon. engraving

Note The women wear fashionable outdoor dress. Sleeves were at their widest in this year, making capes, cloaks and mantles the most popular outer garments.

Head The daughter wears her waved or frizzed hair in a low knot under a boat-shaped hat, trimmed with birds' wings, or a whole bird in flight, and a spotted veil. Her mother wears a bonnet (now favoured only by older women) decorated with large upstanding bows and a spotted veil.

Body Both wear high-collared day dresses, the daughter's demonstrating the fashionable gigot sleeves and a flared skirt. Her mother's cape is made of silk or cloth decorated with braid and ribbon, and edged with fur or beaded braid.

Accessories Both have fashionably long parasols, and the daughter's shoes or boots show the current style of pointed toes and high heels.

147 The Bayswater Omnibus (detail), 1895
T.M. Joy

Note The large gigot sleeves of the middle of
the decade were matched by broad-collared
capes or cloaks, and wide-brimmed 'picture'
hats. Clear stones were popular for tiny brooches
and pins, in the form of crescents, stars, hearts,
birds and animals. Some fastened pendant
watches.

Head and Body The fashionable woman,
dressed for city travelling, wears a wide-brimmed
hat, a high-collared day dress of striped fabric,
probably silk, and a cape or cloak, with wide
frilled collar.

Accessories She wears short day gloves,
probably of suede, and holds a long parasol, with
fashionable frilled edge. Her bow-shaped
brooch is probably of paste stones, with a
pendant pearl.

148 The Bayswater Omnibus (detail), 1895
T.M. Joy

Note The businessman wears correct dress for
formal day and city wear.

Head He has very short hair and a heavy
moustache and wears a curly-brimmed top hat.

Body His dress consists of a high starched
winged collar with spotted bow tie; a frock coat
with braided edges; a high-buttoning waistcoat;
and narrow trousers.

Accessories He wears pointed boots and spats
(popular with frock coats from 1893) and has a
metal-framed business bag. The long furled
umbrella was, in this decade, a fashionable
alternative to the cane. A signet ring was now the
only fashionable form of jewellery apart from the
tie-pin. Gloves of fawn kid or grey suede were
usual with frock or morning coats, but he may
have removed them while reading his
newspaper.

149 Fashionable ball dress, 1895
Anon. engraving

Head The women's hairstyles demonstrate a new tendency towards fullness around the face and in the knot at the back, achieved by waving, and sometimes even padding the hair. The only ornaments are perhaps an aigrette or an ornamental comb.

Body Silk dresses feature low-set balloon sleeves, echoing the daytime gigot. Bodices are heavily boned, with pointed waists. Flared skirts have trains, which have to be held up while dancing. The men wear full evening dress, with starched shirts. Lapels are revived for dress coats after 1893.

Accessories The women's long gloves, usually of suede, fasten with up to twenty pearl buttons. Their shoes, usually satin for evening, have very pointed toes and Louis heels. Fans are still very large.

PAS de QUATRE

Why do they call it a Pas de Quatre?
'twould puzzle a sage to know.
It's you & I, & I & you, as up, & down
we go.
What does it matter whoever the rest,
however they twist & twirl?
Whether they dance, or whether they prance,
or whether they waltz in a whirl?
Never a thought of any one else, as we
go to & fro.
Why do they call it a Pas de Quatre?
'twould puzzle a sage to know.

Why do they call it a Pas de Qua...
I think I'm beginning to k...
What of the hands that hold & lo...
as up & down we g...
What of the feet that rise & fall...
patter along the flo...
For two are yours & two are mine.
& two & two make four.
What of the eyes that meet & p...
as we go to & fr...
Why do they call it a Pas de Qua...
I think I'm beginning to k...

Cosmo Monkhouse.

132

'Princess.'
Very stylish **Black Silk Tea Gown**, handsomely trimmed with Beige Lace of
very new design, 4½ guineas.
Orders by Post carefully executed. Patterns of all goods Post Free.

150 Tea-gown, 1895
Anon. engraving

Head The model still wears her hair in the small bun or knot and frizzed fringe of the first half of the 1890s.

Body Her tea-gown is of silk, trimmed with lace. The tea-gown was an easy-fitting, unboned, leisure garment, first introduced in the late 1870s, to give respite from the cuirass bodice of day and evening wear. Initially, it was almost indistinguishable from a dressing-gown, but it became more elaborate in the 1880s, as day wear became more severe. By the late 1880s, it was often worn as an informal dinner dress. Although usually without a waist seam, it always included some fashionable features. Here, the wide yoke, huge gigot sleeves, pointed waistline, and hip-moulding, trained skirt are typical of the mid-1890s.

151 Alfred Austin, 1896
L. Ward

Note The Poet Laureate is in fashionable country clothes.

Head The bowler hat is low crowned and curly-brimmed.

Body He wears a high winged collar, Norfolk jacket and matching knickerbockers, probably of heavy wool tweed. The Norfolk jacket had a distinctive box pleat at the centre back and on each front large patch pockets, concealed vertical breast pocket, and a matching belt, which buttoned at the front waist (those of the 1890s usually had a shoulder yoke). Generally made of thick wool, its warmth and comfortable fit made it ideal for country and sporting wear. It was fashionable throughout the last quarter of the century.

133

152 In the holidays, 1897
Anon. engraving

Note Middle-class families in fashionable but informal seaside wear.

Head Straw sailor hats are popular for men, women and children,
alternatives being soft-peaked caps for men, more dressy wide-brimmed
hats for women, and cotton sunbonnets for little girls (copies of those worn
by countrywomen).

Body and Accessories For women, a tailored jacket, blouse and skirt
(left) are an alternative to day dresses, but both feature high collars, gigot
sleeves, narrow waists and flared skirts. The older girl wears a calf-length
version of adult dress, but the younger ones complement their sunbonnets
with loose, yoked dresses or overalls, based on the country man's smock.
Their brothers wear jerseys and open-legged knickerbockers. Men favour
informal suits and two-tone brogue shoes.

153 Max Beerbohm, 1897
W. Sickert

Note Max Beerbohm wears fashionable casual dress. Shirt collars grew higher in this decade, reaching three inches by 1899. The reefer jacket was distinguished from the lounge by its straight front edges. Originally a yachting coat, it was adopted in the 1860s as a town overcoat. In a shorter, more fitted form, it soon developed as an informal jacket, usually for outdoor wear.

Head He has short hair with a centre parting, a fashionable alternative to the side parting. A clean-shaven face was favoured in 'artistic' circles.

Body and Accessories He has a high standing collar and his spotted silk tie is worn with a 'four-in-hand' or 'Derby' knot, with its distinctive horizontal border along the top and bottom edges. He also wears a high-buttoning waistcoat; a double-breasted reefer jacket; contrasting trousers, probably of flannel; and pointed shoes.

154 The Duchess of Portland in fancy dress, 1897
Anon. photograph

Note Fancy dress balls became increasingly popular during the century. Many outfits revived fashions of previous eras, chosen according to the taste of the day, but however detailed the reconstruction, they always revealed the fashionable features of their own time.

Head and Body Here, the Duchess is dressed for the Devonshire House Ball as the Duchess of Savoy. Her outfit is vaguely 'antique', the pointed waist and hanging sleeves deriving from mediaeval dress, her ringlets, wired neck ruff and jewelled girdle all elements from the sixteenth and seventeenth centuries. Her curved décolletage, puffed sleeves, heavily-boned and fitted bodice and flared skirt are typical of evening dresses in the mid-1890s.

Accessories Pearls were popular in the 1890s as in the seventeenth century.

155 Boulter's Lock, Sunday Afternoon (detail), 1898
E.J. Gregory

Note Middle-class families at leisure on the river.

Head and Body Surprisingly few of the women wear practical blouses and skirts. Most wear more elaborate day dresses and hats. Although several still have full gigot sleeves, the girl in the foreground has adopted the new style, introduced in 1897, featuring narrow sleeves with just a small puff at the shoulder head. Also typical of the late 1890s are the frothy trimmings of lace and frills, particularly half way down the skirt, where they mark a new flare towards the hem. The men generally wear peaked caps, shirts and white flannel trousers. Stripes are popular for caps and blazer jackets.

Accessories Japanese paper sunshades are still a popular accessory.

137

156 Woman in cycling dress, 1899
B. Partridge

Note The craze for cycling in the 1890s necessitated more practical styles. Many women wore a simple blouse, tie and skirt, with sailor hat. Others ventured divided skirts, and a minority adopted a wider version of men's knickerbockers.

Head The woman's hair is waved and padded and swept into a chignon on top of the head. She has a low-crowned, curly-brimmed hat, probably of felt.

Body She wears a scarf or tie in a loose bow; a tailored jacket, with wide lapels, emphasizing slightly gathered sleeves; a blouse and perhaps a waistcoat; and wide knickerbockers. The typical country man now wears a straw hat, scarf, and loose informal jacket. He still ties his trousers with yarks, and wears heavy boots.

Accessories Stockings, high-heeled lace-up shoes with pointed toes and short gloves are worn for cycling.

157 Feminine Pinpricks, 1899
Cleaver

Note The woman in the centre wears a frothy and undulating day dress in the new style which appeared from 1897, a reaction against the severe tailored forms typified by the dresses of the women in the background.

Head Her hair is rolled and padded to form a high cushion round the head, topped by a small knot on the crown. A wide-brimmed hat is tied with veiling under the chin and she wears a scarf or jabot of veiling or lace.

Body The dress is of lightweight, clinging silk, trimmed with lace, frills and bows. Narrow sleeves, with small puffs at the shoulder and a pintucked lower sleeve extend over the hand. The skirt is shaped to fit snugly over the hips, and then swell out below the knee to a wide hem, with bias-cut pleats forming a swirling train at the back.

158 Fashionable walking dress (detail), 1900
Anon. engraving

Note The emphasis is on height, achieved by the padded hair and plumed hats, puffed shoulders, narrow, fitting costumes, and high-heeled boots and shoes. Nevertheless, padded busts and hips and heavily-boned, long-fronted stays create an S-shaped silhouette, completed by the flowing skirts.

Head The women's hair is rolled and padded with a knot on top. Their wavy-brimmed hats are trimmed with feathers, or (left) in ermine to match the outfit.

Body They wear long fitted pelisses of cloth or velvet, trimmed with fur; high wired collars; wide lapels (left); narrow sleeves with small shoulder puffs; and skirts with short trains, cut to flare out from below the knee.

Accessories They carry matching muffs with attached metal-framed purses, decorated with tassles and a posy of artificial flowers (left).

Select Bibliography

The following publications deal with fashionable dress and accessories. Specific aspects of nineteenth-century dress (e.g. occupational, rural and civic) are dealt with in more general works, and are listed in *Costume: A General Bibliography* by P. Anthony and J. Arnold, published by the Victoria and Albert Museum in association with the Costume Society. Articles and reviews of new material can be found in *Costume,* the annual journal of the Costume Society, and in *Dress,* the journal of the Costume Society of America.

Adburgham, A., *A Punch History of Manners and Modes, 1841-1940,* Hutchinson, 1961

Adburgham, A., Introduction to *Victorian Shopping,* David and Charles, 1972

Adburgham, A., *Shops and Shopping 1800-1914,* Allen and Unwin, 1964 and 1981

Arnold, J., *Patterns of Fashion I (c. 1660-1860)* and *II (1860-1940),* Wace, 1964, Macmillan 1972

Blum, S. (ed.), *Victorian Fashions and Costumes from Harper's Bazaar 1867-1898,* Dover, New York, 1974

Blum, S. (ed.), *Ackermann's Costume Plates: Women's Fashions in England 1818-1828,* Dover, New York, 1978

Buck, A., Victorian Costume and Costume Accessories, Herbert Jenkins, 1961

Buck, A., 'The Costume of Jane Austen and her Characters' in *The So-called Age of Elegance,* The Costume Society, 1970

Buck, A., 'The Trap Rebaited, Mourning Dress 1860-1890' in *High Victorian,* The Costume Society, 1968

Byrde, P., *A History of 19th Century Fashion,* Batsford, 1992

Byrde, P., *A Frivolous Distinction: Fashion and Needlework in the Works of Jane Austen,* Bath City Council, 1979

Clark, F., *Hats,* Batsford, 1982

Cunnington, C.W., *English Women's clothing in the Nineteenth Century,* Faber, 1937

Cunnington, C.W. and P., *The History of Underclothes,* Faber, 1951, revised 1981

Cunnington, C.W. and P., *Handbook of English Costume in the Nineteenth Century,* Faber, 1959 and 1970

Davis, R.I., *Men's Garments, 1830-1900,* Batsford, 1989

Evans, J., *A History of Jewellery 1100-1870,* Faber, 1953 and 1970

Flower, M., *Victorian Jewellery,* Cassell, 1951

Foster, V., *Bags and Purses,* Batsford, 1982

Gernsheim, A., *Fashion and Reality 1840-1914,* Faber 1963, reprinted as *Victorian and Edwardian Fashion: A Photographic Survey,* Dover, New York, 1981

Gibbs-Smitt, C., *The Fashionable Lady in the Nineteenth Century,* H.M.S.O., 1960

Ginsburg, M., *An Introduction to Fashion Illustration,* Victoria and Albert Museum, 1980

Ginsburg, M., *Victorian Dress in Photographs,* Batsford, 1982

Holland, V., *Hand-Coloured Fashion Plates 1770-1899,* London, 1955

Hope, T. and Moses, H., *Designs of Modern Costume Engraved for Thomas Hope of Deepdene by Henry Moses, 1812,* Introduction by J.L. Nevinson, Costume Society Extra Series no. 4, 1973

Irwin, J., *Shawls,* H.M.S.O., 1955

'A Lady', *The Workwoman's Guide,* 1838, reprinted by Bloomfield Books, Doncaster, 1975

Laver, J. (introduction), *Costume Illustration: The Nineteenth Century,* H.M.S.O., 1947

Manchester City Art Galleries, *Women's Costume 1800-35,* Manchester City Art Gallery, 1952

Manchester City Art Galleries, *Women's Costume 1835-70,* Manchester City Art Gallery, 1951

Manchester City Art Galleries, *Women's Costume 1870-1900,* Manchester City Art Gallery, 1953

Moore, D.L., *Fashion Through Fashion Plates 1771-1970,* London, 1965

Newton, S.M., *Health, Art and Reason, Dress Reformers of the Nineteenth Century,* John Murray, 1974

Rhead, G.W., *History of the Fan,* K. Paul, 1910

Rock, C.H., *Paisley Shawls,* Paisley Museum and Art

Galleries, 1966

Swann, J., *Shoes*, Batsford, 1982

Walkley, C., *The Ghost in the Looking Glass: The Victorian Seamstress*, Peter Owen, 1981

Walkley, C., and Foster, V., *Crinolines and Crimping Irons; Victorian Clothes: How They Were Cleaned and Cared For*, Peter Owen, 1978

Waugh, N., *The Cut of Men's Clothes 1600-1900*, Faber, 1964

Waugh, N., *The Cut of Women's Clothes 1600-1930*, Faber, 1968

Waugh, N., *Corsets and Crinolines*, Batsford, 1954 and 1972

Glossary and Select Index

Note This lists costume and textile terms mentioned in the captions, with a definition where this is not included in either text or caption. The numbers in brackets refer to plates where selected examples of the item listed can be studied. (Basic garments such as *bonnets, shawls, top hats* etc. appear too frequently to be included in this system.)

Aesthetic dress (125) (127) (128)

Aigrette a tuft usually of feathers, but sometimes of flowers or jewels. (149)

Apollo knot a knot of hair on the crown of the head, topped by vertical loops of stiffened, plaited hair, often secured by Glauvina pins (q.v.). (40) (42) (46)

Basques tab-like extensions below the waist of a bodice. (69) (109)

Bavolet a curtain of fabric attached to the back of a bonnet to shade the neck. (61)

Bedgown a short, loose, wrap-over gown, often worn as a jacket by country women. (16)

Beret sleeve a short, very wide, puffed sleeve. (46) (47)

Bertha a deep collar falling as a continuous band from a low neckline. (51) (60) (66)

Bishop sleeve a long, full sleeve, gathered to the wrist. (86) (91)

Blazer a flannel sports jacket with patch pockets. Usually striped or brightly coloured, hence the name. (155)

Blonde lace made from undyed silk. (41) (42)

Bloomer dress (69)

Blouse (144)

Blucher boots men's half boots with straight tops and front lacing. (79)

Boater see *Sailor hat.*

Bobbin lace an openwork mesh made by interweaving threads wound on bobbins. (68) (87)

Bowler a hard felt hat with a bowl-shaped crown and curled brim. Called a Derby in the USA. (100) (124) (151)

Breeches (1) (68) (128)

Brocade a woven fabric, with elaborate patterns created by the introduction of additional threads of a different yarn or colour. (54) (108)

Broderie anglaise coarse, openwork embroidery, the large holes overcast with stitching. (75) (83)

Bullycock (Billycock) hat (52)

Burnous mantle a loose form of mantle with a tasselled hood. (84)

Busk a flat rod, inserted into the front of a corset to stiffen it. It was usually made of wood or whalebone in the early part of the century, and of metal from the 1860s. (14)

Bustle (2) (24) (40) (109) (130)

Cape a short cloak. (146)

Chapeau bras a crescent-shaped opera hat, which could be folded flat. (11)

Chatelaine a metal waist ornament with attached chains from which were suspended domestic accessories (e.g. keys, scissors, scent-bottle). (141)

Chatelaine bag a bag hung from the waist. (122)

Chemise a female undergarment consisting of a long, loose, low-necked, short-sleeved shirt, worn next to the skin. It was made of linen or cotton. (14) (40)

Chemisette in the first half of the century, a high-necked, sleeveless muslin half-shirt, worn as a fill-in for low-necked dresses; by the 1860s, a long-sleeved blouse. (14) (25) (32)

Chenille a furry looking silk thread with a long pile. (86)

Chesterfield overcoat (140)

Clocks patterned areas on stockings in the region of the ankle. (14)

Cornette a bonnet-shaped cap, tying beneath the chin. It was sometimes pointed at the back. (14)

Court dress (28) (87)

Crinoline a petticoat distended by hoops of cane, whalebone or steel, introduced in 1856. (85) (88) (96) (98)

Cuirass bodice a heavily whaleboned bodice, extending over the hips in a point front and back. It was named after a form of body armour. (109) (120)

Damask a heavy woven cloth with a reversible pattern produced by alternating plain and satin weaves. (65)

Dandies (9) (24) (36) (43) (58)

Disposition, à a term applied in the 1850s to ready-patterned skirt flounces. (75) (78)

Drawers (14) (47) (60)

Dress coat a man's formal tail coat, cut square across the waist. (19)

Dressing gown (20) (119)

Epaulette an ornamental shoulder-piece in the form of a short cap to the top of the sleeve. (92)

Falls a form of closure for trousers, breeches, and pantaloons, by means of a falling flap at the front, which buttoned to the waist. (1)

Fichu-pelerine a pelerine (q.v.) with scarf-like extensions hanging down at the front. (44) (45)

Figured fabric a fabric woven with a pattern, but without additional threads of a different yarn or colour (compare *Brocade*). (54) (65)

Frock coat a man's skirted coat of about knee length, characterized by its straight front edges. (21) (24) (26) (105)

Gaiters protective leggings fastening with buttons or straps and extending over the foot. (52)

Gaiter bottoms a term applied to trouser bottoms where the side seams curve forward, producing a flared front to accommodate the foot. (58)

Gauging a technique of gathering skirts, by which the fabric is finely pleated, together with its lining, and sewn to the bodice at alternate pleats. (63)

Gigot ('leg-of-mutton') sleeves sleeves with very full puffed shoulders, but tapering to a narrow wrist. (36) (38) (48) (146)

Glauvina ('Glorvina') pins ornamental hair pins with detachable heads. (See *Apollo knot*).

Gore a triangular-shaped panel in a skirt, adding width at the hem, without fullness at the waist. (97) (145)

Half boots short boots, reaching just above the ankle.

Hessian boot a knee-length boot with a heart-shaped peak at the front, often decorated with a tassel in the centre. (4) (9) (19) (23)

Jabot an ornamental frill on the front of the bodice. (122) (126)

Jersey a knitted top, originally worn by sailors, but adopted by women and children in the 1880s. (80) (152)

Knickerbockers baggy breeches, usually gathered just below the knee. (119) (151) (156)

Lappets long bands attached to a cap or headdress and hanging down over the ears. (28)

Louis heels strictly a heel continuous with the sole, but used to describe a curved heel, set well under the foot, as found in eighteenth-century French shoes. (149)

Lounge jacket a short jacket, worn informally. When accompanied by matching waistcoat and trousers, it became a lounge suit. (91) (145)

M-notch lapel an M-shaped opening at the join of collar and lapel, found in men's coats between 1800 and 1855 (and in evening coats until the 1870s). (9) (10 (19)

Mancheron a short, flat oversleeve. (5) (17) (49)

Mantle at the beginning of the period, a cape with scarf-like extensions; by the 1820s it had become a loose-fitting wrap, half way between a coat and a cloak, with wide sleeves or armhole slits. There were many individually named variations. (2) (59) (69) (138)

Marie Stuart bonnet or cap a cap cut with a distinctive dip in the centre front, imitating the heart-shaped caps worn by Mary Queen of Scots. (33) (35)

Mentonnière ('chin stays') a ruffle of tulle or lace at the top of bonnet strings creating a frill around the chin. (50)

Mittens (48) (54)

Mourning coat a tail coat with curved front edges. Originally a riding coat worn in the morning, it became general day wear. (6) (34) (43) (81)

Morning dress (96) (97)

Mousquetaire hat a low-crowned, wide-brimmed hat with a feather plume, inspired by those of seventeenth-century musketeers. (78)

Norfolk suit (151)

Pagoda sleeve a sleeve which was tight to the upper arm and flaring below the elbow. It became very wide between the years 1857 and 1860. (78) (83)

Paletot the French term for overcoat, it was applied in the mid-century to short loose coats, usually without a waist seam. (88) (90)

Pannier part of a skirt or overskirt which is looped up in a puff on the hips. (108) (129)

Pantaloons a form of very tight-fitting legwear, usually made of stretchy fabric or soft leather. (6) (9) (19) (36)

Patent leather a very glossy leather made from hide coated with layers of varnish or lacquer.

Peg-top (usually applied to sleeves or trousers) cut wide at the top and tapering towards the bottom.

Pelerine a very wide, cape-like collar. (41) (44) (48) (56)

Pelisse a woman's fitted overcoat. (5) (15) (18) (45) (158)

Pelisse dress a dress cut in imitation of a pelisse (e.g. with lapels and/or a belt) popular in the late 1830s and 1840s. (50)

Pinking the raw edge of fabric cut in zigzags or scallops. (78)

Piping the insertion of a fabric-covered cord into a seam to stiffen it, the tube of fabric being all that is visible. (61) (63)

Plastron a loose panel of fabric inserted down the centre front of a bodice, creating the effect of a waistcoat. (129) (130)

Pointing decorative lines of stitching on the backs of gloves. (140)

Polonaise a bodice with attached overskirt. An eighteenth-century form, revived from the mid-1860s onwards. Those of the late 1870s were so long as to be almost indistinguishable from a dress. (103) (118) (122)

Pork-pie hat a small round hat with an upturned brim almost flush with the crown. (88)

Post-boy hat (136)

Princess dress a style of dress without a waist seam, perhaps called after Princess Alexandra. (121) (122)

Pump a light shoe, usually low-cut, with flat or low heel. (23)

Reefer an informal jacket, usually double-breasted and with straight front edges, derived from a yachting coat. (153)

Reticule an early form of handbag, usually in the form of a simple rectangle of fabric fastened with a drawstring. (24) (45) (52) (140)

Rouleau a trimming consisting of a puffed or padded roll of fabric. (31) (39)

Sailor hat a low-crowned, narrow-brimmed straw hat. (144) (152)

Sandal a flat shoe with ribbon ties around the ankle. (15) (22) (40)

Sevigné bodice a bodice decorated with horizontal pleats caught by a vertical band in the centre. It was named after the Marquise de Sevigné (1626-96). (46)

Shawl collar a collar continuous with the lapels. (43)

Smock (52) (68)

Smoking cap (123)

Spats short gaiters, reaching just above the ankle. (148)

Spencer a woman's short-waisted, long-sleeved jacket. (16) (21) (31)

Spoon bonnet a small bonnet with sloping brim and cut-away sides, creating a spoon shape. (89) (93)

Stays (14) (40)

Stock a made-up, stiffened neck band, fastening behind, with or without a bow in front. (6) (34)

Stocking purse a tubular purse of knitted silk or cotton, the coins being inserted through a slit in the middle and secured in the ends by metal rings. (78)

Stomacher a panel of fabric, in the shape of an inverted triangle, inserted between the centre front edges of the bodice. Popular in the seventeenth and eighteenth centuries it was often imitated in the nineteenth. (28) (120)

Sunbonnet a bonnet with a very deep bavolet (q.v.), worn by country women to protect them from the sun. It was usually made of printed cotton gathered on to half hoops of cane or whalebone. (152)

Swiss belt a wide belt with a double point centre front. (92)

Tablier, en lines of trimming on a skirt front arranged in an inverted 'V' to imitate a front opening. (50)

Tail coat see *Dress coat* and *Morning coat.*

Tea-gown (150)

Tie-back skirt a skirt made with internal tapes passing between the side seams at the back, so that the fabric is drawn closely to the hips and legs at the front, and the fullness concentrated at the back, usually in a train. (118) (120) (121)

Titus, à la a term applied to hair worn short and tousled, in the style of the Roman emperor of that name. (1) (2)

Toe spring the elevation of the toe of a shoe above the ground. (81)

Top boot a tall boot with the top turned down to show the paler lining. (24)

Top frock an overcoat in the style of a frock coat, but usually with wider lapels and cuffs. (105)

Toque a hat, usually small, with little or no turned-up brim. (44) (126) (140)

Tucker a frill of muslin or lace worn inside a low neckline. (The term was sometimes applied to a more substantial fill-in.) (27) (66)

Ugly a folding sunshade worn at the front of a bonnet, and consisting of a band of silk (usually blue) distended by half hoops of cane. (73)

Ulster (111)

Undersleeves (62) (83)

Vamp the front part of a shoe upper, covering the toes and part of the instep. (15) (20)

Vandyking zigzag edgings, supposedly imitating the pointed lace collars and cuffs of the seventeenth century, as depicted in portraits by Van Dyck. (29) (39) (42) (120)

Victoria sleeve a sleeve puffed at the elbow (49) (59)

Warp-printing the printing of warp threads of a fabric before weaving to produce a blurred pattern. (72)

Watered silk – (moiré antique) a corded silk pressed between heated rollers so that the crushed cords reflect the light in wave-like patterns. (55) (99)

Wideawake hat (71)

Winged collar a standing collar with the two front points turned down. (135)

Yark a cord used by country men and labourers to hitch up their baggy trousers below the knee. (79) (156)